Luke Harding

INVASION

Luke Harding is a journalist, writer, and award-winning foreign correspondent with *The Guardian*. Between 2007 and 2011, he was the *Guardian*'s Moscow bureau chief. The Kremlin expelled him from the country in the first case of its kind since the Cold War and in the summer of 2022 put him on an official blacklist.

He is the author of eight previous nonfiction books: *Shadow State: Murder, Mayhem, and Russia's Remaking of the West*; *Collusion: Secret Meetings, Dirty Money, and How Russia Helped Donald Trump Win*; *A Very Expensive Poison: The Assassination of Alexander Litvinenko and Putin's War with the West*; *The Snowden Files: The Inside Story of the World's Most Wanted Man*; *Libya: Murder in Benghazi and the Fall of Gaddafi* (with Martin Chulov); *Mafia State: How One Reporter Became an Enemy of the Brutal New Russia*; *WikiLeaks: Inside Julian Assange's War on Secrecy*; and *The Liar: The Fall of Jonathan Aitken* (the last two cowritten with David Leigh).

Two have been made into Hollywood movies. DreamWorks' *The Fifth Estate*, based on *WikiLeaks*, was released in 2013. Oliver Stone's biopic *Snowden*, adapted from *The Snowden Files*, appeared in 2016. An award-winning stage version of *Poison*, written by Lucy Prebble, premiered in 2019 at London's Old Vic theater. Harding's books have been translated into thirty languages. He lives near London with his wife, the freelance writer Phoebe Taplin, and their two children.

INVASION

INVASION

The Inside Story of Russia's Bloody War
and Ukraine's Fight for Survival

Luke Harding

VINTAGE BOOKS
A Division of Penguin Random House LLC
New York

A VINTAGE BOOKS ORIGINAL 2022

Copyright © 2022 by Luke Harding

All rights reserved. Published in the United States by
Vintage Books, a division of Penguin Random House LLC,
New York, and distributed in Canada by Penguin Random
House Canada Limited, Toronto. Simultaneously published
in hardcover in Great Britain by Guardian Faber Publishing,
an imprint of Faber & Faber Limited, London.

Vintage and colophon are registered trademarks
of Penguin Random House LLC.

The Cataloging-in-Publication Data is available
at the Library of Congress.

**Vintage Books Trade Paperback ISBN: 978-0-593-68517-4
eBook ISBN: 978-0-593-68518-1**

Author photograph © Christopher Cherry

vintagebooks.com

Printed in the United States of America
10 9 8 7 6 5 4 3 2 1

CONTENTS

N

BELARUS

POLAND

Pripyat

Chornobyl•

•Lutsk

Hostomel
Bucha □ Ky

•Lviv

•Ternopil

Ivano-Frankivsk•

Dniester

•Vinnytsia

Southern Buh

Prut

Chernivtsi•

MOLDOVA

Odesa

ROMANIA

Annexed by Russia in 2014

Controlled by Russian proxies
before the invasion on
February 24, 2022

Limit of Russian advances
March 24

Ukrainian counteroffensives
September 6–12

•••••• Limit of Russian-controlled
area September 20

0   100 miles

0   100 km

Izmail

Snake
Island

Ukraine, 2022

R U S S I A

Sumy

Kharkiv

Poltava

Donets

LUHANSK

Cherkasy

Sievierodonetsk

Slovjansk

Lysychansk

Bakhmut

Luhansk

Avdiivka

DONBAS

Kropyvnytskyi

Dnipro

Dnipro

Donetsk

Zaporizhzhia

DONETSK

Nikopol

Enerhodar

ZAPORIZHZHIA

Mariupol

kolaiv

Kherson

KHERSON

SEA *of* AZOV

RUSSIA

CRIMEA

B L A C K   S E A

INVASION

ONE

The City

There had been peace at one time,
and now that peace was dead.
—MIKHAIL BULGAKOV,
The White Guard

It was the evening before everything changed. The Ukrainian novelist Andrey Kurkov had invited me for dinner. A few friends, he said, and borsch. We had first met earlier that memorable winter—a pleasant meal in a Georgian restaurant in Podil, a neighborhood in the lower part of Kyiv next to the Dnipro River; a glass of red in a boutique café near the old city. The date was now February 23, 2022. It was 8:15 p.m., and I was late. I stopped in a shop, bought a bottle of Kolonist port from a winery in Odesa, and hurried to Kurkov's flat.

These meetings happened under the shadow of war. The news—which I was writing for my newspaper, *The Guardian*—was alarming, terrible even. A week earlier, Russian-backed separatists had shelled a village in Ukrainian-controlled territory next to the pro-Russian regions of Luhansk and Donetsk. The missile had landed in a school gym. Mercifully, no one was killed, but the eight-year conflict in the east was heating up.

Humor was essential in these dark times. Kurkov sent me a meme via WhatsApp. It showed Fyodor Dostoevsky's head floating surreally in a hole in the school's wall, peering at the rubble. Around the great nineteenth-century Russian writer were soccer balls, a mural depicting a jungle, and a climbing rope. Kurkov was an agreeable companion, the author of many playful and magically luminous books, and Ukraine's most celebrated living writer. Also, remarkably, he was an optimist.

I, by contrast, was increasingly gloomy. The omens pointed in one scarcely believable direction: Russia was about to invade Ukraine.

Vladimir Putin had a long-standing interest in Ukraine. In 2014, he responded to a pro-European uprising in Kyiv by annexing Ukraine's Crimean Peninsula and coordinating a counter-rebellion in the Donbas, a region subsequently controlled in part by Russia-installed rebels. By the end of the decade, it had grown into a brooding obsession.

The crisis had been growing since autumn 2020 like a fog rolling in. First, Putin had sent troops, tanks, and armored vehicles to Russia's western border with Ukraine and to Belarus, a brother state that Moscow had practically absorbed. The vehicles bore a curious white symbol: the letter *V*.

Next, Putin had issued a series of demands so imperious and swaggering you could only marvel at their audacity. He sought nothing less than the annulment of the security infrastructure that has governed Europe for the three decades since the Soviet Union's 1991 collapse. Further, he wanted the Biden administration to guarantee Ukraine would never join NATO, the United States–led military alliance set up in 1949 to contain the Soviet Union.

Additionally, Russia's president demanded that NATO take its forces and equipment out of European countries that had once been Cold War satellites: Romania, Bulgaria, Poland, the Baltic states. These countries had joined NATO after 1997; now Moscow wanted to wind the clock back. Putin's apparent goal was to re-create the USSR's sphere of influence that had existed across the European continent behind what Winston Churchill called an "iron curtain."

This zone encompassed Belarus and Ukraine—"historic" Russian lands, as Putin saw them—unjustly separated from Moscow by Bolshevik blunder and Western meddling.

Diplomatic attempts to appease him—a trip to Moscow by France's president, Emmanuel Macron, and the offer of a superpower summit from the White House—had gone nowhere. Meanwhile, new Russian tactical battalion groups assembled on Ukraine's borders. Satellite images revealed an array of lethal modern weapons: Sukhoi fighter jets, Buk anti-aircraft missile systems, short-range artillery, fuel and transport vehicles.

On that Monday, two days before my borsch invitation, Putin held an extraordinary summit of his security council, Russia's top decision-making body. His spy chiefs, senior government colleagues, and foreign minister all gave their support for a plan to recognize the Donetsk and Luhansk "people's republics"—DNR and LNR—as independent. It was a bizarre display of fealty in Moscow. Whatever misgivings council members may have had were left unsaid.

Putin's decision pushed the button on a broader Russian military intervention in Ukraine, which has been a sovereign state for thirty years. The DNR and LNR claimed territory in the Donbas that was under the control of Kyiv's pro-Western government, led by president Volodymyr Zelenskiy, a former TV star. An unsuccessful eight-year dialogue—named after Minsk, the Belarusian capital—over the status of these Russian-controlled zones was over. A terrible succession was dawning.

Putin was seeking to resolve these political questions of lordship and allegiance, language and identity, using tactics familiar from Russia's dark past: bombs, destruction, and the murder of civilians. Over the last decade, Russia had leveled Aleppo and other Syrian cities and demolished Grozny during two Chechen wars, the second as Putin came to power in 2000.

The immediate enemy this time was Ukraine, as well as its Atlanticist leadership. But the war that would play out in 2022 would be bigger and more epochal, a moment in which the world was forever transformed. Germany's chancellor, Olaf Scholz, called it a *Zeitenwende*—literally a times-turn, a turning point in history. It would mark the end of a period of relative peace that began in 1989 with the fall of the Berlin Wall.

To paraphrase Lenin, there are decades where nothing happens, and weeks where decades happen.

Russia's invasion would become the largest armed conflict on European territory since 1945: an attempt by one nation to devour another. From everywhere other than Moscow, it looked like a classic imperial raid against a refractory onetime colony. Putin's justification for his adventure seemed preposterous. His aim: to "denazify" and to "demilitarize" Ukraine, a country led by a Jewish president.

More plausible was the axiom that without Ukraine, Russia could never be an empire or a great power. There was the threat of example, moreover. Ukraine was home to millions of native Russian speakers. If it could become a successful Western-style democracy where critical voices were allowed, then so could Russia.

The consequences of invasion would be transformative, not least for international relations. In a matter of days unthinkable things happened. Sweden and Finland abandoned neutrality; Germany, pacifism; the United Kingdom, post-Brexit estrangement from European neighbors; Poland and Hungary, antipathy toward refugees. By showing solidarity with Ukraine, the United States and its allies found a role, a new moral purpose, and a collective resilience.

Russia's battle went beyond Ukraine. It was—to a large degree—a proxy war against the West. The *glavniy protivnik* was the United States—the chief adversary in dry KGB language— as well as other democratic governments that had armed the Ukrainians. Washington had sent ammunition and Javelin anti-tank missiles, London the Next generation Light Anti-tank Weapon (NLAW) system, the Baltic states additional hardware. These defensive shipments enraged Moscow.

As conceived in the Kremlin, the war was something else, too: a civilizational struggle. It was more akin to a medieval crusade than the wars of the past century. One ideological foe was decadent liberalism. In the view of the Russian Orthodox Patriarch, Kirill I, who defended and blessed Putin's endeavor, Europe was permissive and anti-family. The conflict's scope extended into a transcendent realm; Russia's armored vehicles were marked with a mystical Z. What the letter meant was unclear. It became the main propaganda symbol of Russia's invasion.

In sum, Putin wanted nothing less than a new world order. Since becoming Russian president in 2000 he had frequently complained about the post–Second World War international system. It led to American hegemony and triumphalism; to disastrous Western interventions in Iraq and Afghanistan; and to blatant encroachment by NATO into Russia's neighborhood, he said. Ukraine had become an anti-Russian project, Putin added, hatched by the CIA.

This state of affairs had become intolerable. It was time to end it. Russian foreign ministry officials were evasive about how this might come about. They promised a "military-technical" answer.

The dinner was special. Kurkov and his British wife, Elizabeth, had invited a handy group of guests: Brazil's ambassador to Kyiv, who was still in the Ukrainian capital after many of his diplomatic colleagues had fled; the head of the city's medical history museum, which had its own subterranean morgue; and two writers working for *Politico* and *The New York Review of Books*. I apologized for being late. Kurkov brought me a bowl of borsch. It was delicious.

There was honey vodka, Odesan wine, and pork zakusky. Kurkov passed around fascinating material taken from the files of the Bolshevik secret police. The daughter of a KGB general had discovered them in an attic after her father's death. They were source material for Kurkov's latest novel and included records of interrogations—some typed, others written in curling Cyrillic letters. The papers dated from 1917 to 1921, when the Red Army had swept away a short-lived independent Ukrainian parliament based in Kyiv and had reclaimed the city for Lenin's new Union of Soviet Socialist Republics.

Among the files were black-and-white photos of police suspects. They included three young men—one with crimped black hair, wearing a white blouse. Circus performers, the records said. There were portraits of a bourgeois young woman, smiling, debutante-like. And more conventional prison-style mug shots of arrestees with shaved heads. Most, I suspected, vanished into the vortex of the 1920s and '30s. Was history repeating itself a century later, with Moscow once more snuffing out Ukraine's independence with another invasion?

Despite the premonitions, war that evening seemed unreal. Surely, Putin was bluffing. His maximalist posture—on NATO and European security—was a gambit, was it not? The international community had listened politely to Putin's tirades, shot through with familiar anti-Western grudges and paranoia. In theory, Ukraine might join NATO. To say it couldn't would be to violate the country's democratic rights. But—whisper it in Brussels, where the headquarters of NATO is located— nobody expected Ukraine to join the alliance soon, if ever.

Putin, though, appeared to dwell in a strange and unreachable realm. He had gone beyond what you might imagine to be rational considerations of self-interest. The United States, the European Union, and the United Kingdom had threatened the Kremlin with massive consequences should it attack Ukraine. These included a package of devastating sanctions that would destroy Russia's economy if they were enacted. Did Putin really want to return Moscow to a pre-globalized existence sans Visa card payments, Big Macs, and aircraft parts— a sort of gray twenty-first-century USSR?

And then there was Kyiv. It was a colorful modern European city of three million people. With its cafés and restaurants, Bolt cars, and food-delivery guys on pedal bikes laboring up ancient cobbled boulevards, it felt like a cosmopolitan Berlin or Prague. You could order a taxi or an artisanal pizza by app. There was an art-house cinema and an underground bar not far from the French Renaissance opera house. (The bar was down a flight of steps, in an unmarked basement, open Wednesdays and Saturdays by password only.) A contemporary capital, in short, where hipsters navigated the hills on electric scooters.

That evening, on the brink of war, people were out and about as usual. Kyivites had come up with a term for a possible Russian invasion—"Day X"—never quite believing it would happen. I was staying in a hotel on Yaroslaviv Val. The street was close to the heart of the capital. I walked past pavement florists selling tulips from buckets and a violinist, busking in her usual evening spot and playing Edith Piaf's "La Vie en Rose." Mornings, I ate porridge in Paul, a French café frequented by the middle classes. Farther down the road, outside Bessarabia market, a homeless person lay on a piece of cardboard, asking for a mandarin.

It was inconceivable that Russian missiles might soon be landing amid such varied humanity and beauty. Kyiv's art nouveau mansions were painted in the faded colors of a Victorian stamp album: lilac, buff, cerise, and imperial green. My street was home to the Polish embassy. Across the road was the House of Actors, originally a synagogue, built in an imposing Moorish Revival style. Four doors farther along was a late-nineteenth-century building called the Baron's House, a neo-Gothic fantasy with a turret and two demonic gargoyles above the door.

These demons—human body and torso, bat wings, doglike faces—appeared to be in conversation, with each other *and* passersby beneath. They had seen and outlasted war, revolution, and Nazi occupation. Farther down the road was the neoclassical Renaissance hotel. One brick face was unadorned, save for an incongruous recess, carved sixty feet up. A solitary nude female figure sat in this niche, gazing down serenely.

The dinner done, I embraced Kurkov and his wife before leaving to walk home. Their flat, it seemed at that moment, had everything you might wish for in life: love, good conversation, books, paintings, and a tub filled with spring narcissi next to a kitchen window. Why would you ever leave such a place? But like most residents in the city, they had an emergency plan should the worst happen: to set off for their dacha one hour's drive west of Kyiv, in a seven-seater vehicle filled with gas.

Out on the street I took a call from a well-placed contact who had served in Ukraine's foreign ministry. He knew people, information, rumor. It was approaching midnight. The sky was a dark shiny velvet.

The invasion, he said, would begin at 4:00 a.m.

I slept little. The Russian operation began practically on schedule, soon after 4:30 a.m. local time. Distant explosions and the whine of car alarms were heard across the capital. A nation shook itself awake.

What had been foretold by the United States and other Western governments, by military experts, and—late in the day—by President Zelenskiy himself was actually happening. Putin was attacking and invading Ukraine. His apparent goal: the annihilation of a country, a culture, and its citizens. There had been danger signals, intelligence briefings shared among government agencies, diplomatic dispatches, sober assessments in *The New York Times* . . . and yet.

It seemed impossible in the twenty-first century. With imperial swagger, Russian troops, tanks, and planes were on the move. The disaster unfurled on a gray, ordinary Thursday morning, sprinkled by rain. By 5:00 a.m. friends and loved ones were calling each other, peering into their phones, clicking on news updates, and making existential decisions. Stay or flee?

Some packed and got ready to leave. Others took refuge in apartment building basements, wondering if the horror might pass. Alerted by colleagues, I threw on my boots and coat and took the stairs to the hotel's underground garage. The floor filled up with staff and guests. A family arrived. A mother shepherded her two children to safety. The kids perched on chairs. They were carrying coloring books. The war was no longer abstract, a matter for opinion columns and think tanks. It was a bringer of random death, if not to these children, then to others.

By breakfast the scale of Russia's multitudinous military assault became apparent.

Putin's ambitions, it turned out, went beyond the Donbas, where—he tendentiously claimed—a "genocide" was going on. They included pretty much the entire country: east, south, north, and even west. The port city of Mariupol, on the Sea of Azov; Ukraine's second-largest city, Kharkiv, home to 1.5 million people; Odesa and Kherson, on the Black Sea; Ukrainian-controlled towns on the eastern front line—all were being bombed and pulverized.

Russia was clinically targeting Ukraine's defenses: airports, military bases, ammunition dumps. It was shock and awe, done with a ruthless indifference to human cost. Sleep-deprived, it was hard for me to make sense of Moscow's developing war plan, but the bold strokes were visible. An attempted blitz-krieg was under way. The ultimate target was Kyiv and its U.S.-backed government. Putin, you suspected, would wish to kill or capture Zelenskiy and to replace him with a pro-Russian puppet governor and administration.

Amid this ferocious onslaught there were moments of normality. The bombs didn't appear to be close, so I ventured outside. It was cold, just above zero. I wore a flak jacket and a woolly hat. A few residents were walking their dogs. The first queues had formed outside cash machines. Most shops and cafés were closed. But Aroma Coffee had opened as usual, selling croissants and takeout, as if nothing very remarkable had happened.

Among the locals I spoke to that morning, the mood was one of shock, fear, and quiet disgust that Putin—without cause or reasonable pretext—had decided on war. I passed by the Golden Gate, a Soviet replica of an early fortification built by Prince Yaroslav the Wise during the times of Kyivan Rus, the city's early medieval dynasty. Twenty-four hours earlier a floppy-haired guitarist had been singing Oasis numbers in the gardens. Now it was deserted. Its metro station would soon become a bomb shelter.

I turned left toward the old city and its cathedral square. Kyiv's familiar sights were intact. The bells of Saint Michael's monastery tolled the hour, as they had in ages past. The gold-domed cathedral sits across the plaza from Saint Sophia, a second great cathedral that dates from the Byzantine eleventh century. I took a photo of Saint Sophia's baroque turquoise bell tower, just in case. The ensemble of religious buildings is close to the headquarters of the SBU, Ukraine's security service, at number 33 Volodymyrskaya; to the offices of the border guard; and to Kyiv's city police department.

All were obvious targets for Russian bombs. The monument to Bohdan Khmelnytsky, the seventeenth-century Cossack leader, was still in place. Khmelnytsky sat on a black horse across from Saint Sophia, his mace pointing to the northeast, toward Russia.

The square's playground was empty, home now to a few jackdaws and a dog. With scant traffic, the birdsong seemed louder. I walked down Mykhalivska Street toward Maidan Nezalezhnosti, which translates as Independence Square. This was the scene of the 2004 and 2014 uprisings against the country's pro-Russian elites. At its center was a column signifying Ukraine's independence, a gold statue of a woman holding a rose branch perched on top. How long would she remain there? Statues came and went. An empty plinth marked where Lenin once stood, at the bottom of Shevchenko Boulevard.

The Maidan was normally busy with tourists and shoppers, stopping for lunch in the food court of the Globus Mall. They had vanished. A few people waited in the rain for a trolley bus. A coffee kiosk had opened up. I spoke to a customer, Viktor Oleksiivych. "Russia is one hundred percent wrong," he told me. What would he do now? "I'm going to take my grandson out of the city, and then I will come back," he said. "I don't have any weapons, but I'm ready to defend my country."

Viktor said he had phoned his son when he heard the first Russian explosions rock the city's outskirts. He turned on the TV. He had watched Zelenskiy address the nation, introduce martial law, and urge citizens to be calm. "Putin is the aggressor here," Viktor told me. "He's invaded Ukraine because we don't want to live under his strictures, his model." The model—feudal domination by Moscow—was, Viktor said, unappealing.

Another customer, Liudmyla—a young city police officer who had popped out for coffee—said she would carry on. "I didn't sleep last night," she said. "I tried to sleep before work, but I couldn't manage it.

"Cheerio," she added with a grin. She returned to her office.

Three Ukrainian soldiers in uniform joined the Maidan coffee queue. They were cheerful. Oleh Olehovych, a thirty-year-old officer, said he had been summoned at 4:00 a.m. His office was in the center of the city. "Civilians are leaving. But we will stay," he said. Could Ukraine defeat mighty Russia, with its vast airpower and Black Sea navy? "We will smash them," he said. "The military is in good shape; our communications are working."

During these first hours of invasion, shaped by confusion and dread, the nation's fate was hard to predict. Ukraine's armed forces were in better shape than in 2014, when they wilted under superior Russian firepower. Everyone said so. It appeared to be true. On paper, Ukraine had 220,000 troops, plus 400,000 veterans with combat experience, and modern weapons. A smaller force than Russia's, for sure, but these soldiers were motivated, ready to defend homes and families.

And yet the cars streaming out of Kyiv told another story. From early in the day the streets were jammed, as civilians sought a way out—to Zhytomyr, west of Kyiv, and from there to Lviv and the Polish border. Traffic on the boulevards moved slowly and sometimes not at all. A great exodus had begun. It would grow into Europe's largest refugee crisis since 1945. There was no panic as such, but a sense that this newborn war would get dramatically worse.

Reports suggested enemy formations had already crossed the international checkpoint and the border with Belarus. This was two hours' drive and 160 kilometers to the north, beyond the city of Chernihiv. The Russians were trundling Kyiv-ward through a primordial landscape of pine trees and swamp. It seemed Belarus's dictator, Aleksandr Lukashenko, was facilitating war on Kyiv, too, at Putin's personal request.

The war had lent Kyiv a new and frantic tempo. The city moved faster and with greater intensity and purpose than before, as if a million separate atoms had been disturbed and violently shaken. A couple of cars and a yellow municipal bus sped down the Khreshchatyk, rolling past a sign that read: I ♥ UKRAINE. It was 9:00 a.m. We were four hours into invasion day—February 24, 2022. The date, you imagined, would take its place alongside other storied ones—September 1, 1939, and September 11, 2001.

Nearby the Ukrainian national anthem rang out from a loudspeaker inside the trade unions building. Few were around to hear it. The office overlooking the Maidan had played a key role in the uprising eight years previously that saw then president Viktor Yanukovych flee to Russia. The "Heavenly Hundred" road leading up to the main administration complex was lined with shrines to demonstrators shot dead by Yanukovych's security forces.

Since 2014 this European country of forty-three million people had moved in an emphatically pro-EU direction. Its progress had been imperfect but dogged. Putin seemed determined to stop Ukraine's westward integration forever. Paradoxically, his theft of Crimea and war in the east had consolidated Ukrainian nationhood and identity. Differences that once existed melted away. The war made everything simpler. Putin and Russia were the enemy; a struggle for survival had begun; defeat meant subjugation and extinction.

It was Mikhail Bulgakov, in his masterful novel *The White Guard*, written a century ago, who dubbed Kyiv "the City," with an uppercase *C*. Bulgakov had lived on Andriivskyi Descent, a street linking the upper town with Podil. The City, it seemed on that unhappy morning, would endure. It had lasted more than a thousand years. But how much of it would survive? And would Ukraine—some of it, all of it—gain new, harsher Russian masters?

TWO

Lost Kingdom

Siberia
March 2021

And Kyiv, decrepit, golden-domed,
This ancestor of Russian towns—
Will it conjoin its sainted graves
With reckless Warsaw?
—ALEXANDER PUSHKIN,
On the Taking of Warsaw

In spring 2021, Vladimir Putin went on a short vacation. His destination was the snowy forests of Siberia. Accompanying him on this weekend trip to the taiga was Sergei Shoigu, Putin's regular hiking companion. Shoigu had been appointed as Russia's defense minister in 2012, and he was one of the most influential members of the president's inner circle.

Photos released by the Kremlin's press service show the two men relaxing in a blue-skied wilderness of mountains and conifers. Putin took the wheel of a lumbering all-terrain vehicle painted in khaki colors, a *vezdekhod*. Shoigu sat in the front passenger seat. They went for a ride, traversing streams, snowdrifts, and picturesque gullies between pine trees. Putin shook snow from his traditional Russian felt boots.

The two men were dressed in matching sheepskin coats. Neither was exactly young—Putin was sixty-eight, Shoigu sixty-five. Shoigu showed Russia's leader a workshop where he modeled wood. Afterward the minister and the president sat in the open air at a wooden table, drinking tea from metal camping mugs. There were plates of sausage and sauerkraut, as well as a cucumber and tomato salad. "Good. A beautiful location," Putin declared.

It was a bucolic private spot—and, it appears, the place where an extraordinary scheme was discussed. The plan was breathtaking in scope: to reclaim a lost kingdom. Russian imperialists referred to this hallowed place as "Little Russia" or *Malorossiya*. Its modern-day incarnation was Ukraine. It was the second-biggest country in Europe, after Russia—twice the size of Italy and a little smaller than the state of Texas.

Not that Putin held Ukraine in much esteem. He had long believed it to be sub-sovereign, a "cobbled-together country" with six million Russians, according to former Polish foreign minister Radosław Sikorski. Its continued existence more than three decades after the end of the USSR was a growing threat, the president fervently believed. As he saw it, this situation could no longer be tolerated.

We don't know what Putin said to Shoigu, or who else they may have met. One version—told to me by Lviv's ebullient mayor Andriy Sadovyi—is that the pair consulted with a Siberian shaman. The shaman gave the president a prophecy: that he was destined to redeem Russian lands. Banging a drum, he recommended a date for Putin to begin this great and historic task, one that had a mystical significance: 02/22/2022.

This alluring story is unprovable. But the weekend, which also featured a tramp through the slopes to watch wild animals, coincided with several verifiable public developments. The day before he flew off to Siberia, Putin celebrated the seventh anniversary of his annexation of Crimea with a rally at Moscow's Luzhniki Stadium. Crimea's "reunification" with Russia had righted a historical injustice, he told crowds waving white, blue, and red Russian flags.

It was Shoigu who had brought this about. Russian special forces under his command led the 2014 military operation to seize the peninsula. These "little green men" occupied the regional parliament building in Simferopol and other strategic locations. With Kyiv in turmoil, the Ukrainian army had been powerless to stop what was an efficient Russian coup, legitimized soon after via a Kremlin-organized "referendum."

Shoigu followed this successful mission with one in Syria a year later, when Russian forces intervened on the side of President Bashar al-Assad. The move rescued the regime in Damascus, now Russia's closest ally in the Middle East. It was Moscow's first military deployment outside the borders of the former Soviet Union since the Cold War. It exorcised, perhaps, the ghosts of communist Moscow's disastrous foreign war in Afghanistan.

Shoigu was quiet-spoken, a founder of the ruling pro-Putin United Russia party, ambitious, and deeply hawkish. He enjoyed the president's trust. Some saw him as Putin's successor—not that the president indicated any willingness to step down. Critics said Shoigu was an insubstantial person, a yes-man in meetings, and someone who was better at PR than military matters.

The minister appeared to share his boss's strong religious

faith. Largely unnoticed in the West, Shoigu was the first defense minister since the Russian Revolution of 1917 to cross himself in public. He was a devout patriot, loyal to the Russian Orthodox Church and to its patriarch, Kirill, a close Putin ally who had described Putin's presidency without irony as a "miracle of God."

Money flowed into the army's budget, with Shoigu overseeing a major program of modernization and military expansion. Under Shoigu, the Russian army enjoyed unusual prestige. As Andrei Soldatov, an expert on Russia's security services, noted, the Russian armed forces were outside political decision-making during Soviet and imperial times. Now, the general staff in Moscow appeared to be a more significant institution than the FSB, or Federal Security Service, the domestic spy agency Putin used to run and whose cadres he had formerly promoted.

Shoigu took the lead in implementing the Siberian plan. When Shoigu got back from break, he issued a series of orders. Their consequences soon became visible—revealed by a series of car drivers and later confirmed by U.S. intelligence and former White House press secretary Jen Psaki. Dashcam footage showed Russian military hardware, lots of it. It was going south and west, toward Ukraine.

The purpose of this military deployment wasn't immediately explained. But it amounted to a vast demonstration of weaponry: the biggest since Russia's Crimea invasion and war in the Donbas, which was still going on. One video showed a convoy of Msta self-propelled howitzers trundling over the Kerch Strait to Crimea via a railway bridge connecting the peninsula to the mainland.

Another showed armored vehicles in the southwestern city

of Voronezh, about 150 kilometers from Ukraine's border. The units had arrived from all over Russia: Pskov, Dagestan, and the Kemerovo region. They included T-72 tanks previously used in fighting around Donetsk, and a column of "Hurricane" multiple rocket launchers, spotted near Voronezh and parked up next to a motorway bridge under charcoal-colored clouds.

This display might be read as a riposte to Washington. Shortly before Putin's Siberian vacation, President Biden was asked by ABC News if he thought Putin was a "killer." He replied: "Mm-hmm, I do." It might also be read as a warning to the Zelenskiy government, which was refusing to recognize the LNR and DNR as independent political entities, a key Moscow demand.

While striding over the taiga, Putin had dressed up as a wanderer and man of the woods. It was the latest in a series of costumes. Over the years, the president had dramatized many roles for the camera: scuba diver, horseman, martial artist, ice hockey star. Some had wondered whether his lack of self-awareness said something profound about his psychological state.

Putin was also a naturalist. He had flown with cranes in an ultralight aircraft. And—together with Shoigu—he had cradled a (tranquilized) tiger in a forest. (The animal, according to reports, was sourced from a zoo. It died a few days later.)

Ultimately these were merely performances. When he returned to Moscow, Putin took on a persona that had real-world implications. It required no physical prowess. The effort was mental. The consequences—for Ukraine and Russia itself—would be devastating.

Putin became an amateur historian.

. . .

At home in the Kremlin, Putin examined what he called "the Ukrainian question." Working in isolation, he called up books, files, and papers. Putin's usual reading matter was composed of classified reports. This new material was open source. The result of his labor was a five-thousand-word article. It appears to be his own work. His focus was no longer current affairs but the distant past, shimmering like a vision before him.

Published on the president's website on June 12, 2021, the essay is titled "On the Historical Unity of Russians and Ukrainians." Putin lays out his controversial thesis in the first paragraph. He says he is returning to an idea he has long considered to be true: that Russians and Ukrainians are "one people." The word in Russian is *narod*. They are, he writes, a "single whole."

By way of proof, Putin goes back more than a thousand years to the misty origins of Russian civilization. He argues that today's Russians, Belarusians, and Ukrainians are all descendants of Kyivan Rus, or what he calls ancient Rus. The territory encompassed the city-states of Kyiv, Novgorod, Pskov, Lagoda, and Chernigov. All shared the old Russian language, the ruling Rurik dynasty, and Orthodox Christianity, he asserts.

From the outset there are omissions in Putin's version. The founders of Kyivan Rus in the ninth and tenth centuries were Vikings who arrived by river, not Slavs. The word *Rus*— pronounced *Rooss*—means "men who row." Its etymology is Scandinavian. Modern state boundaries and modern national identities were formed much later.

These early Scandinavians, it is true, assimilated into local culture. Kyiv—or Kiev, in Russified spelling—is at the heart of what Putin regards as a proto-Russian world. "The throne of Kiev held a dominant position in ancient Rus," he writes. He cites the city's great king, Prince Vladimir, who was "Prince of Novgorod and Grand Prince of Kiev." It was Vladimir, or Volodymyr, as Ukrainians know him, who in 988 converted Rus to Christianity, a seminal chapter in Russian history. This religious "affinity" continues today, Putin notes.

Putin relies heavily on a twelfth-century chronicle, *The Tale of Bygone Years*, compiled in Kyiv by a monk named Nestor. One subject is an early and possibly Nordic Kyivan Rus ruler known as Oleg the Prophet. Putin quotes Oleg's famous line from the chronicle: "Let Kiev be the mother of all Russian cities."

Subsequently this East Slav princedom fell into "fragmentation and decline," Putin writes. The president blames foreign intrigue for Rus's woes, in the early medieval period and later. There were the Mongols, who ravaged many cities in the mid-thirteenth century, including Kyiv in 1240. And then there were the Poles and Lithuanians, who incorporated what Putin calls "southern and western Russian lands" into an alien Catholic grand duchy.

Harmony with Russia was restored, Putin writes, when the Cossack leader Bohdan Khmelnytsky asked the king of the Polish-Lithuanian commonwealth to defend the rights of Orthodox believers. Unsuccessful, he turned to the Russian tsar Alexei Mikhailovich, who offered protection to his "brothers in faith." In 1654, Kyiv "swore allegiance" to Moscow, Putin recounts.

The areas under Russian control flourished, the president adds. This was broadly the left bank of the Dnipro—much of today's Ukraine. Farther lands were incorporated into a "single unified state" that included Crimea, which Catherine the Great annexed in 1783. This "gathering of lands" came about because of common language, faith, and culture, Putin argues.

In his view, Ukraine was never a real country, he once told U.S. president George W. Bush. Foreign elites sought to promote this "concocted" idea—Poles and Austro-Hungarians in the nineteenth century and Germans in the twentieth. Meanwhile, Ukrainian nationalists exploited "turbulence" in Russia during and after the First World War to proclaim their own independent state—an "inherently unstable" one.

The essay is at its most striking when it discusses the twentieth century. Putin had been accused of wanting to re-create the USSR. This may be true in a territorial sense. The essay makes clear, however, that he reviles the man who established the Soviet Union, and whose waxy body still sits incongruously in a mausoleum in Red Square. Vladimir Lenin is to blame for Ukraine, Putin's essay asserts.

It was Lenin who, in 1922, recognized the Ukrainian Soviet Socialist Republic. By handing Ukraine autonomy, Lenin planted "a dangerous time bomb under the foundation of our statehood." In 1954, Nikita Khrushchev compounded this crime by gifting Crimea to Ukraine. When the Soviet Union fell apart, Ukraine became independent. Russia was, according to Putin, "robbed"—of people, lands, and coreligionists.

Putin returns to a familiar theme in the last part of his article. It amounts to a grumpy denunciation of America and Kyiv's current Western outlook. Under U.S. tutelage Ukraine was an "anti-Russian project," Putin sneers. Contemporary Ukraine is a place where neo-Nazis are indulged, ethnic Russians murdered, "spiritual unity" thrown aside, and multigenerational ties of family and friendship forged in the struggle against German fascism forgotten.

He ends on a menacing note. It is unambiguous, clinically stated. From now on it is Moscow that will determine Ukraine's future.

"I am confident that true sovereignty of Ukraine is only possible in partnership with Russia," Putin warns.

The essay was, by any standard, an extraordinary document. It was arguably the most important text or decree issued by Putin during his long years as president and prime minister. It was a manifesto for upheaval and revisionism.

The article owes a debt to Russian novelist Alexander Solzhenitsyn. In 1990, Solzhenitsyn wrote a pamphlet called *Rebuilding Russia*. It articulated the same Putinite views: that Russia, Belarus, and Ukraine all emerged from Kyivan Rus. Were it not for the "terrible misfortune" of "Mongol invasion and Polish colonization," the people of these "three branches" would still be together, Solzhenitsyn wrote. He decried Ukraine's "reckless" modern "separatism."

Solzhenitsyn added a caveat: "Of course, if the Ukrainian people really wanted to secede, no one would dare to keep them by force."

This, however, is precisely what Putin was now contemplating. His own derivative essay laid out what Eugene Rumer and Andrew S. Weiss of the Carnegie Endowment in Washington called a "historical, political, and security predicate" for invading Ukraine. Ukraine was never a country. Ergo, seizing it was not an act of aggression. Rather, it was an act of restoration, similar to the rejoining of East and West Germany.

Russian commentators agreed on its chilling implications. *Moskovsky Komsomolets* called it a "final ultimatum to Ukraine." It presaged something "very big," the pro-Kremlin paper thought—a declaration of war, almost. Speaking to the radio station Echo of Moscow, sociologist Igor Chubais said it opened a "Pandora's box" that meant the "endless redrawing of borders in post-Soviet space."

Western readers were unimpressed. One Cambridge professor emeritus told me Putin's undergraduate foray into academia merited a 2.2 (roughly the equivalent of a C grade). Experts cited by the Atlantic Council said the article conveyed "nothing new," was "the latest example of gaslighting by the Kremlin leader," and was "an expression of imperial agony." Adjectives included "amateurish," "chauvinistic," "historically incorrect," "distorted," and "condescending." Putin had demonstrated he didn't understand Ukraine, they agreed.

Certainly, the article had myriad flaws. Ukrainians I spoke to in Kyiv were contemptuous. Why should Ukraine answer to Russia if when Kyiv was founded in the tenth century, Moscow was a mere forest or bog? The text also ignored the autonomous Cossack period in the fifteenth, sixteenth, and seventeenth centuries when the areas that would later become independent Ukraine enjoyed a long period of self-government.

The original Cossacks were nomads, freemen and freebooters, according to historian Serhii Plokhy in his masterful study *The Gates of Europe*. They lived off the steppe, beyond settlements, and were bandits, trappers, and fishermen. This brotherhood evolved into an officer democracy. The Cossacks would elect military commanders, known as hetmans, who ran free territories without fixed boundaries.

The Cossack political model was contractual. A chief had

obligations to his subordinates and could, if necessary, be removed. The Hetmanate was a place of mutual rights, in contrast to absolutist Russia. Successive tsars diluted its privileges and identity, until under Catherine the Great it vanished altogether. Cossack ideas laid the foundation for modern Ukrainian statehood.

Putin's argument on Crimea was equally specious. When Catherine's imperial generals conquered Crimea, it was a longtime home to Crimean Tartars. They formed more than 80 percent of the population, together with Cossacks. The indigenous Muslim Tartars—deported by Stalin and persecuted by Putin—were written out of the picture. It was a classic example of what academic Andrew Wilson, writing for the London think tank Royal United Services Institute (RUSI), called "settler colonialism."

What's more, the president mentioned but glossed over the repression of Ukraine's language and literature. In the nineteenth century, Russian authorities enacted strict censorship measures. They feared Ukrainian cultural "separatism" might have political implications. Leading Ukrainian intellectuals were arrested and internally exiled, including the national poet and former serf Taras Shevchenko, who wrote in Ukrainian as well as Russian.

Religious texts, grammars, books, journalism, and even plays performed in Ukrainian were banned. The edicts were only abolished in 1905.

The most remarkable thing about Putin's polemic was what he left out. Nowhere does he consider what Ukrainians might wish for themselves. They seem to float outside his worldview as nonentities, rootless and without agency.

That same summer of 2021, Dmitry Medvedev, Russia's former president, described them as lacking "self-identification." They were, he said, mere "vassals."

Two months before Russia's invasion, I met with Olexiy Haran, a professor of comparative politics at the National University of Kyiv Mohyla Academy. He was a smart, engaging person, overworked during this latest political crisis, and casually dressed in a tracksuit. It wasn't the first time I had interviewed him. Back in 2014, soon after the Maidan revolution, which had driven President Yanukovych from office, we had met at his apartment in a high-rise building in Kyiv's northern suburbs.

Haran, a member of the Maidan's organizing committee, showed off the orange helmet, gas mask, and hammer he had taken with him to protests. (He didn't use the hammer.) He characterized the events that heady winter and spring as a "national liberation and anti-corruption movement." Yanukovych had dumped an integration agreement with the European Union in favor of a deal with Moscow. He behaved "like a Russian puppet," Haran said.

At the time, the professor was upset with some Western liberal opinions. Left-wing Harvard academics had written to him, he said, repeating Kremlin talking points. They had solemnly informed him—the organizer on the spot—that the Maidan was a "coup" carried out by Ukrainian fascists and the CIA. "We are talking about traditional Russian propaganda," he told me with exasperation.

In an open letter, Haran and other experts on post-Soviet Ukrainian nationalism pointed to the heterogeneous nature of the 2013–2014 antigovernment movement. Some of those who took part were nationalists, it was true. But others were liberals, socialists, and libertarians. The first protester to die was Jewish—a sixty-one-year-old builder and grandfather from western Ukraine.

The protests, Haran recalled, were initially peaceful. They had turned violent because of escalating police brutality and murder. Overstating the role of far-right actors ultimately served "Russian imperialism," he said. A few days after our conversation, Putin annexed Crimea in what Haran called a "pseudo referendum."

When we saw each other again, in December 2021, the messaging from Moscow was unchanged. Russian officials said neo-Nazis ran Ukraine, a claim that was nonsensical given the extreme right's poor performance during elections. I took the blue line on Kyiv's metro to Heroyiv Dnipra Station and met Haran on the third floor of a shopping center. We drank tea in a branch of Puzata Khata ("Hut of the Potbelly"), a rustic Ukrainian canteen.

Over the summer, Putin had withdrawn many of the troops he had sent that spring to Ukraine's borders. But he had left the hardware in place. Then, in autumn 2021, Russia's armed forces began a second buildup, bigger and more ominous than the previous one. The soldiers kept arriving. Military training exercises were under way on Ukraine's doorstep. Jets roared in the skies. A Pantsir air-defense missile system appeared in a snowy field next to a local primary school in Voronezh district.

The situation was troubling.

My main question was, would Putin attack Ukraine? Haran believed this to be likely. Having made a series of escalating statements and demands, it would be difficult for Russia's president to back down without presenting concrete gains, he felt. "The rhetoric from Moscow is very dangerous," he observed. Events had acquired a worrying "momentum."

There was also Putin's Solzhenitsyn-like essay on Russian history. Haran was struck by its anti-Bolshevism. Putin had spent the early and middle part of his KGB intelligence career serving the Soviet state. Now he was openly critiquing socialist ideas and Lenin's "nationalities" policy, which sought to eliminate Moscow's cultural domination and saw Ukrainian-speaking children taught in their own language. Lenin classified society along nonethnic class lines, with oppressors and oppressed, Haran explained.

Putin was not the only leader to wonder where Russia's boundaries started and ended—nor the first to convince himself that language equated with nationality. But he was the first in modern times to go right back to Russian imperial thinking. According to Haran, Russia's president was advocating principles first set out in the 1830s by Count Sergei Uvarov, education minister under Nicholas I.

Uvarov wrote a memo for the tsar setting down his thoughts on imperial politics. He came up with three concepts— Orthodoxy, autocracy, and *narodnost*. Haran wrote down these terms in Russian in my reporter's notepad. *Narodnost* was tricky to translate into English. One version was "national way of life"—a spiritual and cultural identity that flowed from the common Russian people, conservative in nature and shared between generations.

Like Putin, Uvarov was obsessed with Kyivan Rus, a holy grail chased throughout Russian history. Reclaiming Kyiv and the "western provinces" for Russia was essential to the imperial project, he believed. Putin, I was told, kept a bust of Nicholas I on his desk. "Putin is espousing the ideology of Russian tsarism," Haran remarked.

These explanations gave some context to Putin's thinking in these anxious weeks for Ukraine. But there seemed additional internal and external factors that might have been driving his behavior.

For a start, there were domestic considerations. Putin's power inside Russia was at its apex. In a mere matter of months, he had wiped out Russia's opposition movement, jailing Alexei Navalny, his biggest political enemy and most persistent critic.

In the summer of 2020, a team from Putin's old spy agency, the FSB, poisoned Navalny in a hotel room in the Siberian city of Tomsk. This team, as it happened, had been shadowing him for years. Their method was ingenious: the secret officers applied the nerve agent Novichok to the opposition leader's underpants. Navalny collapsed on board a flight back to Moscow.

Remarkably, however, he survived. After treatment at a hospital in Omsk and medical evacuation to Germany, Navalny recovered. He exposed the assassination plot with help from Bellingcat, the open-source investigators. Then, in January 2021, he flew from Berlin to Moscow to confront Putin—whom he dubbed "a thieving little man in a bunker."

Navalny may have calculated that his actions—brave, heroic, and maybe even foolhardy—would set off a revolution. As he expected, his arrest at the airport sparked countrywide protests. But Russian security forces quelled this mini revolt by beating up and arresting young demonstrators. The authorities rolled up Navalny's anti-corruption movement, which had released a documentary exposé of the president's lavish palace on the Black Sea. They also disbanded his network of local political offices.

By the time Putin published his essay, Navalny was sitting in a penal colony. His senior aides were in jail or exile. Independent media outlets were being extinguished one by one, like lights fading gradually into darkness. Russian journalists who had investigated the secret fortunes of Putin and his kleptocrat friends slipped out of the country. I knew many of these reporters. We had worked together on the Pandora and Panama Papers leaks.

Russia, it was clear, was entering a new phase of political development. The soft authoritarianism of the early Putin period had given way to full-blown totalitarianism. Dissent in any form was a crime. The Kremlin must have reckoned that in the event of a major war with Ukraine protests would be small in scale and containable, and that its well-oiled propaganda machine would prevail.

Meanwhile, the international situation appeared favorable, from Moscow's perspective. Putin had long regarded the West as weak and irresolute. Over two decades he had tested the United States and its allies with a series of highly provocative deeds. The response was limited and conventional. And so Putin doubled down, with further episodes of rogue behavior.

These shocking acts included the 2006 murder of a dissident ex-FSB officer, Alexander Litvinenko, who was poisoned in a London hotel with a radioactive cup of tea. FSB assassins carried out the hit. Less than two years later, Putin invaded Georgia. It was a dress rehearsal for events in Ukraine. In 2014, he took Crimea and launched the war in the Donbas. The Obama administration imposed some sanctions, but Russia shrugged them off.

Incredibly, Putin and his spy agencies then launched a comprehensive operation during the 2016 U.S. presidential election to help elect Donald Trump. The Kremlin correctly identified Trump as the candidate most likely to divide America and to discredit its democracy. Trump's obeisance to Putin is still not fully explained. Whatever its cause, the United States under Trump retreated from the world, to Russia's advantage.

President Biden tried to establish a more predictable relationship with Putin. In June 2021, they met at a summit in Geneva, Switzerland. Any normalization, however, was short-lived. Russian state media went back to portraying Biden in disparaging terms as decrepit. The proof, per Moscow: the United States' and other NATO countries' bungled withdrawal from Afghanistan.

Surveying the European scene, the Kremlin saw the same familiar signs of division, hesitancy, and poor leadership. Germany was in transition, with the untested Scholz taking over as chancellor from Angela Merkel, Putin's great EU adversary. The Brits were in disarray in the wake of Brexit, a project Moscow and its troll army had encouraged. And Macron—Putin's preferred European interlocutor—was preoccupied with the upcoming French presidential election in April 2022.

Besides, the Europeans relied on Russia to keep their houses warm. The completion of the Nord Stream 2 pipeline—running under the Baltic Sea and bypassing Ukraine—meant Berlin's energy dependency on Moscow was about to hit a new level. The Germans were always pragmatic about trade, Putin probably concluded, despite their professed commitment to human rights.

Haran and I agreed that while the stars all aligned to Russia's geopolitical advantage, this didn't wholly explain Putin's determination to impose his will on Ukraine. We wrapped up our tea meeting and walked off separately.

It was known that Putin did not use the Internet. He considered it a CIA creation. Instead, he relied on briefings from the shadow state in which he had served—Russia's spies and secret agents. What were they telling him about Ukraine? Would its population resist or welcome "Russian liberation"?

The following month, in late January 2022, I took a taxi across town to a nondescript gray office building. It was a Sunday afternoon. There was no sign on the entrance. I was the only visitor. I walked inside, gave my name to a guard, and proceeded through a cage-like turnstile. A silent official dressed in a business suit took me up to the fifth floor.

A sign upstairs proclaimed the office's clandestine function. This was the headquarters of Ukraine's foreign intelligence service, the FISU. Its job was to defend the state from external danger. Russia, clearly, was its main concern. I had come to talk to the bureau's director, Oleksandr Lytvynenko.

Bearded, congenial, English-speaking, and dressed in a wool sweater, Lytvynenko had been doing the job for six months. Ironically enough, he had trained in Moscow, completing a degree in the early 1990s at the federal security service's spy institute of cryptography and communications. He was a versatile person: a political scientist, civil servant, mathematician, major general in the army reserve, and a graduate of the Royal College of Defence Studies in London.

I left my cell phone outside. Lytvynenko invited me into his airy office. In one corner was an old-fashioned globe; we sat across a glass table in brown leather chairs.

Russia's buildup on Ukraine's borders was there for all to see; you could plot it on a map. There was a strategic urgency underlying Putin's machinations that was not fully explained: a sense of haste.

Was he perhaps ill? There had been rumors he was in poor health. Cancer, perhaps? Or steroid addiction, which might explain his puffy cheeks? A neuroscientist had written to me diagnosing Parkinson's disease, based on a review of the president's rare public appearances, in which he had difficulty moving his right arm. During meetings he appeared to be writhing, the doctor said.

Related to this was the more diffuse question of Putin's mental well-being. Most Ukrainians I spoke with thought the president had gone completely nuts. Others, including the distinguished historian of Russia Simon Sebag Montefiore, suggested that he was behaving rationally but within warped parameters.

Ukraine's former prime minister Yulia Tymoshenko shared this view, having negotiated with Putin one-on-one. She described him to me as "absolutely rational, cold, cruel, black evil." "He acts according to his own dark logic. He's driven by this idea of historic mission and wants to create an empire. It comes from a deep inner belief," she said. His objective was to "depersonify" Ukraine, strip it of its identity, she added.

And then there was the issue of ultimate concern, too awful to contemplate. Was Putin crazy enough to launch a nuclear bomb?

The Kremlin was notoriously impenetrable. The president's health records were almost certainly beyond the reach of MI6 and the CIA. Lytvynenko, too, said he couldn't judge whether the president was sick or deranged. He offered a more subtle portrait—of an aging leader, nearly seventy years old, whose isolation from the outside world had grown throughout the pandemic. In normal times Putin met with only trusted aides, in what was an Ottoman-style court. Now these contacts were even more limited.

Putin, it appeared, was terrified of catching Covid-19. He had become the planet's foremost exponent of extreme social distancing. He met members of his cabinet across a comically long table, his underlings seated many meters away. In time, this became a meme—a metaphor for Putin's estrangement from normal human company, and Russia's from the world community.

The president lives in an alternative reality, Lytvynenko told me. He explained: "He really believes Ukraine is a divided society with a Russophobic elite, corrupted and pro-Western. Beneath it is a brilliant population. It loves Mother Russia. And it will meet Russian soldiers with bread and salt"—the traditional greeting for visitors. Putin regards Ukrainians as "rural Russians," the intelligence chief said.

Putin's spy agencies were complicit in this fantasy, he added. Seemingly, the FSB had informed the president that a Russian takeover of Ukraine would enjoy popular support, with little meaningful resistance. This misconception would have large consequences. Putin seemed unaware of his own limitations, and to have surrounded himself with toadies. They confirmed his mythic prejudices.

"The agencies tell him what he wants to hear. It's a usual story in dictatorship. Putin is used to hearing what he wants, just like Stalin and Hitler." Lytvynenko continued: "Putin considers himself to be a brilliant spy." There were "more realistic people around him," including Valery Gerasimov, Russia's top general and chief of the general staff. "Quite a clever person," Lytvynenko said of Gerasimov. But generally speaking, members of Putin's court were imperialists who hated Ukraine.

Putin was not the first notable Russian with anti-Ukrainian biases, he added. He mentioned Solzhenitsyn and Bulgakov, the latter writing unsympathetically about national forces in *The White Guard*. Bulgakov regarded the idea of a Ukrainian state as a "kind of phantasm," Lytvynenko said. It was a folk myth supported by the rural intelligentsia and by peasants—and rejected in Bulgakov's novel by an urban and monarchist elite.

Even Alexander Pushkin was not immune to patriotic thinking. He wrote a poem celebrating Russia's capture of Warsaw and the crushing of an 1830 rebellion by Polish officers. This was a brutal episode that carried an imperial lesson for Kyiv.

Ukraine's situation was now "extremely different," the spy chief told me. Its thirty-year existence as an independent democratic state was a "fact of time," he said. Ukrainian support for NATO grew after Putin annexed Crimea and attacked the Donbas, making peaceful coexistence with Russia impossible. "We can name Putin as one of the fathers of Ukrainian nationalism," Lytvynenko observed wryly.

One of the reasons for the current crisis was ignorance in Moscow, he concluded. Ukraine had a "pretty good understanding" of its neighbor, but Russian expertise on Ukraine, on the other hand, was "very weak." Ukrainians spoke Ukrainian and Russian; Russians didn't understand the Ukrainian language or the country's culture. He added: "They consider us to be a lost province."

We spoke for an hour and a half. It was an illuminating conversation. Lytvynenko acknowledged the military situation was grave: invasion was "absolutely possible," he said. He had a final prediction: "If Putin attacks, he will lose power in one or two years."

War or peace—the decision on invasion seemed to be Putin's, and no one else's.

There was something else. It struck me that one additional factor was at work deep within the Kremlin. More than any other, this consideration may have influenced Putin's thinking.

It was intangible, veiled, a mystery—best visualized as a last battle, fought against a backdrop of clashing armies and shrill heavenly trumpets.

In 2012, Putin appeared in a documentary aired on Rossiya-1, a Russian state TV channel. It was called *The Second Baptism of Rus*. The program began with one of the president's favorite priests, Metropolitan Hilarion of Volokolamsk, delivering a piece to the camera.

The church leader walked along the sandy bank of a river. His location? Kyiv. Russia's Orthodox story began when "Prince Vladimir of Kyiv christened Rus in the waters of the Dnipro," Hilarion said. A new Christian civilization was born. Ever since, the same faith and values had united the *narod* (people) of Great, Little, and White Russia, he added.

The film included one biographical revelation. Putin said his mother had secretly baptized him when he was an infant. She kept the ceremony hidden from his father, also Vladimir, who in the 1950s was a low-level Communist Party functionary. Baptism, in an age of official atheism, "touched me and my family personally," Putin recalled.

True story or artful invention? Either way, there was ample

evidence of Putin's religiosity in his later years and of the collaboration between church and state. Successive patriarchs had secretly worked for the KGB. Now KGB officers who had served in the atheistic Soviet Union were professing loyalty to the Orthodox Church. Both groups saw Russia as the great spiritual guardian of canonical Orthodox Christianity.

They also attached a foundational importance to Kyiv. As Plokhy relates, in 2016, Putin unveiled an eighteen-meter-high statue of Prince Vladimir, complete with cross in one hand and saber in the other. The statue was erected opposite the Kremlin, in the center of Moscow. The foundation stone came from newly annexed Crimea, where, according to Putin, Vladimir was baptized.

Putin was joined at the ceremony by Patriarch Kirill and by Solzhenitsyn's widow, Natalia. I had spoken to her in 2008, shortly before her husband's death at age eighty-nine. She told me he'd felt passionately about Ukraine because it was the home of his mother's family. A week earlier, Solzhenitsyn had dismissed claims that Stalin had unleashed genocide on Ukraine in 1932 and 1933, when millions died of famine.

Her presence at the event was a sign that Putin shared Solzhenitsyn's conservative religious views and his dislike of Western secularism. Putin described Prince Vladimir/Volodymyr as a "gatherer and protector of Russian lands and a prescient statesman." He had "laid the foundations for a strong, united centralized state." Did Putin imagine himself, you had to ask, as a second Prince Vladimir?

Since 2014, the Kremlin and the patriarch had been promoting the concept of "Russian World" or *Russkiy Mir*—a transnational spiritual realm that encompassed Russia,

Ukraine, and Belarus, made up of ethnic Russians and Russian-speakers. This idea suffered a serious blow in 2018, when the independent Orthodox Church of Ukraine formally split from the Moscow Patriarchate.

The Russian Orthodox Church had congregations and property in Ukraine still, including the Kyiv-Pechersk Lavra, a sprawling monastery and cave complex, and one of the country's most important places of worship and veneration. But the church's influence was shrinking as parishes switched sides.

The schism was a further source of grievance for Putin. His invasion was a war of conquest, for sure. But it also had what the patriarch described as a "metaphysical component." It was, as seen in Moscow, a clash between darkness and light, a Manichean reckoning. For Ukraine to be saved, the evils of America and NATO had to be defeated.

In the dimming years of his presidency, Putin seemed preoccupied with his own place in history—and how he matched up with bygone kings and warriors: Ivan the Terrible, Peter the Great, Stalin. What would Putin's legacy be?

One of his heroes was Fyodor Ushakov, an eighteenth-century naval commander and admiral, celebrated for his success in battle. It was Ushakov who had defeated the Ottomans and who consolidated control of Crimea. In retirement he became a monk. And then—during Putin's presidency in 2001—he became a saint.

Ushakov's birthday appears to have held an occult-like significance for Putin as he embarked on his long-contemplated messianic project to reunite Ukraine with Russia. It was February 24, the day Putin picked to invade. With God, the patriarch, and a mighty terrestrial army on his side, victory may have seemed inevitable. The tide was favorable, history his to command.

Only one leader stood immediately in Putin's way. This person had not come from the KGB, or from any part of the system. He was only a former actor.

THREE

Servant of the People

Bankova Street, Kyiv
February 26, 2022

I'm here.

—VOLODYMYR ZELENSKIY

One winter evening, I walked up Hrushevskoho toward a row of government buildings. The Kyiv street is named after Mykhailo Hrushevsky, a historian whose bearded visage appears on Ukraine's fifty-hryvnia note. Hrushevsky was head of the Central Rada, the 1917–1918 parliament that proclaimed Ukraine's independence from Bolshevik Russia, and he was a revered patriot and intellectual.

Subsequent Ukrainian leaders did not always match up to the saintly Hrushevsky. During the years following the country's modern independence, the whiff of scandal was never far away. The accusation, inevitably, was corruption. And in the case of the gangster-like Yanukovych—who was caught cheat-

43

ing in the 2004 presidential election and who returned as president in 2010—selling out to Moscow.

There were other structural issues characteristic of post-Soviet states. Ukraine's oligarchs were so powerful, so unbudgeable, they constituted a permanent shadow government. The courts, prosecutor's office, and anti-corruption bureau were susceptible to political influence. The culture of paying bribes was entrenched. Large private fortunes were hidden offshore. Reform was elusive.

I passed the Verkhovna Rada, the Supreme Council or parliament, and stopped at number 5. It was a damp, cold, foggy day in late January. I showed my passport to a policeman in a dark blue uniform and entered through an ornamental gate. There was a formal garden with a sweeping view over the black Dnipro, and on the left, a turquoise neoclassical palace stood, brightly lit.

This was the Mariinskyi, the Ukrainian president's official residence, constructed in the eighteenth century for the tsar, and subsequently used by governors and as a museum.

I had come to see the palace's latest incumbent, who had been elected in a landslide nearly two years previously. With the threat of invasion hanging in the air, the president's press team had invited a group of foreign journalists for a briefing. Aides escorted us down a long corridor into a ceremonial reception room, decorated in French empire style with a lozenge-pattern floor. There was no lectern; a chair had been placed informally on a dais in front of blue-and-yellow flags.

Exactly on time the president walked in. Of medium height, five feet five inches, perhaps, boyish looking, he was dressed in a black suit and tie with a white shirt. The cameras clicked.

Three days earlier, he had celebrated his forty-fourth birthday. He arrived with a self-deprecating remark. At the time, Covid was racing around Kyiv. "Can I be without mask?" he asked his audience in English.

He nodded, gave us a ceremonial mini bow, and sat down with an "Oof."

Enter Volodymyr Zelenskiy.

I half expected him to remove a bicycle clip from his right ankle. Or to leap onto a stage and do a small theatrical kick in the air. This, of course, was the real president. But close-up it was hard to distinguish him from his alter ego, Vasiliy Petrovych Holoborodko, the fictional president from the hit Ukrainian TV comedy series *Servant of the People*. Holoborodko had done all of these things and more.

Where, I wondered, did Holoborodko end and Zelenskiy begin?

Between 2015 and 2019, Zelenskiy had played Holoborodko on the nation's TV sets. The actor was already well known as a versatile comedian and performer. He appeared in the popular show *Vecherniy Kvartal*, or *Evening Quarter*, and in 2006 won his country's version of *Dancing with the Stars*. *Servant of the People* made him a household name. Zelenskiy's character is a secondary-school history teacher who one day rants about impunity and misrule, themes familiar to every Ukrainian. A student secretly films Holoborodko's classroom outburst, and the clip goes viral online.

Holoborodko stands reluctantly for election after his students crowdfund his entry fee. He wins. As president, Holoborodko is a self-effacing everyman, a genuine and likable guy, unspoiled by fame. He cycles to work, turns up for his inauguration in a taxi, and squabbles with his ex-wife and his family. In office, he is decent and true to himself, an outsider and naif who unexpectedly finds himself bearing great responsibility.

Zelenskiy's friends from Kvartal-95, the production studio he founded, wrote the script. It was a classic fairy tale, a sort of Cinderella with oligarchs. Some of it was shot at the Mezhi-hirya estate outside Kyiv, where Yanukovych built himself a lavish Swiss-style chalet, together with a replica galleon and private zoo. The show was genuinely funny, a collective tonic during a traumatic period of revolution and war in the Donbas.

In 2018, during season three, the show received a cosmic twist, as if penned by the same capricious postmodern gods who gave America and the rest of humankind Donald J. Trump.

Zelenskiy announced he was going to run for president. Actual president—as in, doing the job for real. He registered *Servant of the People* as a political party. When I arrived in Kyiv in March 2019 on a study trip with the German Marshall Fund of the United States, Zelenskiy was leading in the polls. I met his campaign team in a modern office in the Pechersk district, close to the United Arab Emirates embassy. They were agreeable, new faces. About politics they knew little.

Like Vasily Petrovych, Zelenskiy wished to clean up public life. His campaign chief, Ivan Bakanov—later the head of the SBU intelligence bureau—said the candidate wanted to turn Ukraine from a "monster state" into a "service state." That meant repatriating offshore wealth and canceling immunity from prosecution for politicians.

On Russia, Bakanov admitted that Ukraine had an "existential problem." "We are the victim of bullying," he told me. Zelenskiy's solution was to sit down with Putin. As president, he would end the grinding war in the east with Moscow. This peace message worked. In the spring 2019 election, Zelenskiy trounced sitting president Petro Poroshenko, winning 73 percent of the vote.

That was the high point.

Zelenskiy hoped Putin might be appeased. In his first months in office Zelenskiy refused to call the Russian president an aggressor. His new government toyed with the idea of offering possible concessions to Moscow. One was the resumption of the supply of water from southern Ukraine to occupied Crimea, which was stopped when Russia annexed the peninsula in 2014.

This appeasement strategy bore a few results. There were prisoner exchanges in late 2019 and a series of short-lived cease-fires across the "line of control." Ukrainian forces pulled back. But it gradually became apparent that de-escalation wasn't really happening. Instead the Russian side accepted Zelenskiy's concessions and carried on shooting. More Ukrainian soldiers died.

Meanwhile, attitudes in Moscow toward Zelenskiy were beginning to harden. There was frustration that he would not yield to Russian demands in the Minsk agreements—the negotiating process between the two countries, which began in 2014, guaranteed by France and Germany. Putin demanded political recognition of the Donbas separatist enclaves, followed by the withdrawal of heavy weaponry and a cease-fire; Zelenskiy wanted the reverse sequence.

In the face of hardball tactics Zelenskiy took a tougher anti-Kremlin stance. In February 2021—weeks before Putin's fateful Siberian holiday with Shoigu—Ukraine's national security council closed down three TV channels controlled by Viktor Medvedchuk, an influential pro-Kremlin politician and oligarch. The TV stations were broadcasting Russian propaganda, the council said.

Medvedchuk was a Kremlin interlocutor and the most important leader for Russia within Ukraine. Putin viewed the shutdown as a "personal insult," Oleg Voloshin, a deputy from Medvedchuk's Opposition Platform party, told me. Putin was godfather to the oligarch's younger daughter. The authorities put Medvedchuk under house arrest and charged him with treason.

The Russian government decided that contact with Zelenskiy was pointless. "There is a deep conviction that Zelenskiy is a guy whom it doesn't make sense to try to discuss things politically," Fyodor Lukyanov, a foreign policy analyst whom I had known in Moscow, said. Ex-president Medvedev added that Russia had to negotiate directly with the "suzerain"—that is, with Washington.

By the time of our Mariinskyi Palace briefing, reality and comedy drama had parted company. Accommodation with the Russians had proved impossible, a naïve plotline that didn't land in real life. Zelenskiy was facing a geopolitical crisis. It was darker and scarier than anything his TV collaborators might have dreamed up. Many of them, though, had gone from show business into senior government posts.

In the weeks leading up to February 24, 2022, questions swirled about Zelenskiy's political judgment.

In the face of Russian aggression, the international community had shown solidarity with Ukraine. This support went beyond the rhetorical. The United States, the United Kingdom, and others were sending defensive arms to Kyiv, lots of them, flown in to Boryspil International Airport outside Kyiv by cargo aircraft. The Western allies had also raised the political stakes with Putin. The Biden administration had warned of massive consequences; should Moscow launch a full-scale attack, there would be unprecedented sanctions.

Zelenskiy, however, disagreed with Washington about the nature of the Russian threat. It was not a falling out as such but a difference of opinion. His response irked U.S. officials and undermined Western efforts in the face of a looming disaster.

The facts were these: some 120,000 Russian troops had massed on Ukraine's borders. General Mark Milley, the chairman of the U.S. Joint Chiefs of Staff, described the buildup as bigger "than anything we've seen in recent memory." He pointed to "ground maneuver forces, ballistic missiles, and air forces"—all "packaged together" to unleash destruction on Ukraine. If the operation went ahead, there would be heavy casualties in urban areas, Milley predicted.

The White House believed these Russian tactical battalion groups to be a potential invasion force. A Russian attack was "distinctly possible," Biden said. Some of the United States' European allies agreed, though France and Germany were more skeptical. So was the Anglo-American far left, which pointed to inaccurate claims made by Western intelligence in 2002 and 2003 about weapons of mass destruction in Iraq. The Kremlin, meanwhile, said it did not plan to invade Ukraine. It dismissed Pentagon assessments as hysteria.

Zelenskiy acknowledged a large-scale war might happen at any time. But he did not think the recent buildup was different from the tensions that had persisted since 2014. Speaking that January inside the palace, he described the Russian threat as "constant"—an eight-year war pursued against Ukraine and Europe. Ukrainian intelligence sources said Russia was piling pressure on Kyiv, for sure. But they viewed the latest Russian troop movements as part of a longer-term strategy to destabi-lize Ukraine and its internal politics.

Hyping the likelihood of attack ultimately served Moscow's interests, Zelenskiy said. It caused panic, depressed the econ-omy, spooked foreign investors, and ran down the country's currency and gold reserves. Why, he wanted to know, should Ukraine suffer and its "cynical" neighbor be rewarded?

The president, it was evident, had been stung by critics on social media who had compared his Panglossian attitude to the Netflix drama *Don't Look Up*. "We are looking up. We do understand what is happening," he told the assembled press. He added: "Yes, it may happen unfortunately. But you have to feel the pulse on a day-to-day basis." In the same way Biden had a better grasp of D.C., he understood the mood in Kyiv, Zelenskiy said.

One area of friction was the exodus of Western diplomats from the capital. The United States, Canada, and the United Kingdom had moved some staffers and their families to the western city of Lviv, five hundred kilometers away and close to the Polish border. They had suspended consular services. The diplomats had been relocated for safety reasons, U.S. Secretary of State Antony Blinken said. In other words, to avoid being bombed by Russia.

It was my turn to ask Zelenskiy a question. I wondered what he made of the Western diplomatic pullout from Kyiv. "Was this a mistake?"

The president agreed. "Yes, for us it was a mistake. I say this openly," he replied. Zelenskiy said he wasn't convinced by the argument that these were nonessential staff. Under these tense circumstances, everyone was essential. He pointed to the fact that the government in Athens had not pulled out its diplomats from Mariupol, a city with a Greek minority that was on the front line in the east with pro-Russian separatists.

"You can hear the cannon firing. The Greeks didn't take anyone away. This is such an important message." He stressed: "Everyone sees how Biden and the U.S. reacts. These are the captains of the diplomatic corps. The captains should not be leaving the ship. I don't think we have a *Titanic* here."

There was a murmur of relief among the reporters. The *Titanic* line was headline worthy. Zelenskiy left, surrounded by bodyguards who looked remarkably like their counterparts in *Servant of the People*.

In those fateful last weeks before the invasion, was Ukraine the *Titanic*, steaming inexorably toward a Russian iceberg? Or, in fact, was Russia the giant hubristic ship, headed for a nasty surprise?

As I returned to Independence Square and to the Maidan metro station, it struck me that most Ukrainians were happy to accept their president's reassuring posture. The commander in chief's message amounted to the famous Second World War propaganda poster slogan, now printed on virtually everything: keep calm and carry on. Or as Ukraine's deputy defense minister Hanna Malyar phrased it: "Take it easy."

On the streets of Kyiv that January I saw no visible preparations for war. The grandiose Stalin-era buildings that lined the Khreshchatyk, the capital's main shopping and business street, looked the same as when I had first visited Ukraine as the *Guardian*'s Moscow bureau chief, some fifteen years before. I had returned many times to report on the country's fractious politics. And, memorably, to watch Paul McCartney play a concert in 2008. I had stood in monsoon-like rain as Paul sang "Back in the USSR."

Even Kyiv's neoclassical city hall, home to the office of former boxer turned mayor Volodymyr Klitschko, seemed undefended. The head of the city's civil defense unit, Roman Tkachuk, said it would be unwise to tape up windows or pile sandbags next to the entrances of government offices. "This would cause concern," he said when we met. Despite the apparent lack of fortifications, he insisted: "We are ready for any emergency situation. We are highly prepared."

Kyiv had a network of five thousand bomb shelters, including forty-seven metro stations dug deep underground. There was enough space for the city's residents, he said, with purpose-built basements in hospitals, bread factories, and other facilities, plus plans to evacuate the old and infirm. "I will be the last person to leave the city. My family lives here. My mother is here. I'm not going anywhere," he said.

Eight decades earlier, Kyiv's Soviet defenders took a different view. They ran away, but not before booby-trapping the Khreshchatyk, which had been home to Communist Party officials, actors, and the secret police. In September 1941, the Wehrmacht swept in. German officers took over comfortable flats. The buildings were then blown up; the street was burned and destroyed; after the war it was rebuilt.

Modern Kyiv was deploying a less incendiary weapon. It was carrying on as normal. In the affluent Podil district, families strolled among festive lights and skated on an open-air ice rink. There were queues at the October Cinema for a screening of *Stop-Zemlia*, a prizewinning film about the lives of Ukrainian teenagers. Dos Amigos, a Mexican restaurant popular with the creative classes, was full of diners drinking amber beer.

But beneath this insouciance was a growing unease. Residents were making tentative plans about what to do in case of invasion. Mariia Hlazunova, a communications manager at Ukraine's national film archive, said she discussed the topic with her mother over coffee. "My mom said: 'I'm not interested in politics. What would Putin want with me?'" Glazunova added: "People who read the Internet are not so calm. But life goes on. We think about war, but we have to work and we need fun as well."

Zelenskiy skeptics alleged that he lagged behind events, as shown by his semi-row with Washington over the departure of diplomatic staff. "He's always two or three steps behind what is happening. He can't get out of his square box," one former senior Ukrainian diplomat told me. The diplomat blamed Zelenskiy's chief of staff, Andrii Yermak, for offering bad advice. "It's like it's theater, not fact," the diplomat grumbled.

Zelenskiy, it was true, seemed distracted by domestic grudges. That same month Poroshenko, Zelenskiy's defeated presidential rival, flew back to Kyiv from Switzerland. Prosecutors had accused Poroshenko, the owner of the Roshen confectionery empire and one of Ukraine's richest businesspeople, of selling coal to Russian-backed separatists. Western observers saw the case as politically motivated and mistimed.

The most serious critique concerned Zelenskiy's handling of relations with Moscow. During the 2019 campaign, Poroshenko espoused hard-line anti-Kremlin views. At the same time, he was careful not to offend Putin personally or to annoy Russia over Ukraine joining NATO. "Poroshenko played the game in a way that was understandable for the post-Soviet elite," one insider told me. "He knew not to cross Russia's red lines."

Zelenskiy, by contrast, had put NATO membership at the center of his country's foreign policy. By refusing to back down, he was steering his country toward disaster, his opponents said. They argued that he needed to find a pragmatic solution to the standoff with Putin by offering to make Ukraine a neutral state. They argued that the United States and the Europeans would go along with such a declaration—even breathe a sigh of relief.

"The Russians will keep going until Zelenskiy gets the message," Vasyl Filipchuk, a Ukrainian ex–foreign ministry spokesperson, predicted that January. "They want him to stop what they see as anti-Russian rhetoric. A statement on NATO would calm the situation down." The president was worried that a declaration of nonalignment would cause a right-wing backlash and hurt his ratings, Filipchuk added.

They had already fallen. In January 2022, Zelenskiy's approval rating was at 25 percent. The Holoborodko effect was wearing off. His party had experienced parliamentary scandals but was still more popular than his rivals. It looked as if he would be reelected as president in 2024—assuming, that was, that Ukraine and its democracy continued to exist.

The crisis brought Zelenskiy a procession of international visitors. They included Macron and Scholz. There were phone calls with Biden, a meeting with Vice President Kamala Harris at the Munich security conference, and conversations with the European Commission chief, Ursula von der Leyen, and other prominent world leaders.

In early February, I went back to the Mariinskyi Palace for another high-stakes press conference. This time it was UK prime minister Boris Johnson's turn to speak with Zelenskiy. Johnson was glad to swap London for Kyiv, it seemed. At home he faced embarrassing questions about parties held at his office in Downing Street during a period of strict Covid lockdown.

According to Johnson, Russia presented a "clear and present danger." Russia's president was trying to redraw Europe's map and to "impose a new Yalta, new zones of influence." He claimed this zone would include Georgia, Moldova, and other countries. Sanctions against Moscow would come into effect as soon as "the first Russian toe cap" crossed into Ukrainian territory, he promised.

I watched Zelenskiy closely. He was an effective and fluent speaker. But it was hard not to feel he was still somewhat behind the curve of history—struggling to respond to developments, and to the mighty storm bearing down upon him.

The differences with London and Washington were politely papered over. Johnson said a Russian incursion was "imminent." Zelenskiy said it was "possible." But not inevitable. He wanted sanctions now, not later. We made our way out via a back route that took us past the palace's kitchens.

The next days passed in a frightening blur.

The separatists launched intense artillery bombardments. False-flag events took place—a car bomb in Donetsk; a "shell" landing in Russian territory; the evacuation of civilians from rebel areas to the Russian city of Rostov. Then came Putin's meeting with his security council in Moscow.

And then, on February 24—bombs, explosions, fighting outside Kyiv, and a puissant armored raid from many directions. The Russian calculation was straightforward. The capital would fall in a matter of days. The Ukrainians would capitulate. Zelenskiy would flee.

.   .   .

Three days later, a gaunt, unshaven figure emerged into a white dawn. It had been a sleepless night punctuated by bombings and the rumble of attack, percussive blows thundering on the near horizon.

The person looked into his iPhone camera and pressed record.

"*Ya tut*," Volodymyr Zelenskiy said simply—"I'm here."

The president was still in Kyiv. He had failed to take Moscow's brutal hint that it was time to escape.

In the center of the capital, Zelenskiy stood, unbowed and defiant, his voice gravelly. "Good morning, Ukrainians! There's a lot of fake information online that I call on our army to put down arms and to evacuate. So this is the thing: I'm here. We won't lay down our weapons. We'll protect our country because our weapon is our truth. It's our land, our country, our kids, and we will defend all of them. That's it. That's what I wanted to tell you."

He finished: "*Slava Ukraini*! [Glory to Ukraine!]"

Zelenskiy had chosen the backdrop for his intimate forty-second video carefully, shared via his official Telegram social media channel. It was the House with Chimaeras. The art nouveau building designed by the Polish architect Władisław Horodecki is immediately identifiable. Everyone in Kyiv knows it. It boasts fantastic figures and gargoyles. There are elephants, rhinos, antelopes, lizards, toads, dolphins, and mermaids. The address—10 Bankova or Bank Street—is Ukraine's equivalent of 1600 Pennsylvania Avenue or 10 Downing Street.

A hundred meters down the road is the presidential secretariat, a newly sandbagged fortress. Lamps had been switched off, with the compound plunged into dim gray light. The night before, on day two of the invasion, Zelenskiy had made another video address from just outside the complex, accompanied by Defense Minister Oleksii Reznikov, Prime Minister Denys Shmyhal, and Andrii Yermak, the president's chief of staff. They hadn't fled either.

It had been a bruising night. The president had been inside as the Russians invaded, together with his forty-four-year-old wife, Olena Zelenska, as well as their daughter, Oleksandra, who was seventeen, and their son, Kyrylo, nine. At one point, Zelenska looked out the first-floor window of her presidential villa and saw a fighter jet scream past. It was unclear if it was Russian or Ukrainian. When the booms came close, she scurried downstairs with the children and their security detail to the basement.

"The enemy has designated me as target number one, and my family as target number two," Zelenskiy said. "They want to destroy Ukraine politically by destroying the head of state." The president hugged his wife and told her she and the children would be taken to a safe place. And then he carried on with his work.

The circumstances of war transformed Zelenskiy. In the words of *Guardian* columnist Jonathan Freedland, the president became Churchill with an iPhone. His natural abilities—warmth, likability, empathy, a sense of the street-level scale of things—were invested with a moral power. There was something heroic about his decision to stay in Kyiv, regardless of personal risk. It was clear the Russians would kill him if they got the chance. The operation to encircle the city and remove him from the political scene was under way.

Zelenskiy's allure was further enhanced by the unequal nature of his and Ukraine's struggle for survival.

Indeed, it was hard to think of the last time a conflict had

had such good versus evil clarity. There had been nothing like it since the Second World War, more than eighty years before. Putin had launched an imperial invasion, a war of blood and soil, as if the twenty-first century were the nineteenth, an epoch of Great Power squabbles. Ukraine was now involved in an anti-colonial battle for its existence, one with little prospect of instant success. As the political scientist Ivan Krastev put it, Zelenskiy was the leader of a "romantic constellation."

The Russians had overwhelming military superiority: warplanes, tanks, long-range cruise missiles, and nuclear weapons. Plus a well-honed domestic and international propaganda operation.

But Zelenskiy and his underdog team had soft power advantages of their own. If Moscow was closed—a state built on secrecy and lies—Kyiv was open and transparent. Its story was democratic and contemporary, progressive and digital. As the invasion unfolded, it would offer the world a master class in messaging and emotional outreach.

The people around Zelenskiy understood the power of narrative in war: how storytelling was itself a valuable weapon. It could be used to shore up morale at home and to galvanize support abroad, from places far away. Many of the president's advisers had a TV background. They were showrunners, some of them veterans from *Servant of the People*, who were now crafting real-time video updates from Europe's bloody front line.

Zelenskiy and his team were adept at linking Ukraine's current struggle with previous paradigm-shifting battles from history, imbuing the fight with mission and purpose. And they were familiar with pop culture. They presented the war as light versus darkness. In this *Lord of the Rings*–style drama, Russian soldiers were orcs—a word that entered everyday speech—Moscow was Mordor, and Putin an invisible Sauron.

Ukraine's armed forces, by contrast, were warriors of light.

As the world soon discovered, Zelenskiy was a superlative communicator. He was at ease in front of a camera; he took everything he knew from TV and applied it to the conversational idiom of social media. Yes, he was an actor. But it was evident from his iPhone appearances that he believed what he said. He spoke from the heart, an amplifier of the national mood. His public statements were delivered not from above, but horizontally, citizen to citizen, an act of truth-telling amid the fog of war.

The contrast with Putin could hardly be greater.

Eighty-five hours into the invasion, Reznikov tweeted a photo of himself with Ukraine's president. Zelenskiy had his arm casually draped around his defense minister's shoulder. The two men look tired but exuberant. They were not merely colleagues, the picture said, but friends and comrades. Around the same time, Putin met with Gerasimov and Shoigu. They sat at the far end of a long Kremlin table. There were no smiles. It was a chilly encounter with the Führer.

While Putin shrank from the world, Zelenskiy appeared to have grown. As a presidential candidate his interactions could be overlong, and his press conferences sometimes stretched for hours. Now his speeches were punchier. They rarely lasted more than ten minutes, and his words were carefully chosen.

The man who wrote them, I discovered, was a thirty-eight-year-old former journalist, Dmytro Lytvyn. He was little known outside Kyiv: when the war broke out, he had fewer than two hundred followers on Twitter. Lytvyn was an early supporter of the president's and had worked as political analyst for *Servant of the People*. He was a fan of books by Hunter S. Thompson—*Better Than Sex, Kingdom of Fear*—and admired the contemporary Ukrainian author Alexei Nikitin. Lytvyn was initially reluctant to discuss his writing partnership with Zelenskiy. "I don't like to talk much about it," he messaged.

When we met subsequently that April and August, he acknowledged the importance of his work for the president. "It's the first time a MacBook has become a weapon of war," he said, showing off photos of Zelenskiy holding his laptop in Bankova's situation room. Lytvyn was a shrewd observer of Russia. "Objective reality does not control him. He seeks isolation," he wrote of Putin. The Kremlin regime was a mix of North Korea and Nazi Germany, he told me as we drank coffee in the Milk Bar, a popular Kyiv café on Shota Rustaveli Street.

Before he joined the administration, Lytvyn worked as a columnist for *Levy Bereg*, a weekly newsmagazine named after the left bank of the Dnipro River. He was unimpressed with Ukraine's veteran politicians and its pre-Zelenskiy governments, in particular that of Poroshenko. "They don't have democratic feelings," he said.

Zelenskiy, by contrast, worried about ordinary people, Lytvyn said, regardless of whether they were "big or small." "He isn't just a leader; he's a historical leader. He feels his responsibility," he said. He added: "He has a presence. You always feel when he is there." Zelenskiy was "*dusha companii*," another aide told me—a magnetic personality at the center of any gathering, the one who picks up a guitar and sings to the room.

When Moscow's invasion started, Lytvyn moved into Bankova, with its network of tunnels. He slept in a room close to the president's. The facilities were basic: one shower for a hundred staff members. (Zelenskiy has his own.) His work as a speechwriter soon became an essential part of the war effort.

The ideas and the emotions behind Zelenskiy's speeches came from the president himself, Lytvyn said. He explained: "You talk to him. He has a lot of ideas. He says what he wants. He suggests a concrete form of words." Lytvyn would put together a draft. Sometimes the president would approve it. On other occasions, he would make changes if he thought the meaning wasn't clear enough, tapping away directly into Lytvyn's MacBook Air. "In his speeches emotions are the most important things," the ex-journalist stressed.

Serhiy Leshchenko, another former reporter turned wartime adviser, described Lytvyn as Zelenskiy's literary and creative assistant. He was a "co-artist," a joint executive producer in a Netflix-style blockbuster. "Dima [Lytvyn] collects the president's ideas each day. He then translates them into prose," Leshchenko said. One day the theme might be the barbarism of Russian soldiers, the next, Ukraine's need for defensive weapons from the West.

Lytvyn was available to Zelenskiy 24/7. As Kyiv came under fire from Russian artillery, he would eat meals in a subterranean canteen. There was no cell phone reception, so the canteen's landline—an old-fashioned phone mounted on a wall—would ring. Sometimes it was the president's office calling. A cafeteria worker would answer and shout across the room: "Is there a Lytvyn here?"

When Russian troops began shelling the Zaporizhzhia nuclear power plant—raising the specter of a Chornobyl-style nuclear disaster—Zelenskiy sent a security guard to wake his speechwriter. It was 3:00 or 4:00 a.m., Lytvyn recalled. "The president told me: 'We have to say something about this.' He was very concerned. It was an emotional moment. He worked on the text." Zelenskiy was determined to avoid the mistake of the Soviet politburo, which kept silent about the 1986 disaster for days afterward.

The president's crafted phrases could be memorable. Addressing the Russian people in Russian, just hours before Putin sent in tanks, Zelenskiy said his country did not wish war but was prepared to defend itself—its freedom, the lives of its people, and its children. "We know for sure we don't need war. Not a cold one, not a hot one, and not a hybrid one. But if we are attacked, we will defend ourselves. And when you attack us, you will see our faces, not our backs," he said.

There was another arresting quotation when foreign countries offered to take him from Kyiv to safety. Turkish president Recep Tayyip Erdoğan put a team on standby to exfiltrate Zelenskiy to Istanbul, I was told. The U.S. government also said it could help get him out, should the need arise to relocate the government to western Ukraine or to Poland, according to a senior U.S. intelligence official quoted by the Associated Press. The president's reply: "The fight is here. I need ammunition, not a ride."

Zelenskiy liked poetry, Lytvyn said. His speeches employed verse-like passages, marked by repetition, dramatic pauses, and vivid similes. Standing in a thick sepia fog outside the House with Chimaeras four weeks into the invasion, the president compared the marauding Russian troops to "otherworldly" and "hellish" creatures. They had arrived by "land, sea, and sky." They were "monsters" who "crawled and swam, burned and looted, attacked and tried to kill," he said, pointing at the surreal figures behind him. Dehumanizing language? Perhaps, but understandable given the breakdown for Ukrainians of the boundaries between reality and nightmare.

Lytvyn said Zelenskiy had thought of the "chimaeras" analogy and had insisted on filming the speech outside. He selected the camera angle. The president's on-set decisions were explicable: he was a professional, after all. They sometimes exasperated the Ukrainian commandos assigned to protect him from Russian assassination. A guard can be seen patrolling uncomfortably up and down in the rear of the shot.

"You must know Zelenskiy is not a bunker man. Even in the first weeks, he didn't sit in it," Lytvyn said. The president insisted that he visit different places, including the front line, making "the security men very stressed with him," the speechwriter added.

Zelenskiy's monologues became essential viewing. Their audience was local—and global. There were updates from the battlefield, a reckoning of victories and defeats. When Ukraine lost ground, he said so. Each night he bestowed awards to members of the armed forces, many of them posthumous ones. These were given to relatives in the same palace hall where in early February I had watched his and Boris Johnson's press conference. The president's bulletins ended with a defiant shake of the arm and the words "*Slava Ukraini.*"

It was hard not to be moved. One German TV interpreter burst into tears. In the first days of the invasion, you wondered if you were being addressed by a future ghost, a dead man walking. Zelenskiy said as much in a conference call with European leaders on February 25, telling them: "This might be the last time you see me alive." His wife, Olena, admitted she had wondered the same, the thought creeping in after they said goodbye.

Those who'd been previously unimpressed conceded he was doing a good job. Kristina Berdynskykh—one of Ukraine's top journalists—tweeted: "I have a lot of complaints against Zelenskiy over his domestic politics. But the way he behaves during this offensive of absolute evil against Ukraine is real political leadership and tremendous courage."

In the West, his public diplomacy was highly effective. His speeches helped to secure external help, military and economic. He flattered, cajoled, pleaded, and reproved. He linked Ukraine's solo struggle against Russia with a wider values-driven fight between freedom and totalitarianism. And he warned that the security of the West was at stake, not just his homeland. If Moscow swallowed Kyiv, it would keep going, biting off further chunks of Central Europe.

That spring the president went on a virtual roadshow. He spoke remotely to democratic parliaments, ranging from Spain and Portugal to Japan and South Korea—more than thirty in all. Each address was tailored to a particular nation. Foreign ambassadors to Ukraine were consulted in advance, Lytvyn told me. The goal, the speechwriter said, was to foster an emotional bond, a sense of shared humanity across time zones and continents, "so we understand each other." Thus, Ukraine's tragedy became universal.

Addressing the House of Commons on day thirteen of the invasion, Zelenskiy linked his struggle against Putin to Britain's against Hitler in the summer of 1940. The mood in 2022 was solemn; the chamber and its iconic green benches full, the

MPs hushed. It was the first time a foreign leader had spoken directly to the British Parliament—a pregnant moment. He laid out the war to date. Russia had begun a "great terror"; cruise missiles had fallen on homes and schools; fifty children had died. Ukraine's dilemma was that of Shakespeare's Hamlet, he said: "To be or not to be."

And then he referenced Churchill's best-known speech, echoing its rising cadences: "We will fight until the end, at sea and in the air. We will continue fighting for our land, whatever the cost. We will fight in the forests, in the fields, on the shores, in the cities and villages, in the streets." Ukraine would never surrender, Zelenskiy said. It would fight on the terricons or slag heaps of the Donbas and the banks of the Kalmius and Dnipro Rivers.

He concluded with the word *veliki*, or "great," binding the two countries together as if by magical incantation: "Glory to great Ukraine, and glory to Great Britain."

It was a brilliant address—grave, powerful, and evocative. In London, his audience rose as one. They applauded. The same phenomenon occurred wherever he spoke, from Nicosia—in divided Cyprus—to Copenhagen to Dublin. Quickly, the Ukrainian flag became ubiquitous: a symbol of solidarity and sympathy. It flew from the top of Berlin's historical museum and from the medieval towers of provincial English churches. Elected representatives wore Ukrainian colors: men, vivid yellow ties; women, blue dresses and yellow scarves.

Sir Jeremy Fleming, the head of the Government Communications Headquarters (GCHQ), the UK government's secret listening station, described Zelenskiy's information operation as "extremely effective." "It's agile, multiplatform, multimedia, and extremely well tailored to different audiences," Fleming said. "One only has to look at the way Ukraine's flag—a field of sunflowers under a sky of blue—is flying everywhere, including outside GCHQ, to see how well the message has landed."

The speeches had a purpose. Zelenskiy made concrete requests for military and economic assistance. He called repeatedly for the West to supply Ukraine with additional weapons: anti-aircraft systems, fighter jets, tanks, armored vehicles, and artillery. Some of this was arriving. He wanted more. He urged NATO to impose a no-fly zone, to stop Russian aircraft from laying waste to residential districts. Zelenskiy demanded further sanctions against Moscow, including a complete oil and energy embargo.

There were other asks. The president requested political support from European governments for Ukraine's accession to the European Union. And he invited countries to take part in Ukraine's postwar reconstruction, urging them to rebuild cities devastated by Russian bomb attacks.

Eight days after his Commons speech, Zelenskiy turned to America, his most important interlocutor and partner. He spoke to a packed auditorium in the basement of the U.S. Capitol building in Washington. As with the United Kingdom, there was a stirring appeal to kinship. The two countries' destinies were intertwined, he told members of the House of Representatives and the Senate. He urged them to remember Pearl Harbor and the "terrible morning" of December 7, 1941, when the "skies were black from the planes attacking you."

He continued: "Remember September 11, a terrible day in 2001 when evil tried to turn your cities, independent territories, into battlefields. When innocent people were attacked from the air. Our country is experiencing the same every day, right now, at this moment. Every night for three weeks now . . . Russia has turned the Ukrainian sky into a source of death for thousands of people."

There were alluring American references. Zelenskiy cited Mount Rushmore and Martin Luther King Jr.'s "I Have a Dream" speech. He showed a powerful video compilation, contrasting children playing in peaceful Ukrainian cities with the destruction rained down upon them by Russian missiles. The room went very quiet. Some lawmakers shook their heads or wiped away a tear.

Zelenskiy was, as *The Guardian* remarked, pushing America's most emotive buttons. Two years earlier, he had been inadvertently swept up in Trump's first impeachment. The accusation was that the then U.S. president had pressured Zelenskiy in a telephone call to dig up dirt on Hunter Biden. President Biden's son's work for a Ukrainian energy company had become a matter of partisan controversy. In January 2021, Trump was acquitted in the Senate. The saga was forgotten.

Zelenskiy wrapped up by appealing to President Biden to close the skies over Ukraine. "I wish for you to be the leader of the world. Being the leader of the world means being the leader of peace," he said. The auditorium burst into bipartisan applause. The no-fly zone was not imposed, amid fears this might lead to a direct military conflict between NATO and Moscow. But over the coming weeks, the U.S. administration would allocate unprecedented sums to Ukraine, by April reaching $33 billion.

Zelenskiy was all things to all people. Before the Greek parliament, he talked of Mariupol. Addressing Helsinki, he spoke of Molotov cocktails, hurled during the 1939–1940 Winter

War by brave Finns against Soviet invaders. Addressing Australia, Zelenskiy reminded his audience of MH17, the Malaysia Airlines plane shot down by Russia in 2014 above eastern Ukraine, in which 298 people died, 38 of them Australian. To the Swedes, he cited the common colors of the national flags.

The president's wartime transformation extended to his wardrobe. The suit and tie disappeared. Henceforth Zelenskiy sported a dark green T-shirt and zip-up fleece jacket. As Jonathan Freedland noted, this was the uniform of a civilian volunteer. It carried a civic message: that the president was an ordinary citizen, an anti-tsar, struggling with the burdens of war like everyone else. Soon his entourage began wearing the same tactical clothing, made by the Ukrainian fashion brand M-Tac.

The president's features altered, too. The stubble he grew in the first few days of the attack became a beard. Ukrainians responded positively to these changes. Orysia Lutsevych, manager of the Ukraine forum at the London think tank Chatham House, said Zelenskiy's previous TV career explained why his new persona was so readily accepted. Viewers were used to seeing him play different roles. They were therefore able to view him as a "commander in chief in a T-shirt"—a shape-shifting feat that eluded conventional politicians.

"They know he can transform. He's like metamorphosis Zelenskiy," Lutsevych told me. "He's a modern-day statesman who came from entertainment. He's in his element. People around him understand the power of narrative during a war." Zelenskiy's speeches "resonated" well inside Ukraine. They helped the country overcome the horrors brought about by invasion and gave an "incredible boost" to morale, especially to those risking it all on the battlefield, she said.

Sociological data appeared to bear this out. Some 80 percent of Ukrainians believed their homeland could repel Russian aggression. A similar number—78 percent—were confident things were going in the right direction. Before the invasion those figures were reversed, with only 30 percent holding this view. Zelenskiy had imbued his people with a sense that they would win, even if this victory—as he conceded—would take time.

Did all this make the president a new Churchill? Lutsevych thought the British premier was more charismatic and ego driven. Another of my favorite Ukrainian political analysts, Ihor Todorov, described this comparison as "a bit much." "I'm a fan of the cult of Churchill. But, really?" he said. He conceded the war had transformed Zelenskiy. The president's wife, Olena, had much to do with the passionate tone of his addresses, Todorov suggested.

A month into Russia's invasion, Zelenskiy was arguably the most popular politician in the modern world, feted for his integrity and bravery. He had supporters everywhere, from Oslo to Auckland. And it was growing clear Putin had made a mistake. Several, in fact. He had underestimated Zelenskiy's personal qualities. And his assumption that most Ukrainians would welcome their rescue by Russian troops was proving a ludicrous fantasy. Further, Putin had misread Western unity and resolve.

The Russian president apparently assumed Ukraine's survival depended on one man. Remove Zelenskiy and the state would topple. As former prime minister Yulia Tymoshenko put it to me when we met in her office in Podil, Russia was fighting an entire nation. On the morning of the invasion, peacetime political grudges and rivalries vanished, she recalled. Shaken, she and other party leaders met with Zelenskiy and pledged their support to him and to the Ukrainian army. "We hugged and shook hands," she said. "Everyone knew we should stand until the last."

Getting rid of Zelenskiy was proving harder than the Kremlin imagined. The advancing Russian soldiers did not receive the cheers their commanders had led them to expect. Ukrainians greeted them instead with sly fury. As soon as the first enemy tank rolled into view, they surreptitiously reached for their phones.

FOUR

Fire and Sword

Chornobyl
February 24, 2022

When a bullet hits a person, you hear it.
It's an unmistakable sound you never forget,
like a kind of wet slap.

—SVETLANA ALEXIEVICH,

Zinky Boys: Soviet Voices from the Afghanistan War

It was early morning, not quite dawn. A large column of vehicles began trundling over a pontoon bridge. For two months their Russian crews had been involved in armored exercises inside Belarus. Now they were going to war. Or, as Putin put it, they were about to take part in a special military operation to free Ukraine from Nazis.

No one was there to witness this noisy arrival. The bridge across the Pripyat River led to a densely forested zone, strangely devoid of life. Hidden somewhere in the trees were deer, elk, wolves, and a few bears. There were no humans, however. The only natural sound came from blue tits and sparrows, flitting and chirruping among pine trees and birches.

Thirty-six years earlier the area had undergone a great cataclysm. The disaster was so terrible—so vast and enduring in its consequences—that a special exclusion zone was established. It encompassed 260,000 hectares, about the size of Luxembourg. It was abandoned and strictly off-limits to unapproved visitors.

Even the dead were sequestered. Once a year, around Easter time, relatives were allowed in to visit the graves of their loved ones, located in villages and towns where residents had once lived full and busy lives. Now, they left flowers and promptly departed.

The Russian military convoy made speedy progress. By breakfast time on February 24, 2022, it had reached a giant, otherworldly-looking steel dome. Concealed inside this sarcophagus was a damaged reactor. Staff working nearby in a suite of gray office buildings heard gunfire and explosions. Visible through the windows were green infantry vehicles marked with the letter *V*.

Within minutes enemy soldiers had swarmed into the facility and subdued its occupants. Those taken hostage included 169 Ukrainian national guardsmen and 103 technical staff whose job it was to monitor radiation levels. The bad news was relayed to President Zelenskiy's administration in Kyiv, a mere 130 kilometers to the south. Putin's troops had captured the Chornobyl nuclear reactor.

It was an astonishing act of recklessness, committed without regard for the safety of the local and regional populations.

The Kremlin also seemed cruelly indifferent to the fate of its own forces. It was unclear if Russia's young soldiers were aware of Cold War history and of Chornobyl's toxic legacy. Most were born well after the April 1986 disaster, when reactor number 4 exploded, sending radiation far and wide. The accident contaminated parts of Belarus, Ukraine, Russia, and Western Europe, including Scandinavia.

Tanks in a still highly dangerous nuclear disaster site were something new.

According to Yevhen Kramarenko, head of Ukraine's exclusion zone state agency, the Russian army used Chornobyl as a command center. It brought in fifty armored vehicles and around twelve hundred service personnel. They immediately began looting—stealing the computer servers used to take radiation readings, as well as microwaves and coffee makers. The station was forced to use diesel generators after the Russians damaged a high-voltage line and cut off the power supply.

Gerasimov, Putin's chief of the general staff, must have known the risks. Nonetheless, he routed part of his massive invasion force aimed at Kyiv through a forbidden nuclear area. His troops followed orders of extraordinary stupidity. They made fortifications in several places, including an underground kitchen. They even dug trenches within the Red Forest, the most radioactive zone of all.

Soil had lain there for four decades, undisturbed. The soldiers now shoveled it into berms and built foxholes. This was tough physical labor. They sucked in lungfuls of radioactive dust containing nuclides. All would feel the consequences, Kramarenko said, some in months after their Chornobyl deployment, some in years.

The bulk of Gerasimov's army kept going. It headed south on a smooth asphalt road. After thirty kilometers, Russian troops reached the Dytiatky checkpoint, on the edge of the Chornobyl zone.

Tourists had once lined up there to visit the site and the

ghostly city of Pripyat, built for Soviet nuclear workers. A yellow sign still read: CHORNOBYL ICE CREAM.

One of the passing soldiers fired a large-caliber round into a bus shelter. It left a gaping hole in the wall. Another raked the checkpoint control booth window with a row of bullets. The convoy threw debris onto the shoulder: food-ration cartons, empty tins of tuna, and cigarette packets, all scattered among empty bottles of spirits and used ammunition.

By day two—February 25—Russia's advance was a vast surging cavalcade. Locals watched this triumphal procession go past. One of them was Vasiliy Davidenko, a bearded sixty-eight-year-old ranger who worked in Chornobyl's exclusion zone nature reserve. He lived in the nearby village of Prybirsk. "On the second day, 1,700 vehicles went through my settlement," he said. "We counted them. They moved in four lanes."

The skies above the forest were thronged, too, he recounted. "There were combat and Mi2 transport helicopters flying continuously above us in formation. They shook the windows of my house. The Ka-52 helicopters flew extremely low, one hundred meters from the ground, dipping up and down."

Davidenko said a group of Russian soldiers from Siberia stopped to chat. They were young and "very dirty," he said.

They asked: "*Batya* [Pop], how are you living?"

He replied: "We are fine here, thanks very much."

For the first few hours those executing Putin's war plan must have felt they were taking part in a rustic camping adventure. The surrounding wilderness is known as Palieski. It is a place of swamps and mini lakes, marsh grasses and rivulets, gulls and swans. When the soldiers parked for the night, in sandy clearings, they could fashion tank shelters from the branches of fir trees and sit beneath the stars.

Davidenko and other residents may have seemed friendly. The impression was deceptive. The ranger said he quickly hid his valuable possessions in the forest: four cars, three snow-mobiles, a couple of canoes, and a boat. He then took out a slim white cell phone and made a series of calls. He passed on details of the advancing party—its location and types of per-sonnel carriers. There were mostly *Boyevaya Mashina Pekhoty* infantry fighting vehicles—BMP-183s and 108s, he said.

The Russians rolled on serenely for another twenty kilo-meters. Up until this point, the invasion was proceeding with textbook ease, a casual Friday romp, almost. According to Ukrainian intelligence, the Kremlin had not communicated its operational aims to those carrying out the plan. The intent must have been obvious to all: they would seize Kyiv in a light-ning attack.

But the Kremlin had failed to take into consideration the geography of its invasion route: a web of narrow roads with thick forests on either side. Moving in mass formation would turn out to be a mistake. It would have a decisive impact on the operation's outcome.

Ukrainian assault troops moved quickly to set up defensive lines in and around Kyiv. They built checkpoints and firing positions, blocked roads leading into the city, and laid down tank traps. An airborne brigade scrambled to meet the Russian invaders head-on.

The brigade struck in the town of Ivankiv. The Ukrainians ambushed the tip of the Russian column, destroying several vehicles and killing and wounding their operators. A fierce battle erupted.

Ivan, a Ukrainian soldier who participated in the intense fighting in the Kyiv region, said Russian troops were stunned when they came under hostile fire. They had been led to believe the locals were harmless Slavic brothers, ready to welcome them. The Ukrainian army would offer little or no resistance, they had been told.

Instead of bread and salt, Putin's warriors encountered universal hostility.

"We greeted them with fire and sword," Ivan said.

"The Moscow plan was blitzkrieg. Russia has the second-biggest army in the world. They didn't expect much from us," he told me when we met in April on the edge of the Chornobyl exclusion zone. He added: "We stopped them. It became hell for Russians. Some abandoned their vehicles and ran off. They underestimated the patriotism and courage of our soldiers."

Ivan—known by his nickname "the Frenchman"—acknowledged that Russian forces were superior. The Ukrainians, however, possessed advantages that came from fighting at home, he said, emphasizing: "We knew the locality. They didn't know how to orient themselves." The Russians may have had a larger volume of artillery. "We used ours more accurately. We were better able to target the coordinates of our opponents," he said.

There were other differences, too. Ukrainians had a democratic command. Ivan said his senior officer cared about his men and stayed cool under shelling. The Russian military, by contrast, suffered from the drawbacks of a totalitarian system. The army was inefficient and corrupt. Promotion was based not on merit but on connections in Moscow. A lack of trust meant operational details were kept hidden from the rank and file. All of this led to poor morale.

Additionally, the Ukrainian soldiers knew exactly why they were fighting, Ivan said: to defend their homes and families.

"At times we were under tremendous Russian pressure. But we Cossacks don't go on our knees for anybody, except for our mothers and the national flag. This is our land. We are independent. The war is a fight for European values. We don't want to be part of Russia or some SSR." He continued: "It's Kyivan Rus. Kyiv is the mother of cities, not Moscow."

Over the next few days, the Russian convoy on the ground grew into a lumbering supercolumn as reinforcements arrived from the direction of Chornobyl. At one point it was sixty-four kilometers long.

Thousands of interlinked vehicles churned through the zone of alienation, taking the contaminated dust with them. Their adversaries operated in much smaller, highly mobile units. At nighttime, Ukrainian fighters on quad bikes rode through the forest on either side of the road leading toward Kyiv. They were able to approach the enemy unseen, in the phantom manner of partisans, stealing toward their targets.

One unit of thirty Ukrainian special forces soldiers and drone operators dramatically stalled the Russian advance. The unit's name, Aerorozvidka, translates as "airborne intelligence"—or spying from the sky. It was made up of volunteer IT specialists and hobbyists who designed their own machines. They had been active since the start of the war in the Donbas in 2014 and turned to crowdfunding and personal contacts to get hold of components prohibited for export to Ukraine, such as U.S.- and Canadian-made advanced modems.

The air reconnaissance team's soldiers went into battle with sophisticated gear: night-vision goggles, sniper rifles, and remotely detonated mines. They carried drones with thermal-imaging cameras and other similar devices capable of dropping small 1.5-kilogram bombs. Video from one of these weapons shows a bomb falling daintily from above. It smothers a Russian tank in an outsize explosion.

The unit's commander, Lieutenant Colonel Yaroslav Honchar, said that on the first night his men destroyed two or three vehicles at the head of the convoy. "After that it was stuck. They stayed there two more nights and eliminated many vehicles," he recalled. The same drone network fed live data to Ukrainian artillery positions using Elon Musk's Starlink satellite system.

The Russians responded by splitting their column into smaller parts. The same hit-and-run team attacked its supply trucks, Honchar said. This left those at the head of the echelon without heat, oil, bombs, and gas, crippling movement toward the capital. And, Honchar added, "it all happened because of the work of thirty people."

Some Russian armored brigades got through. By early March they had taken Ivankiv and Antonov Airport, close to the northwestern Kyiv suburb of Hostomel, and they seized the neighboring garden suburbs of Bucha and Irpin.

These deadly nocturnal attacks must have demoralized Russian soldiers. Enraged, they began hunting for Ukrainian *rozvidnyky* or "spies" among the communities now under occupation. Davidenko said they interrogated civilians in his village and confiscated cell phones.

"They searched our clothes in case we had written something down and hidden it," he said. Five young people were taken away from his village and didn't come back.

Other locals ran off when they heard the sound of firing. Yulia Mikhailenko, age twenty-eight, said she fled with her daughters Camilla, six; and Zlata, one; and her mother, Zoia, from their home in the village of Khocheva, just south of the exclusion zone. It is a place of farmsteads and geese and chickens pecking the ground next to a dirt track.

The women hid in the woods for a week. It was a cold and hungry experience, Mikhailenko said. She went back to her house to fetch medicine when one of the girls came down with a fever.

She found five Russian soldiers living there. They had kicked in the front door and moved in. "The house was a mess. Our clothes were all over the floor. I told them: 'You can see children are here. Why did you do this?' They looked a bit guilty and stared at their boots. They ripped down the electricity cable and took my telephone, laptop, and flash cards."

The soldiers looted crockery and a frying pan from the kitchen. On the household fridge one of the group had scratched: "Glory to Russia." There was more graffiti on an outside wall. The word "Ukraine" had been painted in green Cyrillic next to a monkey smiley face with an X-style cross for a mouth. Its apparent message: Ukraine should submit and shut up.

Whatever the meaning, it was clear Putin's juvenile invaders had a warped idea of Ukraine. Their commanders had told them they were involved in a mission to root out fascism. According to the Kremlin, the war was a necessary continuation of the USSR's 1941–1945 fight against Hitler's Germany. Its modern-day soldiers were seen as successors to the generation of Soviet men and women who had sacrificed so much, and whose valor had become a latter-day state cult.

This fantastical thinking was apparent in their invasion strategy.

At times it appeared the Russian army was engaged in a

clumsy homage to the glorious past, its battlefield tactics a grandiose historical reenactment. The overlong armored columns sent from Belarus to take Kyiv were reminiscent of the Red Army's tank-led assault against Berlin in April 1945, carried out by Marshal Zhukov under pressure from Stalin. The operation, however, was executed without sufficient supporting infantry, causing a large number of Russian casualties.

As the British historian Antony Beevor suggested, Putin's military approach was "atavistic." His forces in Ukraine committed the same errors as "the Russian army" had eighty years before. They even copied the way their Soviet predecessors had attached odd bits of iron, including bedsteads, to their turrets in the hope that anti-tank weapons would explode prematurely. It was as if Ukraine's arsenal of modern U.S. Javelin anti-tank missiles and Turkish-made Bayraktar drones did not exist.

The president's distorted view of history and his obsession with the Great Patriotic War against Hitler contributed to Russia's "extraordinary blunders" in its Ukraine campaign, Beevor told *Der Spiegel* magazine. Other observers agreed that Putin, the former spy, combined martial tendencies with utter ignorance about military matters. "The fact that neither Putin nor his defense minister were ever soldiers is very evident," David Omand, the former head of the GCHQ British intelligence service, told me dryly.

Putin was not the first civilian Russian ruler to micromanage a military campaign. His predecessors had done the same. They included Nicholas I—the tsar whom Putin admired, and whose meddling in the Crimean War contributed to Moscow's defeat. Nicholas II had also taken personal control of the Russian army in the First World War, with catastrophic results.

And Stalin had directed his generals in World War II, having ignored intelligence that the Nazis would attack.

The Kremlin really had taken capitulation for granted. According to Zelenskiy, Putin expected to hold a victory parade on the Khreshchatyk within days of pushing the button on war. The idea was to raise the Russian flag above the Maidan. A Ukrainian army official later said parade uniforms were discovered in an abandoned Russian military vehicle outside Kyiv. Everything was prepared for a further act of nostalgic Soviet cosplay.

Putin's gravest mistake in the spring of 2022 was to misread the unyielding mood of the Ukrainian people. He underestimated the national will to defend. It was a remarkable failure for a man who considered himself to be a superb intelligence professional.

There were further twentieth-century echoes here, too, including of the Prague Spring. In 1968, Warsaw Pact troops taking part in the invasion of Czechoslovakia were told by the politburo they would be greeted as heroes and liberators. Instead they faced months of stubborn resistance; there were no flowers, only tears and curses.

In analogous fashion, Russia's high command in 2022 had misled its own combatants on land, air, and sea about Ukraine's capabilities. They were now discovering the bitter truth.

Aleksey Golovensky was flying his Sukhoi Su-30SM fighter jet above southern Ukraine. It was a week after the invasion had begun, and the Russian pilot was on a spy mission. The major had made regular sorties from his base in the Crimean town of Saky, taking him along the Black Sea coast and the Sea of Azov. The route was picturesque. It looped over Crimea's white table-shaped mountains and a sandy isthmus linking the peninsula with the mainland, seen from above as a bright ribbon.

Saky, on the west coast of Crimea, had a storied past. President Franklin D. Roosevelt and Winston Churchill landed at its airfield on their way to the February 1945 Yalta Conference. The U.S. leader emerged from the Sacred Cow, his Douglas military transport plane. Stalin greeted him on the tarmac. Their meeting at the Livadia Palace determined the fate of postwar Eastern Europe. It fell under Soviet dominion.

Eight decades later, Putin was seeking to redraw Europe's borders, not through Great Power negotiations but via sullen force. Golovensky's squadron had been informed of the invasion on February 23. His task, he said, was to support landings by Russian marines from the sea and to identify potential Ukrainian military objects. His plane carried two missiles and three or four FAB-250 bombs.

Seven reconnaissance flights had taken off without incident. Golovensky was an experienced pilot who, in 2018, participated in Russia's destructive air campaign in Syria. As he later explained, Moscow had confidently assured him that nothing could go wrong when he was in Ukrainian airspace.

"They assured us we could fly safely. We were told Ukraine's air-defense systems were old, weak, and didn't work. There was no reason to worry."

On March 5, Golovensky was flying at an altitude of 6,500 meters above Mykolaiv Oblast. Below him was a patchwork of black earth and steppe, villages and gold-domed churches. The Inhul River was visible to the right.

And then an explosion.

Two rockets slammed into his twin-finned two-seater plane.

Golovensky and his navigator managed to catapult from the burning wreckage as it hurtled toward the ground. They landed in a field, where Ukrainian soldiers captured them. The major, dressed in his orange pilot's flight uniform, put his hands up and suddenly became a prisoner of war.

Speaking a week later at a press conference in Kyiv, together with his colleague and another downed Russian pilot, Golovensky acknowledged he had been deceived. His bosses had misled him about the state of Ukraine's capacity to hit back. Russia was unable to establish air domination, as had been expected. This made it harder to patrol the skies and spot enemy movements.

"Why they sent us to our deaths, like meat or cannon fodder, is a mystery," Golovensky said. "It turns out Ukraine's anti-aircraft defense works very well."

On the third day of the invasion, a bizarre encounter took place in Ukraine's northeastern Sumy region, close to the border with Russia. The situation was wholly unexpected, and rather surreal. A Russian military vehicle stood on the side of a highway. It had conked out, a deadly purveyor of war no more. Four soldiers stood around it in the road.

A Ukrainian driver whose dashcam recorded the scene pulled up to the hapless group and wound down his window.

"Looks like you guys broke down?" he shouted.

"Out of fuel," a soldier replied.

"Can I tow you back to Russia?" the driver said.

The group laughed nervously.

The driver continued: "Do you know where you are going? To Kyiv, I fucking imagine."

"No, no," the Russians said sheepishly. It seemed their destination was unknown.

The invaders asked for news. The driver said the war was going well—for Ukraine, that was. "Everything is on our side. Your guys are surrendering nicely, because they also don't know where they are going. I asked the entire column of people like you and nobody has a clue where they are heading."

The driver set off again, down an avenue of birch trees and past another stranded vehicle—this one a Russian tank.

Not all Russian vehicles broke down, of course. But the roadside exchange illustrated a problem that would dog the Russian army in the early weeks of its invasion and long afterward. Ukraine is a huge country. As Russia's armed forces pushed deeper into the countryside, supply lines stretched farther and farther. Sometimes they snapped entirely. Problems arose with fuel, food, water, and warm clothing.

Many soldiers said their commanders had informed them they would spend only four or five days in Ukraine. They were given rations commensurate with this brief deployment. Quite often this food ran out, leaving the soldiers hungry and listless. Their officers had no suggestions for how to solve this problem, other than to loot and steal from Ukrainian homes.

In addition to logistical issues there was something more profound working against Russian military success in Ukraine. It was unclear to ordinary soldiers what they were doing there. An air of abstraction enveloped Putin's military-ideological project, despite bellicose "debates" on state TV. The soldiers were initially told they were taking part in exercises and only briefed at the last minute that they were being thrown into the front line.

Their official mission was to "denazify" Ukraine. But this objective was a little tricky to comprehend. What did a Ukrainian neo-Nazi look like, and how might you spot one?

Another roadside exchange demonstrated the absurdity of this assignment.

Artem Mazhulin, a thirty-one-year-old English teacher from Kharkiv, said the Russians entered the suburb where his uncle Viktor and aunt Valentyna lived in the town of Kupiansk. The couple's home in northern Ukraine was just forty kilometers from Russia. It was undefended and of little strategic importance. The soldiers were continuing west, probably toward Kharkiv.

Artem said an armored personnel carrier drove by his uncle's yard soon after February 24. The Russians sitting atop it addressed Viktor as "*batya*"—pop. They noticed his pigeons and asked if he bred them. He said he did and then asked them why they had been sent in armed groups to thunder around Ukraine.

One soldier said cheerfully: "We came here to kill Banderivtsi."

The term *Banderivtsi*—or Banderites—was a staple of Kremlin propaganda, a bogeyman term used to denigrate Ukrainians as fascist. Stepan Bandera was the leader of a militant World War II Ukrainian nationalist organization, the OUN-B. He was a controversial figure.

Some embraced him as a hero for his struggle against Soviet Russia. Others viewed him as a Nazi collaborator and anti-Semite, pointing to atrocities carried out by OUN-B members, especially against Poles and Jews. Arrested by the Germans, Bandera spent most of the war in Sachsenhausen concentration camp.

State media in Russia used the term to describe all modern-day supporters of Ukraine's independence. It was cynical and inaccurate. The Ukrainian far right has done badly in elections and was unrepresented in parliament. And, unlike in Russia, in the Ukrainian government power could change hands, as Zelenskiy's 2019 victory showed.

Further, Zelenskiy was Jewish. As he explained to CNN's Fareed Zakaria, his relatives had suffered during the Holocaust at the hands of the Nazis. Four of his great-uncles died while fighting alongside the Red Army. The Nazis killed his great-grandparents when they set fire to their village. Zelenskiy's grandfather Semyon was a captain in a Soviet infantry unit. He was the only survivor from a terrible time, later settling in the southern Russophone town of Kryvyi Rih, where Zelenskiy grew up, the son of university academic Oleksandr and his engineer wife, Rymma.

Viktor was unimpressed with the soldiers. He replied: "Where the fuck do you see Banderivtsi? There are no Banderivtsi here."

An equally irritated Valentyna told the Russians to get off her front garden. "You are destroying my flower beds," she said.

Artem Mazhulin continued talking to his relatives by phone while they were living under Russian occupation. He said the flower-bed conversation did not surprise him. "Since 2014 the Russian government has been brainwashing its citizens. They try and make them believe Ukraine is not a real state and say fascist monsters have captured it," he observed.

Measuring morale inside the Russian army was not an easy task. Russia's parliament prohibited the military from posting on social media. This was after open-source investigators used online photos to identify the Russian soldiers in 2014 who had smuggled the Buk anti-aircraft system that downed Flight MH17 in eastern Ukraine.

But there was ample evidence that some soldiers were unhappy. There appeared to be a difference between the professional solders who swept in from Crimea and their counterparts in the northern theater, some of them boy-conscripts and reservists. A number from this latter group were captured, and videos of interrogations appeared. Though their statements were made under duress, themes nevertheless emerged. The most compelling: that their military superiors had tricked them about the nature of the operation. A particular phrase used was *oni obmanuli nas*: they duped us. Many said they did not support the war and wished to go home.

A few souls abandoned their vehicles and started tramping back to Russia on foot.

The Kremlin's military plan in northeast Ukraine turned out to be as quixotic as its doomed attempt to capture Kyiv.

The primary target was Kharkiv, the former capital of Soviet Ukraine and an urban center of 1.4 million people. In 2014, Moscow had unsuccessfully tried to instigate a pro-Russian rebellion in the city, the kind that had taken root in Donetsk and Luhansk. It bused in activists and provocateurs from the Russian city of Belgorod. One briefly raised the Russian flag above Kharkiv's main administration building.

When I reported from Kharkiv in 2014, I wrote about the

funerals of two Putin-supporting youths shot dead in a clash with Ukrainian nationalists. The mood was febrile. There were confrontations in front of the city's Lenin statue, Ukraine's largest, in Freedom Square. Pro-Maidan demonstrators daubed it with graffiti. Anti-Western protesters defended the statue with tents and a vigil.

Their counter symbol was an orange-and-black-striped Saint George's ribbon, used by the Kremlin to mark victory day over fascism. The statue was pulled down later the same year.

Putin may have reasoned Kharkiv's strong ties with Russia meant it would accept a hostile military takeover. The city was Russian-speaking. It was just forty-two kilometers from the Russian border. Many residents had close family living in Saint Petersburg, Moscow, and other Russian cities.

Some of Kharkiv looked much like a communist theme park, ready for reabsorption by the motherland. It had the enormous central cobbled square where Lenin had stood, formal neo-classical Stalinist architecture, and a tank and aviation works. Visiting in the early 1930s, the English travel writer Robert Byron described it unflatteringly as "without feature except for a good modernist post office and the Palace of Industry."

In recent decades, Kharkiv had grown into a vibrant modern European city. It was a cosmopolitan center of learning, home to thousands of students, some of them foreigners from Asia and Africa. There was a new zoo, designed by a German architect, with ostriches, tigers, and zebras. Kharkiv had a Ferris wheel and green parks. It was clean. People moved to Kharkiv for higher education and often stayed, building careers and raising families. Its late mayor Hennadiy Kernes—who died of Covid in 2020—was known to be corrupt, but his pride in the city and determination to make it beautiful were genuine.

Kharkiv was therefore a major test of Russia's war of conquest: Could occupation be enacted here and made to stick?

Russian tank columns followed the same route as the hardcore Putin activists who had been sent in eight years previously. The troops crossed the international border from Belgorod and advanced toward the north of the city. Residents woke on invasion day to the sound of bombardment. Some took cover in the city's underground stations; others sheltered in their flats. At night there was intensive shelling.

Early on Sunday, February 27, the Russians tried to seize Kharkiv. Light military vehicles penetrated the northern suburbs. They passed the Peremoha metro station, the final stop on the city's green line, and headed toward the center. A convoy rolled through residential areas and down Saperna Street in the Shyshkivka district. Soldiers crept alongside their Z-marked armored vehicles, sometimes opening fire.

Within hours, the Russian plan unraveled.

Ukrainian troops counterattacked, hitting them with small-arms fire and grenade launchers. There were skirmishes southeast of the city and in the center. A group of Russian soldiers took refuge in an empty school close to the Traktornyi Zavod metro station. There was fighting on Shevchenko Street, home to bars and cafés. Machine-gun rounds boomed across a children's playground dusted with snow. Vehicles burned.

By evening, the assault had been repulsed. The city was under local government control again.

The Ukrainian successes included a destroyed armored column and the capture of several prisoners, including a driver and a young machine gunner. Kharkiv's future going forward was uncertain. But it appeared already by late February that the Russian military had overreached.

Russia's general staff responded to this setback with lethal fury.

It began pounding the city from afar. Artillery, Grad missiles sent from truck-mounted launchers, Kalibr cruise missiles, cluster bombs . . . all rained down upon Kharkiv like a demonic hail. There was no longer much pretense that Moscow was seeking exclusively military targets. The bombing was indiscriminate. Shells fell on apartment buildings, schools, kindergartens. They came through the ceilings of people's kitchens. The goal was to sow fear and terror.

It was a curious way of saving Ukraine's Russian-speaking population, one of Putin's ostensible war aims. Those dying—on street corners, or while in a line for bread—had grown up with Russian as their native language. They were being punished for not welcoming their liberators in the way Russia's president had demanded.

"Many people in Kharkiv are Russian nationals. He counted on their loyalty. He didn't get it," Maia Myronova told me by cell phone, speaking from a metro station in the Malyshev factory district, where she said she was sheltering with around one thousand people, plus cats and dogs. "We are feeling Putin wants to kill us totally. It's awful," another resident, Halyna Padalko, said, adding that the morning-to-evening shelling made the windows in her apartment "shake and vibrate."

The city's suffering would be gruesome.

A few days after Russia's unsuccessful incursion, Oleh Saienko was at home with his girlfriend, Dasha. Their sixth-floor apartment was in a quiet neighborhood, at 197 Klochkivska Street, a short walk from the botanical garden. Around noon Oleh, a software engineer, heard two explosions. Russian missiles had struck immediately outside.

Oleh went to his balcony. He peered out. A rocket protruded from the pavement: gray, sleek, and incongruous. It had landed between a playground and a store where civilians had been queuing for groceries. Below was a scene of horror. The blast blew the leg off a woman. Survivors dragged her, pale and shocked, to a doorway, while her leg lay in the street. She died soon afterward. "Most people thought Russia wouldn't bomb the city. Now they are scared," Oleh said.

The shelling prompted a great exodus from the city. Artem Mazhulin said he spent three nights hiding in a basement with thirty others, mostly women, children, and elderly people. One of them was an electrician who fixed the power supply, allowing people to charge their phones. On day four, Artem and his brother decided to leave. They walked through empty streets, pitted on both sides of the road with tank tracks, until they reached the railway station. Later that night they got on a packed train. They went west, together with students from India, Pakistan, and Nigeria.

Frustrated in its ambitions, Russia moved its offensive operation into a new phase. Attacks on the civilian infrastructure—in Kharkiv, Kyiv, and elsewhere—intensified. They were not accidental. They were a deliberate mechanism intended to cause panic and to force capitulation. Moscow targeted Kharkiv's regional administration building, a Soviet edifice from 1954; the neoclassical court of appeal; and the Stalin-era regional headquarters of the intelligence service. Shells fell on the Assumption Cathedral and among the attractions and kids' rides in the city's Gorky Park. They killed car drivers, other civilians, and a fifteen-year-old boy who had been helping to feed zoo animals.

Some of this mayhem was self-defeating. Russian forces de-

Heart of Darkness

Bucha
February 2022

No animal can be as cruel, so exquisitely
and artistically cruel, as man.

—FYODOR DOSTOEVSKY,
The Brothers Karamazov

For the residents of Bucha, February 24 began with the sound of explosions. By 7:00 a.m., thick charcoal smoke was billowing in the sky above Antonov International Airport. The Russians had hit it with a cruise missile. By midmorning there was unambiguous proof that a large-scale assault was under way, and Putin's invasion was happening a few kilometers to the north of the garden suburb of Hostomel, right outside the gates of Kyiv.

The scene looked like something from a war movie. Russian attack helicopters flew imperiously over dachas and winter-bare orchards. They were too many to count—twenty, thirty, maybe more—moving rapidly in a clatter of rotary blades.

This air armada kept course toward Hostomel. Its mission: to secure the airport so it might be used as a bridgehead for an attack on the capital.

The helicopters swept over a hangar and shot up the giant aircraft inside. The Antonov cargo plane *Mriya* was the world's largest and a symbol of Ukrainian prestige and aspirations. It caught fire. Russian airborne troops leapt out of the helicopters and tried to secure the airfield. Its Ukrainian defenders downed at least one enemy Ka-52 and damaged two others. By evening Russian paratroopers had fallen back to nearby woods.

The next day, units from the Russian armored column, which had traveled via Chornobyl, entered the airport and established control. But the operation could scarcely be counted a success. By this point Ukrainian forces had shelled the runway, making it unusable for the Ilyushin military planes, which were meant to bring troops—thousands of them—from inside Russia to swarm Kyiv.

The Russian land invasion force continued its advance, albeit more slowly than anticipated. It rolled through Hostomel to Bucha. This wasn't the first time a besieging army had marched along this route. A century before, in 1918, soldiers fighting for the Ukrainian independence leader Symon Petliura had come this way on horseback, carrying sabers and blue-and-yellow flags. They were to drive out Kyiv's Hetman Cossack government.

In *The White Guard*, Bulgakov describes the giddy arrival of Petliura's army in the "half-asleep" forests near Bucha:

The snow-covered pine-trees, tall and straight as masts, awoke to the thunderous sound of waves of six-inch shells. Two rounds landed near the large settlement of Puscha-

Voditsa, shattering all the glass in the windows of four snowbound houses. Several pines were reduced to splinters, sending fountains of snow cascading many yards into the air.

Bulgakov's scene was playing out again.

Bucha had retained much of the special character it had when the novelist and playwright used to stay in the town, spending summers in his family's dacha there. The pine trees and resin-scented groves attracted visitors from the big city. Bucha was a green enclave, popular with young families and weekenders, and home to 28,000 people. It was a short commute by car or train to Kyiv, thirty-five kilometers to the south. And it was prosperous.

On February 27, Bucha's new Russian masters appeared. On the first day they seemed civil, friendly almost, one resident, Viktor, said. They went past his house in military vehicles, two abreast. Viktor spoke with a pair of soldiers who said they had come all the way from the Siberian republic of Buryatia, in Russia's Far East.

They told him, "We have an order to seize the Ukrainian president."

That morning, a snake of Russian vehicles set off south toward Irpin, the city that marked the administrative boundary between the capital itself and the larger Kyiv region. The one-hundred-strong column belonged to an elite airborne unit.

The Russians turned into Vokzalna, or Station Street, Bucha's central avenue. We can only guess their mood. It was a suburban scene: on either side were cottages and family homes, their neat gardens visible behind green wooden picket fences. Dogs barked. There was birdsong; a line of leafless lime trees; electricity poles; a grass shoulder and curbstones painted yellow and black. At number 36, a Christmas wreath still hung above the door.

It was a long alley. And the perfect location for an ambush. The Ukrainian army had been tracking the slow-moving *V*-marked column. It now set about destroying it—smashing up first one vehicle, then another, and then everything, with immaculately lobbed artillery strikes. Ukrainian soldiers told me the Russian marines who escaped the first wave of bombing tried to reverse their vehicles and turn around, desperate to get out.

Many didn't succeed.

The street was transformed into an inferno of burning armored personnel carriers and Kamaz trucks: a charred, labyrinthine confusion. Several residential properties were accidentally hammered as well, their roofs and walls shattered as if by a giant fiery fist. There were dead and wounded combatants; the smell of fumes and diesel hung in the air.

When I visited in April, the fire and smoke had dissipated. But the road was still a spectacular mess, a hellscape of broken and contorted armored vehicles that looked painted by Hieronymus Bosch. The skeletons of these machines were strewn about. A blue-and-white-striped shirt, worn by airborne troops, hung from a gun turret, as if awaiting its owner's return. Sleeping bags and Russian uniforms were scattered on the tarmac amid twisted tank treads and a slew of rubbish.

A few plucky locals ventured out, peering at the damage. One man recorded a remarkable video on his cell phone. "Dima! Guys! That's what is left of my house. Those faggots came to our land! Burn in hell, motherfuckers! They came here and went back to hell. I don't believe it. It's all in Bucha," he said, cursing some more as he walked through a smolder-ing avenue of death. He added: "Ukraine armed forces—good job! Well done, guys."

The counterattack set back Russia's mighty invasion plan. Over the next few days, Ukrainian forces pushed the Russians out of Bucha and raised the Ukrainian flag over the town hall. Residents were able to breathe a little easier.

For a brief period, Vokzalna Street became a macabre attrac-tion. One local who visited was Volodymyr Cherednichenko, a twenty-six-year-old electrician. His home was a short walk away across the railway line that led to Kyiv. He lived on Ivan Franko Street, a rustic alley of detached cottage homes, named after a celebrated Ukrainian poet, on the tranquil southern edge of town.

Volodymyr was not a soldier. In 2014, his father, Serhiy, had participated in the battle against Russia's separatist prox-ies in the Donbas. Volodymyr developed a teenage fascination with weapons and uniforms. When his father died in 2021, the young man found solace in talking to his dad's comrades who had served on the eastern front line. Volodymyr had a roman-tic yearning to defend his country and to have adventures of his own.

On Vokzalna Street, Volodymyr clicked a few photos on his cell phone of the Russian wipeout. He sent them to a young woman he knew, a civilian volunteer.

It turned out to be a terrible mistake.

On March 4, the Russians returned to Bucha. This time they were better organized. The city became a strategic base in their attempt to capture Kyiv.

It was now evident to Moscow that its "special operation" could not merely target Ukraine's so-called neo-Nazi government. To win, it had to defeat a hostile civilian population, too. The debacle on Vokzalna Street had taken place because locals had given intelligence to the Ukrainian army, Russian strategists must have deduced. Therefore civilians were also the enemy. Any cell phone was a dangerous weapon. Any man of military age was a potential combatant.

The Russian army reentered Bucha from the north and west. It advanced cautiously, moving street by street. According to residents, a *zachistka*, or "sweep operation," took place. Its chilling purpose was to identify potential "traitors." That meant veterans of Kyiv's anti-terrorist operation in the Donbas, members of territorial defense, and police and local administration officials, plus those suspected of holding pro-Ukrainian views. This last category was so amorphous it could mean anybody.

In some parts of Bucha, Russian internal police units conducted the sweep. In other areas, it was left to regular troops. On March 3, the Russians rolled into Ivan Franko Street in a *Mad Max*-style cacophony of vehicles. The soldiers constructed a checkpoint at the bottom of the road, complete with a tank. They were based about two hundred meters from where Volodymyr lived with his mother, Nadezhda, and aunt Natasha Oleksandrovna at number 5A.

Soon afterward, the family heard a loud banging outside. Natasha opened the door. Three Russian soldiers were there. "They asked to see our documents and mobile phones," she said. "They didn't beat us. They had guns." Natasha said she and Nadezhda had hidden their cell phones. Volodymyr, her nephew, had no choice but to give his phone to the visitors. The soldiers found the Vokzalna Street images.

"*Ty idyosh s nami*," they said—"You're coming with us."

The soldiers took Volodymyr out into the cold. He was dressed in a T-shirt and flip-flops. Later the same day the women went to the checkpoint and asked what had happened to him. They wanted to give him warm clothes—shoes and a coat. The soldiers directed them to a large yellow-painted house, not far from their own property. Natasha, who was sixty-three, said she clambered up an apple tree, balancing her leg on a branch, and peered over a turquoise wooden fence.

It was a pitiful scene. Her nephew was inside, sobbing. Soldiers were interrogating him. "His arm was broken. It was covered in blood. He was clutching it. They kept asking him where the Nazis were. He was crying and saying: 'I didn't do anything. I don't know anything.'" Other Russians came and went; the building was being used as a military office of some kind. After a number of hours, the soldiers emerged with Volodymyr and said they were taking him away for three days in order to make further inquiries.

Nadezhda hugged Volodymyr and helped him into the coat. She begged the soldiers twice: "Return my son to me." They departed in an armored vehicle, apparently heading into the center of Bucha, where senior officers had set up a headquarters in a commandeered glass factory.

Three days passed. There was no news. In the meantime, the Russians transformed Ivan Franko into a delinquents' holiday home fiefdom. Each Russian crew parked its armored vehicle in the garden of a private house, toppling gates and orchards. They broke into properties and moved in. They looted "everything," Natasha said: the drinks cabinet, TVs, jewelry, underwear, shoes. Bucha's overlords could do whatever they pleased.

In the evenings they would sit on the chassis of a stolen truck cab, smoking, chatting, and watching the street.

For entertainment, the soldiers hijacked private cars. They would mark them with a *V* and drive them madly around the block. Sometimes they would sleep in them. Or they would take potshots at them or flatten them with a tank; a red car belonging to Natasha's friend became a concertinaed wreck. When she told me her story, sitting in a neighbor's kitchen, I wondered if there was an element of proletarian envy to the soldiers' behavior. Bucha was affluent, and the Russian soldiers were not. They stole a Tesla first, Natasha said, and demanded keys to Jeeps.

Any encounter with the Russians could be dangerous, especially after a Ukrainian artillery strike hit the checkpoint, leaving the soldiers furious and edgy. Electricity, water, and gas in the city were cut off. Natasha said she emerged from her house to fetch water from a well with a bucket in one hand and a white flag in the other. She had dyed red hair; friends nicknamed her David Bowie; she looked nothing like a fighter. Even so, a Russian threatened to blow her up with a grenade. She told him she wanted to live.

On another occasion she chatted with her occupiers—a homesick bunch who seemed quite young. Natasha asked one of them how old he was. He said he was eighteen and had a seven-month-old son back in Russia.

"I really want to go home," the soldier told her. "I haven't eaten *pelmeni* [dumplings] for two weeks. They only gave us enough food for three days."

"Why did you come here?" Natasha asked.

The soldier shrugged. "Money."

One night, soon after Volodymyr's disappearance, cries and screams could be heard in the darkness from somewhere nearby.

What had happened to him? Natasha asked at the checkpoint. She was bluntly told her nephew was dead—he was a "corpse." Another soldier, however, said this was a case of mistaken identity. According to him, Volodymyr was alive and had been taken to a no-conflict zone in Belarus. He would be transported back to Bucha once the war was over. For three weeks his mother continued to believe her son would return.

The truth emerged on March 31, when Russian forces pulled chaotically out of Bucha after a monthlong occupation. They retreated north, as part of a much larger withdrawal, as Moscow's forces effectively abandoned their attempt to seize Kyiv. Volodymyr wasn't in Belarus. His body was much closer to home. In a cellar, in fact, at number 6 Naberezhna Vulytsa, barely a three-minute walk from where soldiers had first detained him. They had taken him to the empty property and kept him, for some time at least, in a dank brick outbuilding in the garden.

When I visited Natasha in April, she showed me the spot. The house was once a bright home rented to a family. In its garden were daffodils, a well, a doghouse, and a few trees. Opposite the entrance—shot up, its windows broken—was the cellar. I stepped over broken glass and descended the steps into gloom. There was a bloodstained mattress, a sleeping bag, and a purple cuddly toy.

The room had a powerful smell of death. A ghostly crime scene.

"They made him kneel and shot him in the side of the head,

through the ear," Natasha said. "We found him in a kneeling position." Neighbors carried his body out. They wrapped it in cellophane. A temporary grave was dug at the far end of her garden. It was a rectangular hole, next to a back wall, and rather small. A week later he was exhumed. The family was able to bury him properly.

"We said prayers in Russian," Natasha recalled.

The story of Volodymyr's death haunted me long afterward. It became the stuff of restless dreams. I saw him captive and terrified in the dark. His final moments can be imagined. Fear, despair, loneliness, perhaps hope—and then extinction.

The Ivan Franko Street homicide was not a one-off. It was part of a prolific pattern of murder and predation, seemingly approved at the highest levels in Moscow. It was a grisly fugue taken up not only in Bucha but in every zone of Russian occupation. The killings took place across the Kyiv region—in the neighboring satellite towns of Irpin, Hostomel, Borodianka, in surrounding villages—and far beyond. Around fourteen hundred bodies would eventually be recovered. More than 650 had been shot.

It was, as Ukraine's former defense minister Andriy Zagorodnyuk put it to me, Kremlin policy. There was evidence, he said, of an open order given to different Russian military formations—in effect, a license to kill noncombatants. "We believe it was a policy decision done to terrorize the population. They [Russian units] were told it's okay," he said. "We have seen a number of cases."

The cases included about a dozen people from Ivan Franko

Street, who'd been terminated in cold blood. Brothers Viktor, sixty-four, and Yuri, sixty-two, were left lying in a ditch next to the railway line. The house closest to the checkpoint belonged to Serhiy Havryliuk, a security guard who worked in Kyiv, and his wife, Iryna. She fled on March 5; Serhiy decided to stay behind to look after their two dogs and six cats. It was the last time she saw him alive.

His body was found in the yard. He was faceup, dressed in a dark coat with a thick collar and winter boots. Next to him was Irina's brother Roman and a third, unknown, man. "We couldn't identify him because his face was blown off," Natasha explained to me. He had ventured out to find better phone reception; the Russians, who were spooked by the use of cell phones, gunned him down, she said.

The Havryliuks' house was a phantasmagoric ruin. A shell had incinerated a Russian armored vehicle parked in the garden. The explosion hurled a sleeping bag and a pair of trousers into a tall tree. There were unexploded mortars piled up against a sandy mound-slash-firing position and an empty whisky bottle. The white cab of a truck had three bullet holes across the windscreen.

Farther down Ivan Franko Street, to the east, the Russians had left behind a pottage of blackened limbs—six people, four from the same family, murdered and burned. An older man was discovered long after he was shot inside his home, close to where Volodymyr was locked up.

Natasha said she was aware of the killings that took place during Bucha's occupation, though not their savage number. She said her neighbor overheard two Russian soldiers talking to each other.

"How do we get rid of all the bodies?" one asked.

The second answered, "Don't worry. It's not difficult. Throw them down a well or a cesspit."

These myriad crimes came to light between April 1 and April 3, when Ukrainian soldiers reclaimed the city. They drove through an apocalyptic urban landscape strewn with bodies. A man was found shot dead next to his bicycle. Ukrainian drone footage published by *The New York Times* captured his death. It revealed that he was cycling toward an intersection, unaware that a Russian column was heading his way. In the footage, he dismounts and turns into Yablunska Street. A BMD-4 fighting vehicle opens fire with high-caliber rounds. A second vehicle does the same. Puffs of deadly smoke billow.

At least twelve bodies lay in the same road with gunshot wounds to the head. Satellite images from Maxar, a U.S. company, showed the corpses appeared during the period of Russia's grisly occupation in March. The killings seemed demonstrative. It was a gruesome raptorial display, designed to intimidate those still living and to break their spirits.

Many of the dead had their hands tied together by zip ties or cloth. Five bound bodies were found in the bloody basement of a Soviet-era children's summer camp, in the north of the city. The men had burns, bruises, lacerations, and bullet holes in their legs. Though the scene was lurid, it was possible to visualize what must have happened: they were questioned, tortured, and then shot. In similar fashion, eight bodies were found at the back of the Russian army's base at a private house at 144 Yablunska Street. All were victims of summary execution. CCTV footage showed their last moments, marched away at gunpoint, figures shuffling to their doom.

Women were murdered, too. There were grim instances of

sexual abuse. One took place in Ivan Franko, when a soldier nicknamed "Giraffe" tried to rape a fourteen-year-old girl. Her mother pleaded with him; Giraffe raped her instead. According to Lyudmyla Denisova, Ukraine's ombudswoman for human rights, a group of women and girls were kept prisoner for twenty-five days in a house. Nine became pregnant. In another case, documented by *The New York Times*, a woman was kept as a sex slave in a cellar. Her body—she was shot in the head—was discovered wearing a fur coat. She was naked underneath; used condoms and wrappers were found nearby.

Workers from a local funeral home collected some of the dead. They placed dozens of bodies in a communal pit in the rear of Bucha's Saint Andrew and All Saints Church. This had become necessary because the morgue was full. Only two were members of the Ukrainian military; the rest were civilians.

It was raining when I visited the gold-domed church, steeling myself for what was taking place under a dismal sky. Investigators had begun removing bodies the previous day for forensic examination. Others lay where they had been tossed in a large sandy trench. Plastic sheeting covered the sunken grave area. Mannequin-like limbs stuck out. In one place I saw an arm. Farther along the pit was a foot, encased in a sneaker. More than seventy bodies were recovered.

On April 3, a haggard-looking President Zelenskiy toured Bucha. He summed up what had gone on in the city—genocide. This was an emotive word. It had a grave precedent, not least in Ukraine itself, where citizens had fallen victim in 1932–1933 to Stalin's state-engineered famine. The Polish lawyer Raphael Lemkin devised the term in 1944 amid the systematic murder of Jews during the Holocaust. The word came from the Greek prefix for "race"—*genos*—and the Latin suffix for "killing"—*cide*. It was hard to think of a better description for what the Russians had left behind: a barbarous trail of murdered innocents. In bitterly ironic tones, Zelenskiy invited the leaders of the Russian Federation "to come and see how their orders are being fulfilled." This was not a freelance operation, he suggested.

It was officially directed mass murder.

The soldiers had taken their cue from Russian state media. TV pundits in Moscow had long argued that the very idea of Ukraine should be erased, together with those in it. This demonizing discourse was a staple of talk shows and serious analytical articles. Ukrainians were described as *ne liudi*—unpeople—as well as vermin, rats, and diseased. One expert talked of wiping out "Ukraine-ness." There were calls on social media for the mass rape of Ukrainian women and the killing of "Nazis," researchers found. And then there was Putin's 2021 essay, which said Ukraine was a Bolshevik fiction. Ahead of the invasion, Shoigu made the article mandatory reading at Russian military academies. All of this toxic information had created an environment in which killing Ukrainians became a laudable act.

This was certainly how Ukrainians themselves saw it. "They kill us because we're Ukrainian. If you love your country in Ukraine, you are a fascist. If you love Russia, you are a patriot," one Bucha survivor, Valeriia Lysenko, told me. Russia had lost Ukraine irrevocably because of its actions, she said, asking: "What kind of human being would do this?"

The Kremlin, naturally enough, denied responsibility for Bucha.

It said images of the bodies were fake, part of a U.S. plot to defame Russia. It also claimed Ukrainians had executed

collaborators. Hence the many dead. This predictable coun-
ternarrative was not persuasive, at least not to anybody who
existed outside the noxious influence of the Kremlin. There
was abundant evidence of Russian war crimes: video, satellite
photos, and testimony from those who had witnessed their
once-peaceful suburb transformed into a killing field. In fact,
there were intercepted conversations between soldiers in which
they admitted to relatives back in Russia what they had done.

The massacre at Bucha is one of the blackest moments of our
century. It caused outrage worldwide, with the international
community broadly agreeing with Zelenskiy's assessment that
it was genocide. President Biden called Putin a "war criminal"
who wished to "wipe out the idea of Ukrainian identity." "This
guy is brutal and what's happening in Bucha is outrageous," he
remarked after Bucha's dark secrets came to light. Boris Johnson concurred. So did the parliaments of Poland, Canada, and
the Baltic states. President Macron demurred, arguing that
genocide carried with it a moral obligation to intervene.

Over the following months, a procession of experts visited
the city: war crimes lawyers, detectives, and pathologists. More
than forty countries asked the International Criminal Court
and its prosecutor, Karim Khan, to investigate. Ukraine welcomed the move. The prospect of justice and accountability
seemed remote, however, so long as the war raged and Putin's
regime stood. Few thought it likely Russia's head of state would
stand trial before an international tribunal. Nonetheless, legal
teams began the vast task of piecing together criminal cases.
There were at least ten thousand of them.

Some of these crimes were spontaneous, others premedi-
tated, cooked up in a back office somewhere. When I talked
to Bucha's mayor, Anatoliy Fedoruk, he said the Russians had

brought with them a hit list of forty or fifty people. A bureau-crat had made a deliberate effort to type the document up. They had spelled his name wrong—as "Fedorchuk," an error that may have saved him from elimination. He went into hid-ing and survived.

How would he describe what had happened in Bucha?

"It was a Chechen Republic hunting safari," he told me on the telephone.

Amid this shattered landscape there were immediate clues as to the identities of Putin's willing executioners. Driving north out of Bucha, I followed the devastation. There were burned-out BMP-2 armored vehicles, bullet-splattered cars, and a crum-pled Intersport shopping center. In Hostomel the fighting had engulfed a complex of high-rise apartments on Ostromyrska Street, not far from the airport and an aircraft factory.

The Russians had shelled the Antonov plant as part of their initial assault on the airfield. Many projectiles fell short, though, gouging giant holes in surrounding residential build-ings. At least two civilians were killed. Subsequently, a group of Chechen soldiers took over the mini suburb, which had a school and a post office. They used it as a command post. The Chechens lived for some of March in abandoned flats.

The upper stories gave a good view of a strategic T intersec-tion. To the left was the airport, to the right the road leading to Kyiv, its outskirts some ten kilometers away. A monument to a Soviet test pilot, Valery Chkalov, stood next to a pine grove. In front of the statue a man was trying to tow away his war-damaged Lada. The car seemed a hopeless case. It had no windows. "I can fix it," he told me.

I walked through an alley of ravaged garages into a central square. The complex had belonged to the Ukrainian military up until 2008 and still housed some servicemen and their families. The Chechen fighters had made it their own. They'd painted graffiti on its walls. The piece that intrigued me most had a gnomic flavor: "Better [a] terrible end than endless terror." One hinted at their day of arrival: WOLVES 5/3/2022. Another, using the Chechen word for wolf: CHECHNYA BORZ. A fourth, in big Cyrillic letters: ALLU AKHBAR and AKHMAT SILA—"Glory to God" and "Akhmat is our strength."

This last slogan was a Chechen variant of the old Soviet-era saying: "Lenin lived, Lenin lives, Lenin will always live." "Akhmat" referred to Akhmat Kadyrov, the former president of Russia's Chechen Republic. Putin had entrusted Kadyrov, a onetime rebel, with stewardship of Chechnya following two brutal wars by Moscow against Chechnya's separatist elected government. Kadyrov was blown up in the capital, Grozny, in 2004.

Power was transferred to Kadyrov's son Ramzan. He proved to be a loyal servant—ruthless and brutal. With his assistance, the Kremlin was able to eliminate the insurgency in Chechnya, which had morphed from a constitutional struggle for independence from Russia into an explicitly Islamist rebellion. Kadyrov's fighters took part in Putin's wars: in 2014 in the Donbas, more recently in Syria, and now in Ukraine.

The Chechen fighters deployed around Kyiv did not belong to Russia's ministry of defense. Previous attempts to conscript Chechens and to integrate them into the Russian army failed because of conflicts. The Chechen troops were part of the national guard, known as Rosgvardiya. This federal service was responsible for internal security. It was associated with *avto-*

zaki, ominous police trucks used to carry off anti-government demonstrators from Russian public meetings.

The head of the national guard, Viktor Zolotov, was Putin's former bodyguard from the 1990s and a longtime crony. He was a member of Russia's security council and one of very few people the president trusted. Zolotov was also a friend of Kadyrov's. In 2018, Navalny accused Zolotov of siphoning off money from national guard contracts. Zolotov challenged the opposition leader to a duel and threatened to turn him into "mincemeat." The United States sanctioned Kadyrov and, in March 2022, added Zolotov to the list in connection with his Ukraine activities.

The Chechens sent to Kyiv, then, amounted to Putin and Kadyrov's personal enforcers. Had the capital fallen, their likely role would have been to carry out police functions: keeping public order and upholding the rule of a new pro-Moscow puppet regime. The Chechens had a fearsome reputation. They comprised two battalions and a regiment named after Kadyrov Senior.

Instead, the Kadyrovites were swept up in the disaster that befell Putin's northern army. Not all of these proud wolves made it home. On February 26, Ukraine obliterated a Chechen military column in the vicinity of Hostomel's airport.

Among debris piled up outside a five-story roadside tower block, I spotted the remains of a soldier. Or, more accurately, a torso in a green flak jacket. The stench was unmistakable. In a parking lot were mangled armored vehicles, charred and abandoned.

The Chechens had dug a machine-gun post next to a children's playground. A giant Lipton teapot had been blown into a sandpit. There were splintered Somme-like birch trees. With the invaders gone, besides ghosts, the complex's primary residents were animals: pigeons, dogs, and cats, sniffing at a left-behind sack of potatoes.

"Putin's thugs came to kill us," Misha Kazda, a Hostomel resident, told me as he stopped to check on his daughter's teacher. "This was a nice place to live. Now it's a ruin." His wife, Oksana, added: "We were very afraid." She said she had hid in a basement with a group of civilians. Soldiers ordered them out. "They took our phones and smashed them," she said. "They stole all of our household possessions and fired bullets into the TV."

The Kazdas survived the occupation, but Hostomel's mayor, Yuriy Prylypko, was not so lucky.

On March 7, he set off to meet an aid convoy arriving from Kyiv. A Russian column opened fire on the car he was traveling in with three other men. One of them, Ivan Zuria, was hit in the head and died. Prylypko got out and began running. A Russian soldier shot him from an apartment building. The mayor's bodyguard, Taras Kuzmak, took cover behind an abandoned digger. "They immediately opened fire. There was no warning," Taras said, adding he heard the mayor take his "last breath."

Prylypko was one of around four hundred Hostomel residents who perished or disappeared during Russia's thirty-five-day occupation. The crimes in the city were identical to those in Bucha, with different units moving between the adjoining towns.

Volodymyr Abramov said he met the Chechens on March 4, on Yablunska Street in Bucha. The soldiers were immediately recognizable—some bearded, and with sand-colored uniforms and expensive boots. They returned the next day, asked where the "Nazis" were hiding, and told him to step outside, together with his daughter, Iryna, and son-in-law, Oleh. They made Oleh strip off his shirt and kneel, and then they shot him in the temple, Volodymyr said.

Ukrainian intelligence said the most notorious unit operating in the Bucha area was the Sixty-Fourth Separate Motor Rifle Brigade. Other units were also involved. According to Reuters, an ID card was found in a Russian base on Yablunska belonging to a corporal from the Vityaz security force, which is part of Zolotov's national guard. Locals found a love letter in a house occupied by Russian soldiers. A paratrooper from Pskov, serving with the Seventy-Sixth Guards Air Assault Division, received it from his girlfriend. A soldier from the same division spray-painted his social media handle on a wall.

Regular *kontraktniki* or "contract soldiers" were forbidden from using social media. The rule didn't apply to the Chechens, who filmed themselves inside Ukraine and were fond of self-glorifying posts. Videos show them in Hostomel and in Borodianka, a satellite city fifty kilometers northwest of Kyiv. The chief of Chechnya's national guard unit, Anzor Bisaev, posted footage of himself driving down Borodianka's destroyed central avenue, formerly known as Lenin Street. "Akhmat Sila," he says, echoing the slogan daubed on Hostomel's walls.

Bisaev posed outside what would become an infamous symbol of Russia's invasion: apartment building 359. The nine-story high-rise was not a military building or a secret base. Ordinary people lived there. Nonetheless, on March 3, Russian warplanes targeted it with devastating high-explosive bombs.

A central section collapsed. It crushed and entombed dozens of civilians, some of whom were hiding in the basement.

When I came to see it for myself, Ukrainian firemen were picking through debris with a crane, excavating a twisted mound of metal and masonry. Bodies lay underneath.

One resident, Zinaida Nechiperenko, told me she had come back in the hope of collecting a few personal photographs from her sixth-floor apartment, where she had lived for thirty-seven years. She had done so in vain—it was a gutted wreck. "Nothing is left," she said, sobbing. "Nothing." She was mystified as to why Moscow had behaved like this. "My daughter-in-law is Russian. We understand Russian and Ukrainian. We are all brothers and sisters. I can't fathom how this happened."

Across the road was the city's palace of culture and a bust of Taras Shevchenko. A round had been fired into the nineteenth-century poet's head, leaving a hole. It was a small but symbolic example of Moscow's blueprint for Ukraine—the erasure of national identity. "Russian soldiers want to kill Ukrainian people. They want to kill us and our history," twenty-year-old student volunteer Valentyn Yegorov told me while on a break from clearing away rubble.

"My grandfather used to talk about the Nazis. He lived until eighty-three. I think what we had here is worse," another Borodianka resident, Tamara Vyshnak, said. Tamara said she heard the Russian jets flying low overhead, followed three seconds later by explosions. There was no rationale for bombing the city or its peaceful inhabitants. "I'm not a historian, but as far as I recall, Ukraine never attacked anybody," she told me.

When they arrived, the Russian soldiers were hungry and angry, she said. They broke into her garage and stole her bike, which she used to cycle to her vegetable garden. She conceded she had suffered less than her neighbors—some of whom were killed, while others came back to find their properties in pieces.

During a visit to Borodianka, Zelenskiy likened Putin's invasion to the Nazi onslaught in the Second World War. "Evil has returned in a different uniform, under different slogans," he said. Russia's president had enacted a "bloody reconstruction of Nazism in Ukraine." Ukrainians were experiencing a "terrible déjà vu," Zelenskiy added in a video address filmed in stark black and white against the backdrop of apartment building 359. He invoked the Nazi firebombing of cities—Coventry, Liverpool, and Rotterdam—and the Japanese attack on Pearl Harbor.

The question of whether Putin was Hitler, or Hitler-ish, would be endlessly contested and debated. Was it more accurate to liken his crimes to Moscow's own dictator, Stalin? Or simply to describe Russia as a terrorist state? There were plenty of ironies. Russian bombs had hit Borodianka's history museum. Rescue crews were clearing up the sidewalk next to the museum's portraits of partisans who had been executed by the Germans during the Second World War.

Whatever the parallels, a swirling evil had come to Bucha and to other Kyiv-region towns. And it was clear that Putin wholly approved of the actions of his armed forces. Having accused the Ukrainians of committing genocide in the Donbas—a claim with little merit—he had enacted his own genocide in Ukraine. In April, an ostentatious notice appeared on the Kremlin's official website. The president had granted the Sixty-Fourth Separate Motor Rifle Brigade the honorary title of "guards." The award was bestowed on the brigade for its "mass heroism, courage, and fortitude," the citation said.

The horrors of Bucha came to light only because of Russia's hasty retreat. And because of the city's proximity to Kyiv, where U.S. and European media representatives were based. Reports from Bucha filled newspapers, magazines, and TV and computer screens. The images shocked the public. They galvanized support for Ukraine from Washington and other democratic capitals and hastened the supply of arms to Zelenskiy's forces.

But there were other battlefields that were practically inaccessible to the Western media, and from where little reliable information emerged. A thousand kilometers away from Kyiv, in a European seaside city, Russia was repeating the crimes of Bucha on a vast and unimaginable scale.

SIX

Thermopylae

Mariupol
January 2022

Stranger, make this message clear
to those at home who hold us dear.
We honoured what our country said:
to hold our ground—and here lie dead.
—ADAPTED FROM THE EPITAPH FOR THE
SPARTANS WHO FELL AT THERMOPYLAE (BCE 480)

A surreal performance was taking place inside Mariupol's airport. Ukrainian soldiers made up the audience, sitting on benches in a freezing departure lounge. In front of them a group of amateur actors was staging a traditional mystery play known as a *vertep*. Some characters were familiar to me. I spotted the Devil, an angel, and Death. Death had an impressive skeleton costume and a white scythe. Also a black hood, naturally enough, and dark streaks under the eyes.

Other characters in the play came from international politics. There was a President Biden carrying the Stars and Stripes and an actress with a German flag—Angela Merkel, as I discovered. And an imperious looking individual dressed up in a red costume with a gold crown on his head. Some kind of king? Well, sort of. This was Vladimir Putin. The show ended with the Devil and Death kicking "Putin" in the rear and chasing him off to hell.

The cast sang a stirring song, accompanied by a guitar:

A little bird flew
And brought us some news
That Ukraine did not perish
That Ukraine has risen again

Applause rang out across the hall. There were no passengers: the airfield hadn't been used for flights since before Russia began its war in the Donbas in 2014; the troops were guarding it as a military site. The setting was perfect for the play's folk message of patriotism and resurrection. A colorful 1960s Soviet mural decorated the terminal's upper story; it featured proletarian workers and three soldiers dumping Nazi placards in front of Lenin's tomb. A plastic Ukrainian flag had been hung over the Red Square image, covering up its hammer and sickle.

"Russians have lived for twenty years in a dictatorship. They are happy," Death—actually Olena Chebeliuk, an English-speaking historian from Lviv—told me. It was several weeks before the invasion began, but Olena predicted that if it did happen, Russia would meet stiff Ukrainian resistance. And, in case of occupation, partisan war. "We don't like dictators here. Putin is a bit of a dreamer. He wants to be the most powerful man in the world. If he tries to make a dictatorship in Ukraine, he will fail," Olena thought.

The *vertep*'s cast had traveled from western Ukraine to

Mariupol, the largest city on the coast of the Sea of Azov, in the southeast. It was a thousand-kilometer trip. Recent events made their morale-boosting tour of the front line urgent. U.S. intelligence had warned that a Russian attack was likely. Ukrainian government figures had reservations about this but privately told me that if an invasion did occur Mariupol was an inevitable target—the first place Putin would seek to "liberate."

The city was vulnerable because of its geography and tricky to defend. Home to around half a million people, it was located on the edge of enemy-controlled territory in the Donbas. Since 2014 Russia had effectively controlled Donetsk, the regional capital to the north. Mariupol was a mere fifteen kilometers away from an eastern front line with the DNR. This quasi-border ran across a strip of beach and rolling inland villages. Twenty kilometers farther east was the Russian Federation.

An attack from the east and north was obvious. If Russia could advance from the west as well—moving through Zaporizhzhia Oblast and Berdiansk, say—Mariupol would be encircled. There would be no way out.

Beyond these blunt cartographic facts there was a sense of unfinished business, at least from Moscow's revisionist perspective. I visited Mariupol in April 2014. What the Kremlin called a "Russian spring" was under way. Pro-Russian "separatists" had seized a string of municipal administration buildings with help from undercover Russian agents. They wanted a Crimea-style referendum on the region's future status. This "vote" should see Ukraine's industrial heartland join Russia.

Back in Donetsk, the activists had turned city hall into an anti-Western Soviet hangout zone. I found a wall of tires topped with razor wire, a pensioner waving a Stalin flag, and a caricature of Barack Obama as Hitler. A sound system pumped out schmaltzy Russian disco numbers. On the eleventh floor—you had to take the stairs, the elevator didn't work—there were teenagers in balaclavas and bearded middle-aged men in military jackets. They would become the new DNR Kremlin-backed pseudo-government.

It was evident this Moscow-organized uprising was going in an ominous direction. Prominent local pro-Kyiv figures were being abducted and murdered. A shadowy militia run by a colonel from Russian military intelligence, the GRU, had taken over nearby Sloviansk. Later that summer, a Russian army unit operating secretly inside the Donetsk region would shoot down Malaysia Airlines Flight 17, killing all 298 people on board.

In Mariupol, however, the "Russian spring" wasn't quite blooming the way the Kremlin had hoped. I arrived in the port city the morning after around two hundred pro-Moscow demonstrators had tried to storm the Ukrainian army's headquarters. There had been a five-hour gun battle and two protesters were killed. I found bloodstains, a trail of glass and debris, and shot-up army vehicles. Over at Mariupol's occupied town hall I watched an underwhelming DNR rally blessed by an Orthodox priest. The paltry crowd skewed elderly.

At the time allegiances were divided in Mariupol, a Russian-speaking city and home to many ethnic Russians. "I want to live in Ukraine. I can't bear it when they rip down the Ukrainian flag and put the Russian one up instead," seventy-one-year-old Anatoli Dedenko told me. He added: "Russia is okay. But apart from Moscow and St. Petersburg the place is a dump." His pensioner neighbor Oleksandr Kostelia disagreed.

"I'm for federalization and separation from Kyiv. I'd vote for Russia," he said.

In 2014, the separatists controlled Mariupol for two months until the Azov Battalion and Ukrainian army units threw them out. Azov was a volunteer militia founded that May by Ukrainian nationalist Andriy Biletsky. Its mission was to defend the city from Russian forces. From the outset the battalion was eclectic. It attracted football hooligans, intellectuals, and some fighters with a military background. The Kremlin made much of its far-right origins. After wresting back the city, Azov became a special regiment within Ukraine's national guard. It denied Moscow's allegations that it was fascist, racist, and neo-Nazi.

After Mariupol's brush with secession, the Ukrainian authorities began a major program of investment and European-style renewal. The city flourished. There were new parks and better transport. Mariupol attracted refugees from other parts of the Donbas—artists and entrepreneurs. Its population grew by 30 percent. It became a symbol of Ukraine's superiority to the neo-Soviet DNR; the city, unlike decaying Donetsk, was attractive and prosperous.

Meanwhile, the war on Mariupol's doorstep continued. In 2015, the separatists bombarded the city's eastern left bank with rockets, killing thirty-one people. The Azov Regiment and the Ukrainian army counterattacked. They clawed back a few coastal villages. This meant the DNR could no longer reach Mariupol with artillery. When I returned in late January 2022, shooting was still going on. I found Ukrainian soldiers and sailors tasked with defending the city in good spirits. But they acknowledged that their Russian opponents outnumbered and outgunned them.

This was especially true at sea. Ukraine lost three-quarters of its modest naval assets in 2014, when Russian special forces seized the Crimean Peninsula and the port of Sevastopol. More than half of Kyiv's naval officers defected to Moscow. The Russians eventually handed back an aging Polish-built Soviet warship, the *Donbas*, after disabling its communications systems. It caught fire in 2016.

I met the *Donbas*'s Ukrainian captain, Oleksandr Hrigorevskiy. The command and repair vessel was moored in Mariupol's harbor; we chatted in its control room, poring over maps laid out on a green baize table. How big was Ukraine's Sea of Azov fleet? "Everything you can see," Hrigorevskiy said cheerfully. By which he meant the *Donbas* and two armored artillery boats, the *Ludny* and the *Kremenchuk*, parked alongside and visible through a porthole.

They were little match for Russia's mighty Black Sea fleet, it seemed. This was comprised of a fearsome flagship carrier, the *Moskva*, two modern frigates, several smaller warships, multiple missile boats and landing ships, and four submarines armed with Kalibr cruise missiles.

The Kremlin, the captain told me, had recently annexed the Sea of Azov by stealth, making it a de facto Russian lake. Under a 2003 agreement, Russia and Ukraine shared access. Since 2014, Moscow has controlled Crimea's Kerch Strait, the only way in and out. In 2018, it started impounding Ukrainian civilian vessels. In spring 2021, and largely unnoticed, it began a buildup of naval forces in the Black Sea region to match its deployments on land.

Latterly, Russia had closed the Sea of Azov to Ukrainian boats, citing the need to carry out "naval exercises." When the *Donbas* set off toward Kerch in December 2021, sailing in international waters, Putin's FSB spy agency accused Kyiv of an act of aggression. Once the sea's largest trading port, Mariupol could no longer export grain, iron, steel, and heavy machinery.

In Hrigorevskiy's view, Russia's imperial ambitions "never went away." The Black Sea was always crucial to Moscow and to its empire, he observed. It fought a war against the Ottomans over the Dardanelles and in 1853 launched a conflict with France, Britain, and Istanbul over Crimea—a disastrous one, as it turned out. In modern times the Sea of Azov was an important shipping lane for Russian commercial boats and for warships, too, on their way to Syria. Mariupol was therefore key to Russian maritime control.

We went on deck. Enemy warships were just out of sight on the horizon, the captain explained, adding that at night you could see the Russian port of Yeysk twinkling in the distance, fifty kilometers away. Each morning at 9:00 a.m., his sailors raised and saluted the Ukrainian flag. I watched under a pale raspberry sky as they carried out the ceremony. The ship's dog joined the parade.

"Sir commander, the flag is hung," the first officer said.

"Glory to Ukraine!" Hrigorevskiy shouted.

"To the heroes, glory," the sailors replied.

"At ease. At ease," the captain said.

There was no doubting the valor of the tiny maritime contingent deployed to deter Russian aggression. But I couldn't help noticing the date of manufacture stamped on the *Donbas*'s bow machine gun: 1954. "It's old but reliable," Oleksandr commented. The Russian sea blockade had dealt a death blow to the city's economy. The harbor's cranes had nothing to lift; pigeons outnumbered dockworkers; the entrance arch—marked with the year when the port was founded, 1889—seemed forlorn and without traffic.

Before going to the DNR front line, I picked up a local guide, Anatoliy Loza. Anatoliy was a military volunteer who in 2014 had helped wrest Mariupol back from separatist rule. He was one of many patriotic activists who stayed on. He fell in love with a local woman, Olena; they got married and lived in the city with their small daughter. Anatoliy said young people in Mariupol knew how to fight, but he conceded it would be "tough" to hold back the Russians if they advanced in strength.

Anatoliy thought Russia had not given up on Mariupol, where a minority looked favorably on Moscow. "TV plays a big role. You can get Russian state propaganda channels for free. You have to pay for Ukrainian ones," he told me as we sat in a car repair workshop run by a fellow volunteer. What did he make of Putin? "It's hard to understand his behavior. He's the incarnation of evil. I'm reminded of Dostoevsky's *Crime and Punishment*. If you kill one man you are bad, but if you kill a million you're a hero."

I liked Anatoliy—an idealistic figure in his thirties with wispy fair hair. He asked if I could put him in touch with the British tycoon Richard Branson. He wanted Branson to fund a project he was coordinating to provide free modular houses for Ukrainian "warriors." With the offer of cheap accommodation, they might settle in Mariupol and stop it from being a "gloomy borderland" under permanent threat from Putin's *Russkiy Mir*, he told me.

The Ukrainian military arrived at the workshop, and we set off together for the coastal resort of Shyrokyne, the scene of a bitter battle in 2015, ten kilometers east of the city. "My friend was killed in fighting here," the commander, Yuriy Ulshin, said as he drove us in his jeep on the way to a ruined primary school. Ulshin's nickname was "the Greek"; he belonged to Mariupol's ethnic Greek minority, who had settled along the coast in Ottoman times.

The school's desks were covered in grime. A photo of the class of 2011 lay in the wreckage. There were abandoned crayons and third-year books in Ukrainian and Russian. Beyond a bullet-scarred wall was a view of pine trees and sea. "There is nothing worse than war. Why did Russia do this?" Ulshin said. In 2018, a Russian sniper shattered his pelvis and nearly killed him. "Death happens when you don't expect it," he observed.

We continued to Shyrokyne's seaside holiday complex. It resembled a fantastical trashed theater set. An alley of pulverized apartments led on to a glass-strewn terrace. There was a child's rusted bike, a washing machine, and a twisted hood from a GAZ-53 truck. The ground was pitted with shell holes. The beach was mined. "Two days ago they fired a rocket at one of our cars out on patrol. It missed," Ulshin said.

The Ukrainian soldiers had taken over a sanatorium, now camouflaged with netting. It had a woodshed; washing hung on a line. The separatists lobbed missiles at them from beyond the hillside village of Vodiane, close by, and flew attack drones. As we chatted I heard the whump of an automatic grenade launcher. Morale was high. The platoon lacked heavy weapons; nothing had come from the West except for flak jacket plates sent by the Lithuanians, Ulshin told me, acknowledging: "Apart from us, nobody is going to fight."

We returned to Mariupol in a golden January light. On the left a giant factory loomed over the city. It was a mini-citadel of chimneys, pylons, and smelters. There were Victorian-style brick buildings; smoke floated over railway tracks and the Kalmius River; the plant ranged over more than four square miles. Underneath was a tunnel network. This was the Azovstal steelworks, Mariupol's biggest employer and a workplace for eleven thousand people. The communist-era *kombinat*, or industrial complex, privatized in the 1990s, belonged to Ukraine's richest man, the oligarch Rinat Akhmetov.

I had dinner that night in a cellar tavern on Heorhiivska Street, close to a pedestrian square and to Mariupol's 1960s neoclassical drama theater, a city feature with its Grecian sculptures and portico. The rustic brick-walled restaurant, Natan Ryabinkin, was packed. It was Saturday evening. There was live music; a female vocalist sang in Russian and English.

A group of women got up to dance with each other. Their awkward male partners sat and watched: a universal phenomenon at parties, it seems. Nobody was especially perturbed by the darkening headlines and the threat of Russian reinvasion; the city, clearly, had got used to war and to the sound of gunfire in the near distance. It was determined to enjoy itself.

Thinking about this scene later, I imagined a character from the *vertep* play I had seen in the airport earlier—invisible and dressed in black—joining the throng. The hooded figure holding a white scythe had come to summon men, women, children. It tugged them by the sleeve. At first gently, and then urgently.

Death was about to proceed through Mariupol.

In less than two months the city would cease to exist. At least 22,000 people would perish, according to its mayor, in a modern-day danse macabre.

· · ·

Vika Dubovitskaia was asleep at 5:30 a.m. when the first explosions shook Mariupol. It was February 24. Russian missiles crashed into the city's airfield and air defenses, blowing out the glass from the passenger terminal.

She had never really thought Moscow would attack. "I was ninety percent convinced it wouldn't happen," she told me when we met in the western city of Lviv. After all, she explained, the Kremlin's rationale for invasion made little sense. "I'm a Russian speaker. No one was oppressing me in Mariupol. You could choose whether to send your kids to Russian or Ukrainian language school. I didn't need saving."

At 7:00 a.m. Vika woke up, having slept through the early blasts, discovered the news from a neighbor, and hurried off to the nearest supermarket to buy food and supplies. Two hours later she heard a loud boom. The war had indeed arrived. The separatists were bombarding the east side of the city, the Vostochny district, just as they had during the 2015 rocket attack. Vika's husband, Dima, was away in Poland. She was alone with their children, Artem, eight, and Nastya, two.

Her home had no cellar. As the explosions continued, Vika ripped the bathtub from the wall, turned it upside down to form a protective shell, and told her two children to sit inside, coats on. There wasn't enough space for her, so she sat next to it, waiting for the horror to pass. Later that day the family relocated to a friend's flat on the western side of the city, near the port. There was a basement. It appeared to be a more prudent location.

Across Mariupol, residents were organizing themselves into ad hoc groups and moving underground into shelters: women, children, and the elderly going first. At the start, the conditions were tolerable. There was food and water, Vika said. Then the Russians destroyed the city's power grid. Airstrikes intensified and Russian armored vehicles advanced rapidly. Their offensive came not from the east, as everyone had expected, but from the west. The Russians seized the port of Berdiansk. On March 1, they reached the outskirts of town, blockading the western coastal road out.

Mariupol was besieged. The scenario Kyiv feared had come to pass.

On March 4, the gas pipeline that supplied the city was damaged. The city at a time of snow found itself without electricity and gas. Repair crews tried to fix broken power lines but had to retreat under heavy shelling. The Internet and cell phone connections went down in all but a few areas. Mariupol was in darkness. "The only news you can get is the direction of the bomb. It's unbearable, terrifying," one resident, Diana Berg, posted on Facebook, saying she had lost contact with her relatives.

And thus began what the city's deputy mayor Serhiy Orlov described as "medieval conditions," affecting four hundred thousand people. He painted a grim picture of life and death, of a slow and terrible degradation played out amid constant bombing, snow, and below-zero temperatures, of missiles flung from the sky and fired from warships—a campaign of total annihilation not seen on the European continent since 1945.

With no gas, residents cooked on open fires in their courtyards, heating whatever they had managed to grab from kitchens. The most precious commodity was firewood. Groups roamed around destroyed houses, searching for something to eat. Looting broke out, despite efforts by the Ukrainian military to keep order. Shops were stripped of bread, pharmacies of medicines; residents smashed cars to steal gasoline.

The biggest problem was water. "They are happy that it is cold and snowing. Snow means they have something to drink," Orlov told me a week into Mariupol's blockade, speaking via a blurry satellite connection. Some residents had prudently filled their bathtubs. There were long queues outside a handful of water tankers. Others collected water from springs and puddles and gathered snow from roofs. They siphoned it from defunct heating systems.

"I think about where to find some tea and a drop of sugar," Angela Timchenko wrote on Facebook. Without running water, she said she was struggling to feed her children. "Tell me, is it possible to bake an egg in foil? I have six of them lying around," she mused. It was "frosty outside and fiercely cold"; the bombardment had begun "early today," at 3:00 a.m. "The windows are shaking."

Any journey outside—on foot or in a vehicle—could be deadly. Vika said a Russian shell "blew over" her basement companion when she went out to try and find food, leaving her friend shaken and bruised. After that they stayed underground. Bodies lay on pavements, covered with rugs and sheets. It was dangerous to move them. Survivors interred the dead in makeshift graves, dug opposite their houses and in yards. Corpses were piled outside city hospitals or lay under rubble, unclaimed. Later the Russians dug mass plots in the nearby village of Manhush and other locations.

A list of some of the dead shared by local residents on a Telegram group stretched to more than eleven hundred names. Each told a story. There were a few sparse facts—name, address, manner of death, burial place:

Lubov Afanasyeva, 88, died of hunger and cold, buried next
to house
Ivan Mykolaevych, 37, airstrike on house, buried in the yard
of his house
Andriy Vadimovych, 25, shot in a car at the intersection of
Rivna and Zhygulivska Streets
Denys, age unknown, killed by mortar shells on the football
field of school number 34
Oksana Leonidovna, died from shrapnel with her husband,
buried in yard
Lubov Vlasovna, 76, died from hunger and dehydration,
soldiers took away her body from Builders Street 181

And:

Katia Vynnychenko, twelve, died on March 15 together
with her mom, from a direct hit
Myroslava, one year and six months, died along with her
grandmother Svitlana Chervertakova and other relatives.
Their kitchen destroyed, March 29, 2022, in the railway area

There were so many dead the city authorities were forced to
excavate a twenty-five-meter-long grave. "We couldn't identify
everybody," Orlov admitted. The situation, he told me, was
apocalyptic: 1,170 dead by March 9, with 47 placed in the
mass burial site. "Half of those killed by Russian bombing are
Ukrainians of Russian origin," he noted bitterly. If the city did
fall, it would become a "ghost place." "There is no Russian
Mariupol. It's going to be a desert," he said.

Mariupol's air defense no longer worked. And so Moscow

bombed with impunity. "They have used aviation, artillery, multiple launchers firing Grad rockets, and other types of weapons we don't even know about. This isn't simply treacherous. It's a war crime and pure genocide," Orlov said. He added: "A lot of districts are devastated. They are dropping half-ton bombs from the sky. Putin means to capture Mariupol whatever the human cost."

It was hard to disagree with Orlov's grim analysis. Russia's martial tactics in spring 2022 were familiar from previous gruesome Kremlin conflicts and from the darkest moments of the Second World War, when German bombers laid waste to enemy cities. Mariupol—occupied by the Nazis from 1941 to 1943—was becoming another Warsaw or Gdansk, a new and terrible Stalingrad, a modern Guernica.

Moscow had acted similarly in Chechnya and, starting in 2015, in northern Syria as part of its campaign to support President Assad. In both cases Russian aviation flattened whole urban areas, turning them into rubble. The goal was to terrorize the civilian population and to make them flee. It was cynical yet effective. This sort of operation was part of a military doctrine known as strategic bombing.

It would become the signature tactic of Russia's war in Ukraine, especially as Putin shifted focus to the Donbas in April 2022 following his failures to capture Kyiv and Kharkiv. Yes, there had been early losses of men and matériel. But in Mariupol, and in other eastern cities, the Kremlin sought to win through sheer mass—a grinding lethal superiority. Entire cities were razed. Russian troops then moved through the rubble and planted a flag on the ruins.

Strategic bombing was conducted against nonmilitary sites: hospitals, schools, and residential buildings, some of them used by Ukrainian defenders, others not. It was deliberate and systematic. "Putin has a sick imagination. He intends to destroy Ukraine so he can have Ukraine without Ukrainians," Orlov said.

By way of evidence, Orlov reeled off a list of Russian targets in Mariupol. They included numerous private apartment buildings, the main administration service building, the Priazov state technical university, and the six-hundred-bed maternity and children's hospital number 3, bombed by a war plane on the day we spoke. Survivors including mothers-to-be were led out across a burning brown moonscape. Ghostly ash fell from the sky. The missile left a ten-meter-wide muddy crater.

The strike killed three people. They included a pregnant woman and her baby, who died in the hospital. Seventeen were injured. Zelenskiy called the attack genocide. The White House described it as barbarous; the U.S. House of Representatives in Washington passed an aid package and a bill to ban Russian oil exports. None of this international outrage had an impact on the orders given by Putin to his commanders. They amounted to the following: keep going, well done.

The operation to smother the city continued. More than 2,600 buildings would be destroyed, wholly or in part. From bombed ruins came the sweet-sickly smell of human decay, the basements where civilians had sought refuge now so many charnel houses.

It was becoming obvious that to stay in Mariupol meant death, sooner or later. Residents considered escape. But how? Many did not have cars. Some did, but there was little fuel and they risked punctured tires from shrapnel on the road. The journey was theoretically possible, but led to an enemy checkpoint: the Russian column parked on the western edge of the city. There was continuous shelling and a high risk of being shot.

International organizations and the Ukrainian government tried repeatedly to arrange humanitarian corridors. More often than not, these evacuation attempts failed. Russian shooting had destroyed most city council vehicles. Two weeks into the siege there were twenty-one municipal buses left, Orlov said, out of a hundred—enough to evacuate 2,000 to 3,000 people, from around 200,000 who wanted to get out. Plus, the Russians had mined the road.

Despite the "suicidal" odds, Diana Berg and her husband, Sasha, decided they would try to leave. They drove out of the city, past two checkpoints, then, at the nearby town of Nikolske, through a phalanx of twenty Russian tanks and armored vehicles. "One turned its canon toward us. But for some fucking reason it didn't fucking shoot us," she said. It was a "miraculous" journey, and one that left her feeling shaken and guilty for friends and neighbors left behind.

Those without cars had fewer options. Vika Dobrovitskaya and her children got a lift to Mariupol's drama theater after hearing reports that families would be evacuated by bus. The buses never arrived. After two hours of waiting in the cold, Ukrainian soldiers ushered her into the building, together with around three hundred others. It was March 5. More than 1,200 people were already crammed inside, most of them women and children.

Vika had last visited the Dramteatr, as it was known, as a small girl. She had watched a performance of *The Nutcracker*. The theater's underground space was full. One of the company's actors, Damir Sukhov, showed her a place to stay on the first floor. "We lived in the corridor between classical columns. There were thick walls," she said. "It was very cold." Damir advised her to cannibalize the wooden scenery and use it to sleep on.

Other families slept in the auditorium, as well as in the makeup room and in two underground cellars. The stage area was warmer but more vulnerable, she said, situated beneath a flimsy roof. Within two days, another 1,500 people took shelter in the building. She had nothing to feed her children other than the snacks she had with her: apples and biscuits. "They wanted to eat. You feel guilty," she said.

Over the next week conditions improved a little. The soldiers brought food, including frozen fish and chicken, which were cooked on an open fire at the rear of the theater. Only children were allowed to eat. Friends or volunteers—known as *druzhniki*—looted a shop and brought warm clothes. They also organized patrols. The Russian word for children—*dyeti*—was painted outside in giant white letters, visible from the air.

The Russians understood the Dramteatr was Mariupol's biggest civilian facility. They had taken over the surrounding districts and set up an observation post in a branch of the PUMB bank, 250 meters away, Vika said. Meanwhile, she moved sleeping spots and went with Artem and Nastya to a projector room in the front of the building on the second floor.

Anatoliy Loza, the local guide who had shown me around in January, called me several times from inside the besieged city. Initially he was upbeat: Mariupol would not fall! By the time we spoke again, during the second week of March, he was desperate. He had concluded he was unlikely to survive. "Can you save my wife and children?" he asked. I apologized and told him the world was watching Mariupol and talks over evacuation were going on. On March 12, he called just after midnight. I could hear nothing but the sound of wind whipping over the Sea of Azov.

It was the last time he rang. Later, Anatoliy did not appear on the lists of the dead or the living. Like so many, he was lost in the vortex.

March 16 began much as usual for the residents of besieged Mariupol. It was a cold, clear morning—but at 9:45 a.m. there was a bright flash, a ball of fire, and an explosion. A Russian warplane dropped a laser-guided bomb on the Dramteatr. The missile crashed into the rear of the building. It fell obliquely, slicing through the right side and detonating inside the crowded stage area.

The blast flung Vika Dobrovitskaya against the wall. "I put my daughter on my shoulders and grabbed my son's hand. He told me: 'I'm tired of running.' I had hurt one side of my face but didn't notice. It was the adrenaline. My only thought was to get the kids out," she said. They ran down the stairs, together with other survivors, and exited into the street, the burning and smashed building now behind them.

It was unclear how many people perished in what was one of the most egregious crimes in Russia's war—three hundred, Zelenskiy said initially, though the figure was revised to six hundred. Those at the front of the building and basement appear mostly to have survived. All the people in the back area and the right wing of the theater died. That included pregnant women accommodated in the dressing rooms. The field kitchen was obliterated, too, together with those who had been waiting nearby for warm water.

Rescuers tried to help. One of them, Dmytro Yurin, said he heard an enormous explosion and saw the theater had been blown up. "I heard cries and screams," he told me. "There were bodies and bits of bodies. I pulled one woman out, then a girl, then a boy. The boy's legs didn't move. He was screaming. My hands were shaking. I was covered in blood."

Nearby a woman lay motionless, Dmytro said. Family members were pressing on her chest, attempting to resuscitate her. There was a child standing next to her, saying: "Mom, don't sleep." The woman was dead. Dmytro went back to his flat on Prospekt Myra, a few hundred meters from the theater, swallowed some pills, and lit a cigarette. He decided to escape Mariupol. Three hours later he set off.

Dmytro's plan was ingenious. An amateur fisherman, he had spent time with his father catching a local mullet known as *pelengas*. He put on his fishing waders, tied two garbage bags around his socks, and made an improvised buoyancy vest using four five-liter plastic bottles tied together with string. He took a path he knew to the seafront and plunged in.

The water was cold. Dmytro swam out 150 meters. He went in a westerly direction, parallel to the shore. "My teeth were chattering. I hid behind one of the bottles so no one could see me," he said. He bobbed past a Russian position at Rybatske and staggered out of the water at the village of Melekyne. An elderly couple took him in. They gave him vodka and borsch. The next day he got a bus to Berdiansk and traveled from there to safety in Lviv.

One Mariupol family exited by taking the same beachside route. They waded through the water to avoid mines. Another man, sixty-one-year-old Ihor Pedin, walked to Zaporizhzhia together with his dog, Zhu Zhu, an astonishing 225-kilometer trek to safety. Many people, though, remained inside the city. They were stuck.

The siege stretched into weeks, and then a month. One place became a holdout and sanctuary: an unvanquished blue-and-yellow island amid an ocean of seething red.

Yaroslav, an eighteen-year-old graduate of Mariupol's metallurgy institute, began an apprenticeship on February 20. His workplace was the Azovstal steelworks, which loomed over the Kalmius River and the city's left bank. The industrial zone was vast.

Five days later, when Russia invaded, the plant opened its doors to anyone who needed somewhere to shelter.

On March 5, as bombs fell on his neighborhood, Yaroslav moved in. His new "home" was a workshop that manufactured rails for train tracks, located in an isolated part of the site. Yaroslav fashioned himself a bed. Two older employees became his companions. A strange new life began.

For the hundred thousand or so residents living on Mariupol's east side, Azovstal was a natural place of shelter. A deep network of Cold War bunkers offered some protection from Russian missiles. After Moscow's failed attempt in 2014 to seize Mariupol, the plant's management refurbished thirty-six bomb shelters. It brought in reserves of food, as well as generators. Workers were instructed to fill industrial tanks with water.

Soon the factory's underground chambers began to fill up. Workers, their families, and neighbors whose flats were destroyed moved underground. Most expected to stay for a couple of days. A week at most. They brought with them

essentials—diapers, formula, plus documents and blankets—
and clothed themselves in company jackets branded with the
logo METINVEST.

The factory also had a military aspect. Mariia Khodova
said her husband, Serhiy, a territorial army volunteer, was told
soon after the invasion to report to Azovstal. "We didn't know
why. It was a bit of a mystery," she said. Serhiy said goodbye
to his wife and their nine-year-old daughter, Sofia, and to his
mother-in-law, Tatiana. He went off to the plant, disappearing
into its twisting passages.

The Azov Regiment had taken over part of the complex in
preparation for a Russian assault. It stockpiled food, medical
supplies, weapons, and ammunition. The factory was built to
withstand a nuclear strike and was a logical spot for a defensive base. In Yaroslav's workshop there were two half-ton bar-
rels of what Ukrainians called "technical" water, not suitable
for drinking. "We helped the soldiers carry it," he said. This
would become Azovstal's main water supply when bottled
water ran out.

To begin with, civilians consumed their own food. Once it
was gone, Azov fighters provided civilians with something to
eat—canned goods and dried rations, Yaroslav said. He said
he passed the time by playing dominoes and talking about life.
"We spoke to people. We discussed everything," he told me,
speaking in Russian over the phone. There was little expectation that they would get out of Azovstal alive as days rolled
into weeks. "Hope was small," he admitted.

Over time, provisions for everyone dwindled. Olena Chekho-
natski said she fled to Azovstal at the start of the war together
with her husband, Yehor, and their sons, twelve-year-old Artem
and seventeen-year-old Dmytro. By the end the adults were eat-

ing one tiny meal a day and feeding scraps to their dachshund, Spike. Two cups of macaroni went into ten liters of water, and that "soup" fed thirty people. The children ate twice. Mothers warmed water by holding candles beneath metal cups.

There was no Internet or electricity, just a small radio. The Chekhonatskis used car batteries to power LED lights. They played games: chess, backgammon, cards, and a Mariupol monopoly set. Going to the toilet, located up on the ground floor, was risky. They tried to sleep as much as possible. "When you are asleep, you don't need to eat," Yehor explained. Families slept on wooden bunk beds or on beds constructed from pallets and plastic foam.

The Chekhonatskis' two boys were initially traumatized, though gradually they adjusted to their subterranean world. They made friends; the older kids taught the younger ones, *The Guardian*'s Emma Graham-Harrison reported. A four-year-old who could scarcely read the alphabet when they arrived learned to do math, and to write and read well. The exact number of civilians in Azovstal was unclear—between three hundred and one thousand, Mariupol's mayor estimated, including thirty children and a four-month-old baby.

Fire was constant. The Russians dropped bunker-buster bombs. The shelter's walls shook; plaster fell off the ceiling; a blast dislodged a generator, which stopped working. A three-ton bomb demolished a five-story building directly above one location where civilians were hiding, blocking its two exits; soldiers dug them clear the next morning.

By mid-April, the Russians had captured most of Mariupol. They destroyed the *Donbas*, the command ship I had visited in January, and pushed the city's Ukrainian defenders into three pockets. The biggest was Azovstal. Another was the port area and the Primorskiy district. A third was the Illich steel- and ironworks, in the north of the city.

The Illich plant, even larger than Azovstal, was a base for the Thirty-Sixth Marine Brigade, the second unit tasked with protecting Mariupol, in addition to the Azov Regiment. One of the Ukrainian marines stationed there, twenty-five-year-old Hlib Stryzhko, told me the Russian army surrounded the site. They had superior firepower: artillery; attack drones, flown in groups of five; and aircraft, he said.

On April 10, a Russian tank fired at his observation position. "I was in a third-floor stairwell. I flew two floors down. The walls came down on top of me. I couldn't open my eyes. I thought I was dead. Then I heard my radio."

Medics pulled Hlib from the rubble, severely injured. The explosion fractured his pelvis, jaw, chest, and nose. He was taken to a field hospital. Three days later, the brigade abandoned the factory. One group escaped in darkness and managed to cross to Azovstal and join up with fighters there. A second contingent tried to break through enemy lines and got captured. The Russians entered his ward—Hlib couldn't see them but heard their voices. They took him and the other patients prisoner. Hlib spent a few weeks in a DNR hospital in Novoazovsk before his release in late April in a prisoner swap. The Russians brought in a TV crew but offered no treatment, he said.

The Kremlin had almost but not quite created the land corridor it had long craved, connecting occupied Donbas with Crimea. Only Azovstal held out. The Russian army did everything it could to wipe out those inside. It bombed the factory continuously. It carried out air strikes every half hour, as if dropping fuel-air explosives was a quotidian affair. It deployed phosphorus munitions. A shell killed four people who had gone up to the surface for a cigarette.

For both Kyiv and Moscow, the fate of those inside Azovstal had profound significance. It was a place where two rival narratives collided. For Ukrainians, the Azovstal defenders were a symbol of resistance and pride, of defiance and national heroism. Their refusal to yield was compared to the Greeks who fought the Persians in the Battle of Thermopylae in 480 BC, demonstrating extraordinary bravery against impossible odds, and ultimately fighting and dying to the last man.

Alongside Bucha, Mariupol was also spectacular proof of Russia's war crimes. This mass murder was so blatant, it behooved the international community to do something, Kyiv argued. As Zelenskiy put it, speaking to the Belgian parliament, Mariupol was now the "most horrific place in Europe." "It is hell. It is a catastrophe everyone knows about, the whole world." He lamented: "Nobody is determined enough to help stop it."

For Putin, capturing Mariupol was evidence that his military operation in Ukraine was succeeding after his unexpected failure in February and March to topple Kyiv's government. It was crucial to the fiction Russia's president had told his own citizens that the war was being conducted to "de-Nazify" Ukraine. The Azov Regiment had historical far-right links. Its members, from the Kremlin's perspective, were actual Nazis. If they were captured, state TV might exploit them for propaganda purposes. The goal—not quite achieved—was to "liberate" Mariupol in time for May 9 and the Kremlin's annual Red Square victory parade, commemorating the Soviet Union's defeat of Hitler.

Never mind that Putin's scorched-earth methods were

themselves a chilling display of twenty-first-century fascism. As were the deportations, murders, and rapes. Mariupol's mayor, Vadym Boichenko, noted that the Nazis killed ten thousand residents during their two-year occupation of the city. The Russian military more than doubled this figure in just two months, Boichenko said. It destroyed around 90 percent of Mariupol, transforming the city into "ash."

By late April, it was clear breaking out of Azovstal would be impossible. Speaking to Shoigu, Russia's defense minister, Putin said it was not necessary to storm the complex. "There is no need to climb into these catacombs and crawl underground," he said. Instead, he recommended a blockade "so that a fly can't get through." The nearest Ukrainian government–controlled territory was a hundred kilometers away. A deal of some kind with Moscow seemed the only option to save the lives of those inside.

As the world watched Mariupol's agony, the Azov brigade released a video of some of the families living underground. A soldier hands out sweets. The children—seventeen of them, ranging from babies to teenagers—look wan after nearly two months inside Azovstal. One woman said there was almost nothing left to eat. All wanted to go home. Their camp, at the end of a white-painted corridor marked with the sign DEYTI, resembled a youth hostel, with towels and clothes hanging on a line. One child was engrossed in a coloring book.

It was a pitiful scene.

"Please get us out of here. We want to breathe fresh air, to see the sky," a woman said. "You can't imagine what life is like. A cup of tea with sugar would be happiness."

A boy added: "We want to leave, to see sunshine again."

Putin was sufficiently confident in the outcome of the siege to allow a UN-brokered cease-fire. Over four days, beginning May 4, civilians gingerly emerged from their dungeon and boarded a series of evacuation buses. Around three hundred people exited: women, children, Azovstal employees. The Red Cross supervised. Russian TV showed a scene of order as troops and a black-robed Russian priest escorted civilians along a humanitarian corridor.

The actuality was different. The Russians had shelled previous evacuation attempts, killing one Azov soldier in April as he tried to drive civilians to safety. Two others died when a drone spotted and bombed them. Those who emerged in May found themselves subject to a new kind of horror, as the apprentice Yaroslav was about to discover. Russian troops carried this out in all areas that fell under their control: from Mariupol to Kherson to the Donbas. It had a name: filtration.

Yaroslav was one of the last civilians to exit Azovstal. He said he emerged from the catacombs to find his home city "utterly destroyed." He walked for two kilometers along the river embankment to a Russian checkpoint, past rubble and dead dogs. The soldiers told him to put his hands up and said they would shoot him if he tried to go anywhere. Another unit transferred him to a filtration camp in Bezimenne, a DNR-controlled village ten kilometers east from Shyrokyne, the one-time frontline village. Men in balaclavas escorted him to a tent and told him to strip, then checked him for patriotic tattoos. They took fingerprints.

The experience was terrifying, he recalled. His Russian interrogators beat him on the back and kicked him, he said. They confiscated his phone and tried calling his parents. He had warned them not to answer. One of his captors told him: "We will cut your fucking head off and send it to your mother."

Later a Red Cross official stuck his head through the door. The soldiers became a little less aggressive. They eventually said: "You are clean. Go."

Yaroslav boarded a civilian bus to Zaporizhzhia, in Ukrainian government–controlled territory. He went through twenty-eight Russian checkpoints. "I consider myself lucky," he reflected. Yaroslav said his sister and grandparents were taken to the DNR, while a classmate was sent to Russia—one of around forty thousand Mariupol residents spirited across the border. His relatives were marooned, their documents seized and not returned, Yaroslav said, adding that he would not give his last name in order to protect them.

Mariia, whose husband left for Azovstal and never came back, managed to flee Mariupol with her mother and daughter. She reached a DNR police station. "The worst thing was they behaved in a friendly way. They razed my city and gave us biscuits. I tried to hide my hatred for them," she said. The queues at the filtration point were reminiscent of the Soviet Union, she added, with pensioners in one line, and another for cell phone SIM cards from Phoenix, a DNR provider. Many men were taken away and vanished.

The Azov fighters had no illusions about what would happen to them if they surrendered, an apprehension that would turn out to be horribly accurate. They could expect worse treatment than the beatings and psychological pressure meted out to noncombatants. Surrender could mean torture, humiliation, and rape. Possibly execution. The best-case scenario was a prisoner exchange at some future date. On April 20, one soldier was taken prisoner after being knocked out on the battlefield. The Russians suffocated him. Four days later they sent a photo of his body to his mother.

It was against this backdrop that the regiment held a press conference on May 8 via satellite link. Two bearded figures appeared on screen. One was Azov's deputy commander, Captain Svyatoslav "Kalina" Palamar. The other was a senior officer in military intelligence, Lieutenant Ilya Samoilenko. After two and half months underground, Samoilenko's face was porcelain white. He acknowledged the bleakness of their situation. "We are basically here dead men. Most of us know this. That's why we are fighting so fearlessly," he said.

Samoilenko made clear his exasperation. Many people had let them down. They included Ukraine's military high command, which had not tried to rescue them. He was also frustrated with politicians in Kyiv who, over eight years, had failed to adequately shore up Mariupol's defense, and with Western nations whose "weak reaction" to Putin's 2014 land grab had made possible Russia's latest invasion. He also criticized journalists who asked "bullshit" questions about Azov's alleged neo-Nazi proclivities. The regiment ditched its extreme associations long ago, he said.

The garrison had hung on for longer than anybody had expected, inflicting tremendous damage on the enemy and accounting for 10 percent of Russian losses in Ukraine, he added. But Azovstal was now near the end—its defenders out of weapons and lacking basic medicines to treat the wounded, lodged in a hospital "built from scratch." They couldn't abandon their injured, he said. Or the bodies of their dead. After so much sacrifice, those still living wanted an "honorable" way out. "Our message is: 'Don't waste our effort,'" he said.

I asked Samoilenko about collaborators. There were reports that an ex–Azovstal employee had given the Russians a map of the complex. And that local opposition bloc councillors had helped coordinate the attack on the city. Was this true? The majority of Mariupol residents supported Ukraine, he explained, seeming resigned, while those who helped the enemy acted from fear. "A lot of people are terrified," he said.

Eight days later, Zelenskiy ordered the garrison to surrender. This pragmatic decision was made, the president said in a video address, to ensure the fighters' survival. "We need our heroes alive," he told Ukrainians. On May 16, the first soldiers left—51 badly wounded, some carried out on stretchers, and 251 others. The injured were taken to the DNR hospital in Novoazovsk.

One fighter, Dmytro "Orest" Kozatskyi, posted photos and video he had taken during the siege and its final hours. The images are haunting, but also a gift to posterity. After ceaseless bombardment, the factory's roof is a ravaged metal canopy, bathed in an eerie aquamarine light. Rain washes over the lurid scene. Kozatskyi smokes a cigarette beneath broken gantries and flamboyantly splayed metal railings. There is a chiaroscuro quality about the pictures, the faces of Azovstal's defenders lit by flicking fires, as if painted by a Renaissance master—a Rembrandt or a Caravaggio. "That's it. I am thankful to Azovstal for shelter—the place of my death and life," Kozatskyi wrote on Instagram.

The regiment left fully on May 17, together with a part of the Thirty-Sixth Brigade, local police, and territorial defense volunteers, including Mariia's husband, Serhiy. They had held out for eighty-three days. Russian footage showed a line of uniformed soldiers trudging along a pitted road. Guards in white armbands pat them down; some soldiers limp, others are on crutches. They are loaded into buses and driven away. According to Russia's defense ministry, 2,439 Ukrainian fighters surrendered.

Ukraine's presidential adviser Mykhailo Podolyak sought to celebrate the situation. He praised the Azovstal POWs. They had "completely changed" the outcome of Russia's war and had wrecked its plan to capture the east, he said. Their heroic actions had bogged down Moscow's battalions and delayed Russia's advance into the Donbas, buying valuable time for other Ukrainian units. Azov's warriors had dented the idea of Moscow's military invincibility, he suggested. As the battle in Mariupol came to a close, he reinforced the observation others had made, that Azovstal was a new Thermopylae.

All this was probably true. And yet the fall of Mariupol amounted to a major victory for Putin in his effort to strangle Ukraine. Slowly but surely, village by village, street by ruined street, the Kremlin was gaining ground. It believed it was winning. As Putin saw it, Russia was triumphing not just over Kyiv but over Zelenskiy's coalition of Western allies. Putin was beating Europe, and NATO. Most of all, he was chastening America, Russia's eternal foe.

Pushing the button on war. In the summer of 2021, Vladimir Putin published an essay claiming that Russia and Ukraine were a "single people." He sent armored columns to Ukraine's border and demanded concessions from the West and NATO. On February 24, 2022, Putin launched a full-scale invasion. It was Europe's biggest conflict since 1945. The goal was to seize the capital Kyiv, topple its pro-Western government, and wipe Ukraine from the map. *Courtesy of Uncredited/Associated Press/Shutterstock*

Servant of the people. In early 2022, Ukraine's actor turned president, Volodymyr Zelenskiy, was slumping in the polls. The Kremlin's invasion transformed him into a wartime leader and international celebrity. As Russian tanks rolled toward Kyiv, Zelenskiy refused to leave, telling his citizens in an iPhone video: "I'm here." He persuaded world leaders to provide arms and portrayed Ukraine's struggle as a *Lord of the Rings*–style drama, pitting good against evil. *Courtesy of Facebook/@Volodymyr Zelenskiy*

In March 2022, Russian troops seized Bucha, a leafy middle-class Kyiv suburb. The paratroopers—pictured here, in CCTV images—rounded up civilian men. Eight were taken to a military base at 144 Yablunska Street, interrogated, and executed in a yard. Photograph taken from a surveillance camera in Bucha.

Volodymyr Cherednichenko took a photo of a destroyed Russian column in Bucha. It was a terrible mistake. Russian soldiers found the picture and dragged him away from his crying mother. They locked him in a cellar, and one night they forced him to kneel and shot him through the ear. It was a cold, pitiless execution. *Courtesy of Luke Harding*

Russia's prodigious crimes emerged in April 2022 when Moscow hastily withdrew its troops from the Kyiv region and the northeast. At least thirteen people were murdered on Ivan Franko Street, where Volodymyr lived. These are three bodies found in a neighboring house, close to a Russian checkpoint. *Courtesy of Daniel Berehulak/*The New York Times/*Redux/eyevine*

Mariupol was a flourishing modern European city on the Sea of Azov. Within two months, Russia's army had reduced it to ruins, killing at least twenty thousand civilians. It was an act of genocide, with Mariupol a new Guernica. Russian warplanes deliberately bombed a maternity hospital and theater where hundreds of women and children were sheltering. *Courtesy of Mstyslav Chernov/Associated Press*

A municipal mass grave. With no water or electricity, Mariupol's inhabitants cooked food on open fires. Shrapnel killed many of them. Survivors buried the dead in courtyards and playgrounds. Others were entombed under rubble. *Courtesy of Evgeniy Maloletka/Associated Press/Shutterstock*

Mariia Khodova with her husband, Serhiy, and daughter, Sofia, in happier times. On the day of the invasion, Serhiy reported to the sprawling Azovstal steel factory. A military volunteer, he defended the city until the Russians captured him in May. *Courtesy of Mariia Khodova*

Dmytro "Orest" Kozatskyi is an Azov Regiment soldier and talented photographer. His photos offer an astonishing portrait of life and death in besieged Azovstal. Its tunnels were home to troops and civilians during a brutal Russian bombardment that lasted nearly three months. *Courtesy of Dmytro Kozatskyi/Associated Press/ Shutterstock*

Around twenty-five hundred Azovstal fighters surrendered following orders from Kyiv. In custody, they were tortured, intimidated, and starved. In July, at least fifty were blown up and murdered at Olenivka, a camp outside separatist Donetsk. "Orest" was released in a prisoner swap. *Courtesy of Dmytro Kozatskyi/Associated Press/Shutterstock*

Back to the USSR. In his historical essay, Putin revived nineteenth-century imperial ideas and blamed Lenin for creating Ukraine. And yet statues of the long-dead Bolshevik leader were reerected in the Russian-occupied south and east. It spoke to the ideological confusion behind Moscow's invasion project. *Courtesy of Anton Gerashchenko/Telegram*

Roman Kostenko, a member of Ukraine's parliament and a special forces commander, posing with a destroyed enemy vehicle. Kostenko led the defense of the southern city of Mykolaiv, which found itself twenty miles from the front line and within range of Russian guns. *Courtesy of Roman Kostenko*

The banner reads "Kherson is Ukraine." The first city to fall, Kherson was the only regional capital in Russian hands. Residents protested against their new overlords, calling them orcs. Zelenskiy vowed to retake Kherson, and in August, his forces launched a counteroffensive. *Courtesy of Ukrinform.net*

Boris Johnson and Zelenskiy on one of several walkabouts. The then UK prime minister was a passionate supporter of Ukraine who predicted Kyiv would win and sent anti-tank weapons. He became a cult figure among ordinary Ukrainians, celebrated in memes, paintings, and rap songs. *Courtesy of Uncredited/Associated Press/Shutterstock*

The Biden administration gave more than $12 billion in military support to Ukraine. The delivery of long-range HIMARS played a critical role in enabling a Ukrainian counterattack. The U.S. president didn't visit, but in May, First Lady Jill Biden met Zelenskiy's wife, Olena Zelenska, in the west of the country. *Courtesy of Susan Walsh/Associated Press/Shutterstock*

European allies. Olaf Scholz, Emmanuel Macron, and Mario Draghi on their way by train to Kyiv. The invasion caught France and Germany by surprise. Zelenskiy criticized Berlin's apparent reluctance to supply Ukraine with heavy weapons. Draghi, Italy's then prime minister, led the way in weaning the European Union off Russian energy. *Courtesy of Ludovic Marin/Associated Press/Shutterstock*

A Ukrainian fighter, Slava, taking a break from battle. Slava fought in 2014 and joined the volunteer Donbas brigade when Russia reinvaded in 2022. He parked his armored transporter in the city of Sloviansk and went for a swim in the river. *Courtesy of Anastasia Taylor-Lind/* The Guardian

Apartment blocks in Sloviansk hit by Russian rockets. Ukrainian civilians fled frontline towns and cities to escape indiscriminate bombardment. Some elderly residents stayed, and others returned to their homes when they ran out of money. Air-raid sirens and booms became a part of daily life. *Courtesy of Anastasia Taylor-Lind/* The Guardian

In March, Putin said his new war aim was to "liberate" the Donbas. Moscow succeeded in conquering all of Luhansk Oblast, including Sievierodonetsk and Lysychansk in neighboring Donetsk Oblast. This was a slow and costly advance. By summer, it ground to a halt. *Courtesy of David Guttenfelder for* The New York Times/*Redux/eyevine*

In March, Russian forces seized the Zaporizhzhia power plant, Europe's largest nuclear facility, and the adjoining city of Enerhodar. They made the site a military base and used it to hurl rockets across the Dnipro River. Moscow shelled the plant to disconnect it from the Ukrainian power grid. Putin was blackmailing the United States and Europe, whose gas supplies he turned off. *Courtesy of Ed Jones/AFP via Getty Images*

Putin dreamed of staging a victory parade in downtown Kyiv. It didn't happen the way he imagined. Ukraine highlighted his failure by exhibiting destroyed Russian hardware in the square outside Saint Michael's monastery. His war in Ukraine was one of the twenty-first century's biggest strategic blunders. *Courtesy of Sergei Supinsky/AFP via Getty Images*

In September, Ukrainian troops launched a stunning counteroffensive in the northeast and south. They recaptured a string of towns and villages around Kharkiv and squeezed enemy forces dug in around Kherson. Russian soldiers ran away as the Kremlin's invasion unraveled. *Courtesy of Telegram/@kuptg*

SEVEN

The Allies

Kyiv
Spring–Summer 2022

Dobryy den, everybody. I just want
you to know we support you.
—BORIS JOHNSON,
DURING A VISIT TO KYIV, JUNE 2022

There were guards outside the Khreshchatyk metro station, checking names against a list. I gave my details, ducked between a wall of sandbags, and entered a spacious vestibule. An escalator took me deep beneath Kyiv. I went along a subterranean corridor, past white marble walls decorated with floral tiles. Ceiling lamps bathed the station in a calming though unearthly glow.

At last, I reached the platform. It was now the venue for a remarkable press conference. There was a stage, chair, and table with a translation headset. Blue-and-yellow flags formed a backdrop. Ukrainian commandos sat in the front row, together with presidential aides dressed like their boss in somber green

T-shirts. At 7:30 p.m. armed protection officers arrived. Zelenskiy followed, riding down the escalator like a regular Joe.

The president took his place as the last Saturday train service of the day trundled past the platform. The driver tooted his horn; passengers peered out at their citizen leader standing in this surreal scene. This was Zelenskiy's first big press conference since Russia's invasion, two months before. The metro location gave the encounter a sense of theater. The Soviet-built metro was clearly chosen for security reasons, being beyond the reach of Moscow's potent missiles.

After his unsuccessful attempt to grab Kyiv, Putin's battle plan had mutated. He had embarked on an open-ended war of conquest. Its new stated focus was the Donbas.

Zelenskiy, meanwhile, had become the most sought after leader on the planet, the "Justin Bieber of international politics, a pop star, a serial hero," in the words of one admiring diplomat, speaking to *Der Spiegel* magazine. The president's press office received thousands of media requests for interviews, from U.S. networks, European newspapers, and Japanese news agencies. There were too many to handle. Hence an underground press conference to meet the demand.

Two hundred journalists were invited. I got the first question. In light of strange recent video footage showing the Russian leader gripping a Kremlin table with both hands, I asked Zelenskiy why Putin had invaded. Was Putin mad or ill? Or had he gone to war for some other reason? Zelenskiy told me Russia's president had "always wanted to do something like this," adding that much of Russian society shared his prejudice that Ukraine shouldn't exist. "This is a war for Ukraine's freedom, so we can live," he said.

The two-hour briefing gave us, the fourth estate, one stand-out headline. Zelenskiy revealed two important figures were on their way to Kyiv—U.S. Secretary of State Antony Blinken and Defense Secretary Lloyd Austin. They were the most senior American officials to visit since February 24. Zelenskiy said he was hoping Joe Biden might drop by, too, once the security situation improved. The United States was "the leader" when it came to support for Ukraine, he said, together with Britain, and then other European nations.

There seemed little prospect that the U.S. Secret Service would ever allow Biden to travel to Kyiv, I reflected. The journey involved flying to eastern Poland, driving across the border, and typically catching an overnight train from Lviv: the invasion had closed the airports. Ukrainian railways laid on a luxurious carriage for official visitors, and it was an alluring method of travel for sure: look out the window in the summer and you might glimpse a stork nesting atop a utility pole, and dawn breaking over misty villages, with neat wooden dachas and gold-domed churches.

The route was not without hazard, though. Lights were turned off at night to comply with curfew rules. And, put truthfully, to make it harder for Russia to blow up moving trains. Moscow had repeatedly hurled missiles at the Ukrainian railway infrastructure, killing fifty-nine people that April as they waited to be evacuated from the eastern city of Kramatorsk. The prime ministers and presidents who traveled to Kyiv—whether you considered them visionaries or idiots—showed a degree of bravery that went beyond conventional politics.

An anti-Putin coalition took shape in the immediate aftermath of Russia's thunderbolt invasion. The Kremlin had calculated that the democratic world's reaction would be similar to that of 2014, after Crimea: harsh words, minor sanctions, and not much else. Putin believed the West to be decadent, feeble, and in the grip of the same terminal decline that had overwhelmed the Soviet Union in 1991. The West's collapse, Kremlin analysts liked to say, was not far off, an inevitable entropic counterpoint.

In fact, Putin underestimated his opponents' resolve and cohesion, in the same way he wrongly assumed Ukrainians would welcome an occupying Russian army. Inadvertently, he revitalized the transatlantic alliance, which, during the fraught Trump years, had been beleaguered by rancor and froideur. The United States led a coalition that stretched from North America and across Europe to East Asia. It grew to around fifty nations, including the G7, responsible for more than half the world's gross domestic product (GDP).

This pro-Ukraine bloc featured the United Kingdom, the United States' closest ally; the Baltic nations and Scandinavia; the countries of Central Europe; Canada; the big nations of Western and Southern Europe: France, Germany, Italy, Portugal, and Spain; plus Australia, New Zealand, Japan, and South Korea.

In the run-up to war, the White House and Downing Street made sensitive intelligence public. This strategy—dubbed "prebuttal"—went against the grain of intelligence practice. Biden repeatedly warned that Putin was about to invade and that Russia was preparing to launch false-flag chemical attacks—something that ultimately didn't happen, possibly as a result of Washington's preemptive tactics. Overall, the briefings wrong-footed the Kremlin and blunted its disinformation campaign.

EU leaders got the same U.S. briefings. Not all were convinced. The French and the Germans were skeptical. Senior government figures in Paris insisted the Anglo-American view was wrong, that a full-scale invasion was unlikely, and more time for diplomacy was needed. Macron subsequently sacked his military intelligence chief, General Eric Vidaud, for his failure to "master the issues." Germany's foreign intelligence boss, Bruno Kahl, was in Kyiv when Russia's attack began. Kahl had to scramble out of the country by car, a long trip back to Berlin.

Once Russian tanks crossed the border, these differences became a thing of the past. Going forward, Western nations agreed on the *nature* of the invasion. There was no dispute about what happened in spring 2022 and what it fundamentally meant. As Zelenskiy said, this was not a war being waged by Russia against only Ukraine. It was ultimately a war for the future of the world order and for the right to dictate conditions in Europe. A war, then, of ideas.

As Biden put it during a speech that March in Warsaw, the Polish capital, Ukraine's cause was a "new battle for freedom." It was the latest manifestation of a long struggle between "democracy and autocracy; between liberty and repression; and between a rules-based order and one governed by brute force." Framed in these idealistic terms, Ukraine's fight for national survival wasn't particular but universal: not theirs, but ours.

Russia's aggression brought back memories of a communist age, a time when Moscow's tanks rolled into European cities, Biden suggested. He likened resistance in Kyiv, Mariupol, and Kharkiv to uprisings in Hungary, Poland, and Czechoslovakia against Soviet tyranny. The people prevailed in 1989 when the Berlin Wall came down. But in the post–Cold War era, autocracy had revived across the globe, he said, bringing with it contempt for democracy, rules, and the truth.

Rival visions of how the global security system should work clashed. Putin articulated the Kremlin view during a 2007 speech at the Munich Security Conference. He decried a U.S.-dominated international order and said he would no longer tolerate what he called a "unipolar world." His perspective was essentially Hobbesian, with a nineteenth-century flavor: bigger powers could deconstruct smaller ones. Countries were either "sovereign" or "colonies," Putin said bluntly in summer 2022. Ukraine occupied the second category.

The United States and its allies shared a contrasting liberal vision. It was based on human rights and the notion of self-determination. As they saw it, Russia's invasion was a throw-back to a bygone age of violent imperial conquest. It violated a post–Second World War norm that countries did not use force to change sovereign borders. Outside Ukraine, the last time this had happened was in 1990, when Saddam Hussein's Iraq invaded Kuwait. The United States had led invasions of its own, of course—the disasters of Afghanistan and Iraq—but had not sought to change the world's map.

Underlying coalition thinking was a strategic calculation. It said that if Putin prevailed in Ukraine, he would keep going. This seemed highly probable. Biden—whose foreign policy experience stretched back almost half a century and included meetings with Soviet premier Alexei Kosygin—held this view, U.S. officials indicated. In the future, Russia might target the Baltic states, Moldova, and Poland. Beyond that, prime-time Russian state TV included discussions of how the Kremlin could bomb Berlin, or nuke London.

Meanwhile, popular outrage in the West at Russia's aggression helped shape government decision-making, prompting historic swerves in policy. There was a surge of support for

Ukrainians under fire, and admiration for their grit and hero-ism. Ordinary citizens invited refugees to stay in their homes, hung Ukrainian flags from their balconies, went to rallies, and donated money, clothes, and medicine. They demanded eco-nomic sanctions against Moscow and lobbied international companies to exit the Russian market.

Andriy Zagorodnyuk, the former defense minister, told me he arrived at the Ukrainian embassy in Washington, D.C., soon after the invasion to find it festooned with flowers. "We could not get through," he said. He added: "There was a shift in U.S. society. A lot of people were shocked. They could not believe what was happening. There is massive societal back-ing in the U.S. for Ukraine." This sentiment was bipartisan: it united Democrats and Republicans on Capitol Hill at a time of bitter political divisions over the storming of the Capitol by a pro-Trump mob, the Supreme Court's striking down of *Roe v. Wade*, the veracity of the 2020 election result, and much else.

Amid strong public feeling in the United States, high-ranking dignitaries hastened to visit Ukraine. Blinken and Aus-tin were the latest. Speaker of the House Nancy Pelosi visited, too, as did the First Lady, Jill Biden, who met with Zelenskiy's wife, Olena, in the western Ukrainian city of Uzhhorod. Euro-pean guests included Ursula von der Leyen, the president of the European Commission, Spanish prime minister Pedro Sánchez, his Danish counterpart, Mette Frederiksen, plus leaders from Poland, Slovakia, Slovenia, Estonia, Latvia, and Lithuania.

The visits were a show of solidarity. They underscored the fact that Ukraine was still in business as a viable sovereign state, and that Zelenskiy—unlike Putin—had a lot of friends. These emissaries gave press conferences, toured the horror sites of Bucha, Hostomel, and Irpin, and sprinkled positive news.

Blinken, for example, announced the U.S. mission would return to Kyiv from Poland, together with a new ambassador, Bridget Brink, who was replacing Marie Yovanovitch, defenestrated in 2019 by Trump.

The most ardent visitor was Boris Johnson. His trips were tinged with opportunism. They burnished his statesman-like credentials at a time of domestic political woe. As one columnist put it, he enjoyed the comfort of the world stage. At home Johnson was increasingly unpopular. Revelations of lawbreaking in Downing Street—the Covid "partygate" scandal—had caused turmoil inside the country and Johnson's Conservative Party. Loyalists argued that it was the wrong moment to depose Britain's prime minister, given the war in Ukraine and the ongoing threat from Russia.

Set against this critique was the fact that Johnson took Kyiv's cause seriously. Security cooperation with Ukraine had deepened after 2020. The UK trained Ukrainian soldiers, carried out joint paratrooper drills, and helped revamp the ports of Berdiansk and Ochakiv. Days before the invasion, Johnson became the first European politician to discuss aiding the resistance inside Ukraine, on the assumption Kyiv would fall. Subsequently, he pledged £2.3 billion ($2.8 billion) in military aid, a contribution second only to the United States'.

Ukraine—gladly, sincerely—feted Johnson as a new Churchill. Artists painted him as a Cossack warrior, plucking at a bandura, a traditional Ukrainian stringed folk instrument. His features appeared on the sides of buildings, including a street mural I came across in Zelenskiy's hometown of Kryvyi Rih. A council near Odesa named a road after him. There were rap songs that celebrated the prime minister's heroism. One had a thumping chorus line: "Boris crunches tanks like barbaris [a candy]." Mixed in was Johnson's attempt to say "good day" in Ukrainian—"*Dobryy den*, everybody."

Days before his underground press conference, Zelenskiy walked with Johnson through the damp streets of Kyiv. I was in the capital; the visit was secret for security reasons, thanks to recent Russian attacks. Johnson hailed "Volodymyr" and his leadership in making Putin's army retreat from Kyiv. It was, he said, "the greatest feat of arms of the twenty-first century." Locals greeted the British prime minister enthusiastically; they started calling him "*Johnsonyuk*"—an affectionate play on the UK abbreviation. Here, far from London and its seething press, was the adulation Johnson craved. And the hope that maybe some of Zelenskiy's stardust would help him keep his job. A naïve one: that July, a mass ministerial and party revolt forced his resignation.

In the weeks after the invasion, the United States and its allies took practical steps to punish Moscow. The Russian Federation became the most sanctioned country in the world. After thirty years of integration with the global economy—from banks to the technology sector to high street brands and accounting and lingerie firms—there was an abrupt decoupling. It was unprecedented. And history reversing: as if Russia had been tossed back into the drab late-Soviet period, to a time of autarky and precapitalist gloom.

Sanctions fell especially hard on one group closely associated with Russian power: the oligarchs. For years, billionaire businessmen who had made their fortunes in the 1990s had played a successful double game. At home they were loyal Kremlin patriots. Abroad, they were self-made entrepreneurs and philanthropists, with little connection to the Putin regime. To suggest otherwise was to invite an aggressive legal letter. The oligarchs employed expensive attorneys and Western PR firms to enforce this image, regularly threatening journalists at the newspaper I wrote for and others.

Now this fiction had come crashing down. The United Kingdom imposed sanctions on wealthy Russian individuals. They included Chelsea Football Club owner Roman Abramovich; industrialist Oleg Deripaska; Igor Sechin, the chairman of Rosneft and Putin's close ally; and Alexei Miller, the CEO of the Russian state energy giant Gazprom. Plus top Russian bankers: Andrei Kostin, the head of VTB Bank, and Dmitri Lebedev, the chairman of Rossiya Bank. Several had luxury homes in London; their collective net worth was around $15 billion. The European Union froze the assets of thirty oligarchs and more than one thousand Kremlin aides. When several months later a *Financial Times* reporter visited Deripaska's mansion on Belgravia Square, near Hyde Park Corner, they found peeling paint and two dying bay trees by the front door.

The U.S. Treasury department published a similar list. It imposed sanctions on billionaire oil trader Gennady Timchenko, Putin's longtime friend, and on government enablers. They included Kremlin spokesman Dmitry Peskov, his Olympic ice-dancer wife, Tatiana Navka, and a slew of parliamentary deputies. In May the United Kingdom leveled further sanctions on Putin's immediate circle: his ex-wife, Lyudmila; his alleged girlfriend, Alina Kabaeva, a onetime rhythmic gymnast; plus relatives and childhood contacts believed to be proxies for the Russian president's personal wealth.

Additionally, the United States sought to cripple Russia's banking sector. Major Russian banks were disconnected from the Society for Worldwide Interbank Financial Telecommunications (SWIFT). Some of Russia's central bank reserves—$630 billion in foreign currency and gold—were frozen. The United States also barred Moscow from making debt payments using money it held in U.S. banks. The measures pushed Russia into its first sovereign debt default since 1998.

The most significant measures covered energy. Russia is the world's biggest exporter of oil and gas, and the European Union relies on imports for about 40 percent of its gas needs. As Zelenskiy pointed out, European payments for Siberian gas financed Moscow's war machine, facilitating the murder of Ukrainians. During the first hundred days of war alone, Russia earned almost $100 billion (£82.3 billion) from oil and gas exports. The figure was bigger, way bigger, than Western assistance sent to Ukraine.

Putting an end to dependence on Russian gas wasn't easy. The European Union agreed to reduce gas imports by two-thirds within a year. Germany dumped plans to open the completed Nord Stream 2 gas pipeline from Russia. The United States and Canada banned all Russian oil and gas imports. The United Kingdom said it would do the same with oil by the end of 2022, with the European Union phasing out seaborne Russian oil imports over the same period (but not oil sent by pipeline). Europe's break with Russian fossil fuels was partial. A full commodities shutdown was a long way off.

The United States, the European Union, and the United Kingdom also went after Russia's defense industry. They banned the export of dual-use goods—anything that might be used for both military and civilian purposes. The United States tried to disrupt Russian defense supply chains by imposing sanctions on defense companies, on defense research organizations, and on other defense-related entities. It sought to starve Putin's military-industrial complex of critical components. These included aircraft parts: navigation systems, meteorological locators, and smoke detectors.

For Russian consumers, the most visible blow was the departure of international companies. Around one thousand major firms exited. They included Ikea and Apple, Netflix and Nike, Visa and Mastercard, Coca-Cola and Starbucks. Thirty-two years after McDonald's arrived in Soviet Moscow, leading to long queues for Happy Meals, the fast-food chain's golden arches were removed from Pushkin Square and 850 franchises. It was a symbol of Russia's looping journey backward.

The collective impact of sanctions on Russia was staggering, according to Chris Barter, the former head of Goldman Sachs Moscow. "No way did I ever think this decoupling would be possible," he told me. He acknowledged high energy prices offset some of the economic pain but said it was only a question of time before Europe stopped being a commodity customer. Unfortunately for the Kremlin, it would take many years of investment and new infrastructure to reroute Russian gas flows to China and the East, he added.

Many Russian professionals decided it was time to emigrate. They disliked their country's war and its lurch back to a gray, repressed, Soviet-like existence. At least two hundred thousand younger workers—IT specialists and other educated graduates—left. They moved to Yerevan, Armenia; Vilnius, Lithuania; and Tbilisi, Georgia. The exodus was reminiscent of the White Russians who'd fled to Istanbul and Paris after the Bolshevik Revolution. Those who participated in this modern brain drain were "traitors and scum," Putin said.

Would the sanctions make any difference? Inevitably, Moscow found ways of circumventing some of them. It supplied oil at reduced prices to India, for example. Rising hydrocarbon prices offset losses from sanctions. And the rouble quickly recovered its value after Russia's central bank imposed capital controls. At the outset, the United States said sanctions would start at the top of the escalator and stay there. That wasn't the reality. Oligarch sanctions and the broader macroeconomic ones did not prove as successful as predicted, and the Russians were confident they had time on their side.

International condemnation of Putin was less than comprehensive. India was a lead member of a group of countries from the Global South—Africa, Asia, and Latin America—that did not mobilize against Russia. A lot of nations wanted to stay out and remain neutral or thought this was a war that concerned Europe but not them. They did not see any universal principles at stake. This surprised the West. It allowed the Kremlin to intensify its propaganda work and diplomacy inside nonaligned states.

On the political scene, there were few signs of upheaval. Rumors of elite discontent had swirled around Moscow for years, and oligarchs deprived of their yachts and French Riviera mansions were not going to suddenly rise up against Putin. There seemed little prospect of a palace coup. Russian citizens unable to obtain car parts from abroad and forced to pay more for brake pads or cell phone repairs were more likely to blame the West than the regime. The same could be said of falling living standards and rising inflation.

Still, the sanctions had a cumulative effect. Or that was the hope. Bit by bit, they would undermine Putin.

. . .

It was Wednesday, a midmorning in May, when Finnish air traffic controllers noticed something odd. An unauthorized flight was taking place. A Soviet-designed Russian military helicopter had crossed the border from Russia into eastern Finland. The Mi-17 was flying between the towns of Kesälahti and Parikkala, over a landscape of glistening lakes and pine trees. It was an unexpected and menacing presence. The helicopter kept going for about four kilometers, Finland's defense ministry said, before disappearing back into Russian territory.

This was not the first time Moscow had violated Finland's air space. The previous month an Ilyushin passenger jet had deliberately strayed over the medieval town of Porvoo. Finland's neighbor Sweden had suffered similar breaches. Four Russian fighter jets had streaked above Gotland, a strategically located island in the Baltic Sea. A spy plane flew close to a Swedish naval base in the south of the country. And, back in 2014, one of Moscow's submarines was found lurking in the waters off Stockholm's archipelago.

These incursions were not subtle. The Porvoo incident came the same day Zelenskiy addressed the Finnish parliament. He likened Ukraine's military counterreaction to Finland's own war against the Soviet Union eighty-three years earlier, when outnumbered Finnish soldiers fought back against Stalin's winter invaders. It was Ukraine's and Finland's "fate" to share a border with Russia, Zelenskiy said. In case anyone had missed the message, Russian state hackers crashed the websites of Finland's defense and foreign ministries.

The Kremlin, evidently, was unhappy. Putin had explained his war in Ukraine as an anti-Nazi and anti-NATO operation. By invading, Russia was safeguarding its security and preventing NATO's future expansion, the rationale went. In fact,

Putin's war of aggression had the opposite effect. It breathed new life into NATO—an alliance France's president Macron described as recently as 2021 as "brain-dead."

Russia's invasion was a watershed moment for Europe. It transformed the region's security architecture in the most profound way since the 1990s. It dramatically lengthened Russia's western flank with NATO. Finland's border with Russia stretched for 1,340 kilometers. Its future admission into the bloc would pile new pressure on Moscow's already stretched forces. It marked a historic change in Nordic strategic thinking about an old problem: how best to coexist with a hostile and adventurist neighbor. Behind the scenes, the United States played a significant role in persuading Helsinki and Stockholm to drop their policies of neutrality and nonalignment, in Sweden's case going back two hundred years. According to Finnish media reports, in December 2021, the United States shared classified information with Finland's president, Sauli Niinistö. The background briefing was alarming: intelligence showed Russia was about to overrun Ukraine. Biden reinforced the point in a telephone call to Niinistö, citing NATO's open-door policy.

Niinistö was shocked by the U.S. report, according to sources who spoke with him. He trusted its accuracy and understood what this meant for his country's security path going forward. During Soviet times, Helsinki pursued a neutral doctrine known as Finlandization. One political cartoonist described the policy as "the art of bowing to the East, without mooning to the West." Not provoking Moscow meant allowing the Kremlin to dictate much of Finland's foreign policy. This was an uncomfortable act of deference. Supporters saw it as pragmatic: it ensured the nation's survival. Finland didn't join NATO, nor was it a member of the Warsaw Pact; it was an in-between zone, and thus a favorite U.S.-Soviet summit spot.

Officially, modern Finland and Sweden were nonaligned states. In reality, however, this was something of a pretense: the days of equidistance between east and west were long gone. After the USSR's collapse, Finland joined the European Union. It purchased sixty-four U.S. F-18 fighter jets and an arsenal of cruise missiles, and it built up a formidable army of 280,000 soldiers and 900,000 reservists out of a population of 5.5 million. The two countries became NATO partners. They conducted joint military training exercises.

At the beginning of February 2022, Finnish support for NATO was at 44 percent. Putin's actions pushed it to 76 percent. Niinistö unveiled his plan to join NATO the day after Russian warplanes bombed Mariupol's maternity hospital. As the journalist Lauri Nurmi observed, Moscow's invasion "activated our collective memories." For Finns, it was hugely personal. They recalled conversations with their grandparents about the Winter and Continuation Wars, the one hundred thousand young men who had perished defending their homeland, and the grim battle of 1939–1940 in which 10 percent of Finnish territory was lost.

At first the Swedes were more hesitant. At a bilateral meeting that March in Helsinki, Sweden's prime minister, Magdalena Andersson, floated the idea of deeper security cooperation rather than full NATO membership. The Finns made clear they were applying, reversing the power relationship by going first, instead of deferring as usual to Stockholm. Biden— a firm proponent of NATO expansion—wanted both nations to join. Turkey blocked the proposal on the grounds the pair had offered safe havens to Kurdish terrorists, but by the time of NATO's landmark Madrid Summit in June, Ankara had dropped its objections.

For the first time in the modern era, all the Scandinavian countries would be in the same security alliance, with Finland and Sweden joining Norway and Denmark.

In terms of Scandinavia, Putin's gambit, it was fair to say, backfired. Quite spectacularly.

Thirty years after the end of Soviet domination in Central and Eastern Europe, the summit recognized that Moscow was—once again—the Euro-Atlantic community's number one security challenge. Or, put more bluntly, an enemy.

A new strategic doctrine was agreed. Ten years earlier Russia had been described as a partner. It was now seen as the "most significant and direct threat" to the peace and security of NATO members. After a period of naïvety about Putin's intentions—at least from some Western governments—there was a collective recognition of the dangers he posed, not just to Ukraine but to the whole of Europe.

NATO's response was to strengthen its eastern borders. Its secretary general, Jens Stoltenberg, called this new forward deployment the "biggest overhaul of our collective defense and deterrence since the Cold War." More troops were sent to NATO's growing front line with Russia—300,000, capable of being immediately deployed, up from a preinvasion total of 40,000. These NATO soldiers would defend the territories most vulnerable to a Ukraine-style Russian incursion: Lithuania, Estonia, and Latvia. The previous month Latvia's president, Egils Levits, likened February 24 to the Soviet invasion of his country in 1940.

The United States strengthened its position in Europe. It stationed 3,000 troops in Romania, two F-35 fighter squadrons in the United Kingdom, and two destroyers in Spain. There were extra soldiers committed to the Baltic states, and a new permanent base in Poland for the U.S. Fifth Army Corps. "We are stepping up," Biden declared. He quipped that Putin had wanted the Finlandization of NATO, and instead got the NATOization of Finland. Johnson said 1,000 new British troops would be earmarked for Estonia's defense, with one of two new aircraft carriers sent to protect NATO's eastern borders.

All of this was bad news for Moscow. Finland and Sweden's accession meant NATO could enhance its intelligence capabilities in the high north and the Kola Peninsula, where Russia's Northern Fleet was based, including its nuclear-armed submarines. The Arctic—a zone of Russian ambition—was contested. And the Baltic Sea was now a de facto NATO lake. It would be harder for Russia to supply Kaliningrad, its increasingly isolated western exclave, sandwiched between Lithuania and Poland.

Russian officials accused the West of ramping up tensions. There was no acknowledgment that Putin's actions had brought about Europe's stunning remilitarization. Or that NATO had no plan to attack Moscow—whatever Russian state media said to the contrary—and was a purely defensive outfit. Without his 2022 invasion, none of this would have happened. The Russian government refused to see itself as the aggressor. Instead, it was an eternal victim, always reacting, and the author of nothing. In Kremlin-speak, it gave a "mirror answer" to Western crimes.

In the third decade of the twenty-first century, Western nations found themselves in a familiar place. There were echoes of the early Cold War era. Russia's foreign minister Sergey Lavrov lied about practically everything: that was his job. But he told the truth when he said a new iron curtain was "already descending" between Moscow and the West. Cooperation between Russia and the European Union was over, he said, speaking in the Belarusian capital, Minsk.

In his famous "Long Telegram" of 1946, the U.S. ambassador in Moscow, George Kennan, set down his ideas on how the United States should deal with the Soviet Union. U.S. policy "must be that of a long-term, patient but firm and vigilant containment of Russian expansive tendencies," he wrote. He called for countering "Soviet pressure against the institutions of the Western world" through the "adroit and vigilant application of counter-force at a series of constantly shifting geographical and political points, corresponding to the shifts and maneuvers of Soviet policy." The United States sought the "breakup of Soviet power" or its "gradual mellowing."

Washington and its allies had come full circle. Their conclusion was similar to Kennan's. There was no point in engaging with Putin or seeking diplomatic solutions. It was back to the future, and to the all too familiar strategy of containment.

In a grassy clearing somewhere in the Donbas, a group of Ukrainian soldiers prepared a special weapon. It was American: one of a hundred M777 howitzers delivered by Washington to Kyiv. A soldier loaded a shell; his artillery colleagues braced for an explosion. And then it came—a mighty staccato bang that rattled the trees and sucked out the surrounding air, as if a dizzying spell had been cast. Where exactly the shell landed was unclear.

The howitzer was one answer to a demand made by President Zelenskiy in practically every conversation. He repeated it in private phone calls with heads of state, in public sessions including his cavern-held press conference, and in his nightly video addresses to Ukrainians. The plea was simple to understand. It went like this: weapons, weapons, weapons! To have any chance of beating the Russians, Ukraine needed arms, Zelenskiy said, not people taking "tragic selfies." Lots of arms. Heavy ones. And now.

During the first two months of its campaign, the Russian army suffered serious losses of men and matériel. But it was still formidable. It seemed to possess limitless quantities of lethal equipment and ammunition. By summer, the Kremlin's numerical advantages were beginning to tell. The battle for the Donbas had turned into a brutal Second World War–style duel, fought by what Stalin had called the "gods of war"— heavy artillery. And Moscow had more of it, firing ten shells to Ukraine's one.

In order to win back lost ground, Ukraine had to match Russia's terrible firepower. The most pressing need was weapons with long-range capabilities. As things stood, Kyiv was unable to strike back at Russian positions behind the lines while it continued to come under withering frontal fire. It wanted multiple launch rocket systems (MLRS), self-propelled howitzers, and tanks. It also needed warplanes, as many as possible; air defense complexes, to shoot down ballistic missiles; infantry fighting vehicles; and drones.

Ukraine's allies were on the same page, conceptually speaking, about the war in Ukraine: a struggle for values, of light against dark, and so on. On the question of Zelenskiy's extensive weapons shopping list, however, the allies were less united.

This lack of consensus was related to other questions, as the conflict ground on. How might you define Ukrainian victory? Did that mean evicting Russia from the new areas it had occupied since February 24? Or kicking it out from Crimea and rebel-controlled Donbas? And what about the "realist" proposition advanced by the veteran former U.S. secretary of state Henry Kissinger that Ukraine should yield some of its land to Moscow in exchange for peace? In other words, suck it up and agree to a bad deal to prevent further carnage?

As the historian and journalist Anne Applebaum observed, the answer depended on which country you asked. Western policy makers interpreted the war through the prism of the past. But they saw different parallels. The United States and the United Kingdom compared Russia's Ukraine invasion to Nazi Germany's dismembering of Poland in 1939. Putin was Hitler, Kyiv was Warsaw, and February 24, 2022, matched September 1, 1939—the date that marked the outbreak of the Second World War. Poland itself shared this analogy.

In the case of Macron, it was the end of the First World War and the Treaty of Versailles that appeared to mold his thinking. Speaking to French media, he said: "We must not humiliate Russia." Putin should be given an "exit ramp through diplomatic means," he added, with France playing the role of a "mediating power." In his version, Russia was Germany after its 1918 defeat. A humiliating settlement imposed on Moscow would repeat the mistakes of Versailles, and fuel fresh instability and war in Europe.

For Germany and its Social Democrat chancellor, Olaf Scholz, a slightly earlier timeline from history gleamed. Instead of the Führer, Scholz saw the bewhiskered figure of Germany's last emperor and the man who had led his country into the First World War: "I am not Kaiser Wilhelm," Scholz told his coalition colleagues in May, according to *Der Spiegel*. Scholz's fear was that Germany might be dragged into another world war, possibly a nuclear one, if fighting in Ukraine escalated. Critics accused Scholz of ambivalence and abstruseness, not to mention Hamlet-like indecision, over the delivery of German heavy weapons to Kyiv.

One professional historian disagreed with all these comparisons. Sir Christopher Clark, the author of *The Sleepwalkers*, a bestselling account of the origins of the First World War, said the situation in Ukraine was not 1914. Nor was Europe divided into "a binary pair of alliance systems"; in Europe, at least, Russia was isolated. He told *The Guardian*: "A better analogy would be with the opportunist Russian predations of the nineteenth century—most of which we don't know about, because they were at the expense of the Ottoman Empire." The world in general, he added, was "more and more like the nineteenth century: multipolar and unpredictable."

It was certainly true that few foresaw Berlin's dumping of pacifism, one of many formerly inconceivable things brought about by Putin's invasion. Successive chancellors stuck to the traditional policy that Germany would not supply arms to foreign conflicts. Three days after Putin attacked, Scholz made his *Zeitenwende* speech to the Bundestag. He promised to send defensive weapons to Ukraine; to modernize and invest in Germany's underfunded army, with a one-off contribution of 100 billion euros; and to raise defense spending to 2 percent of the GDP. It was a historic turning point. Other EU states boosted their defense budgets as well.

Fast-forward several months and no heavy German weapons had actually made it to Kyiv. How to understand Scholz's apparent hesitancy? There were various explanations. One was the chancellor's habit of overthinking. Another was his party's complaisant relationship with Moscow, symbolized by Scholz's predecessor Gerhard Schröder, who chaired the Nord Stream projects and was Putin's most famous European apologist. Many Social Democrats preferred the party's old Russia-friendly stance; left-wing intellectuals signed open letters calling for peace.

A third possible reason was a misplaced culture of remembrance. The German political establishment typically equated the Soviet citizens killed in the Second World War with modern-day Russians. There was a blind spot with respect to Ukraine. In fact, the Nazis exterminated 6.5 million Soviet Ukrainians; Hitler regarded Ukraine as a colony and a breadbasket that would feed his new Reich. A fourth palpable anxiety was that a choleric Putin might switch off Germany's gas. This last apprehension was proven correct, as it turned out.

Whatever the grounds, Zelenskiy was unimpressed. He made his displeasure known by disinviting Germany's president, Frank-Walter Steinmeier, Schröder's former chief of staff, from visiting Kyiv. Steinmeier conceded his support for Nord Stream 2 was a mistake but denied he had grown too close to Moscow. Some fault must be attributed to former chancellor Angela Merkel, a fluent Russian speaker who understood Putin and his KGB methods but who nevertheless allowed the German economy to become hooked on cheap Russian gas, in what was surely one of the great postwar policy errors.

In June, Scholz, Macron, and Italy's then prime minister Mario Draghi traveled to Kyiv. A grim-faced Scholz inspected a car in Irpin shot up by Russian troops. Back home, Scholz pointed out that Germany had dispatched military gear: 2,500 anti-aircraft missiles, light armored vehicles, and truckloads of explosives. He promised a surface-to-air defense system, plus thirty Gepard anti-aircraft tanks. And much cash. Even so, the perception remained that Berlin did too little, too late. Germany's Social Democratic Party had been slow to recognize that this invasion required a complete reconstruction of its thinking and ideology. Ironically, Germany's Green Party vice-chancellor, Robert Habeck, was quicker to challenge internal shibboleths on nuclear energy, coal-fired power stations, and the transfer of weapons to conflict zones.

On the surface, the anti-Putin alliance was united, including in its backing for Ukraine to become an EU candidate country. Look a little deeper, however, and cracks might be discerned. Within the coalition were two camps. One might be called the "justice" party. It wanted Kyiv to regain all the territory it had lost since 2014. Adherents of this restorationist aim included the United Kingdom, the United States, and Canada, plus the Eastern Europeans, whose populations were understandably anxious about a Russian attack. The Scandinavians, Spain, and Portugal took a similar view.

There was a smaller "peace" group. It comprised Germany, France, and perhaps Italy. These nations believed Russia's wishes had to be eventually accommodated in order to end the fighting and achieve a lasting peace. They were less worried about a Russian invasion of their own countries, and more concerned by the rising cost of gasoline prices and food bills, which the war exacerbated. Linked to this was the business of reelection; Macron won a second term as president in 2022, but then lost his parliamentary majority.

Draghi, a former president of the European Central Bank, showed himself to be more skillful than either Scholz or Macron at weaning his country off Russian energy and in providing direct military support to Kyiv. At the G7, the Italians proposed an innovative cap on gas prices as a way of confronting the Kremlin. Draghi's departure as prime minister after his coalition collapsed over the summer was a blow to Ukraine.

Meanwhile, there was one essential power that might decisively influence how—and possibly when—the war ended. The United States' military and financial capabilities were many times greater than other nations', giving it a unique ability to shape events. The Biden administration had correctly predicted Putin's invasion. Its deft handling of intelligence from late 2021 to early 2022 had enhanced U.S. credibility. Though he got little credit for it at home, Biden's leadership over Ukraine restored U.S. preeminence in the international arena.

There were also mistakes. The administration's analysis of what would happen after Putin attacked was inaccurate. The Pentagon expected the Russian army to take Kyiv and Kharkiv and to realize its objectives within thirty or forty days. Ukraine would live on as a small Western rump state, the thinking went. Consequently, Washington was reluctant to give Zelenskiy sophisticated modern weapons. It feared these would fall swiftly into Russian hands—as had happened in 2021, when the Taliban swept across Afghanistan, scooping up billions of dollars' worth of U.S. military equipment.

Ukraine's unexpected fight back changed the equation. The government in Kyiv sent former defense minister Zagorodnyuk to Washington. He was one of several advisers whose job it was to get the White House to turn on the military tap. Zagorodnyuk was a fluent English speaker who ran a defense think tank in Kyiv, a friendly and impressive person. I got to know him before the invasion. His institute sent out a daily briefing note; it gave a comprehensive account of what was happening on the battlefield and beyond.

Zagorodnyuk made the rounds of all the main Washington, D.C., stakeholders: military, the National Security Council, the Department of Defense, and the State Department. He met with Mark Milley, chairman of the Joint Chiefs of Staff. Zagorodnyuk told me he encountered top-level support for Ukraine's cause. Austin and other senior administration figures thought Ukraine could win; a minority believed this unlikely.

These conversations were wide-ranging. They took place in formal and informal settings. Zagorodnyuk talked about the lessons his country had learned from its years fighting Russians and what weapons were needed to beat them. The Americans, in turn, shared their experiences from other conflicts.

One meeting was with a former government strategist who had been behind Washington's efforts in the Soviet war in Afghanistan. The person told Zagorodnyuk that the delivery of lethal aid made a drastic difference only when a specific number was reached. Every war had its own tipping point. This concept of "critical mass" shaped Ukrainian strategic thinking. The discussion would prove prophetic.

The Biden administration was prepared to furnish Zelenskiy with some of the lethal aid Kyiv required. There were conditions, however. The United States was not seeking to remove Putin from power, a point Biden stressed in an op-ed for *The New York Times*, having previously suggested the opposite in an off-the-cuff remark. Nor would it send U.S. troops to fight in Ukraine: there would be no boots on the ground. The administration was unwilling to supply long-range systems capable of hitting targets inside Russia. This left Russia free to strike Ukraine from its own territory.

Biden's concern was that the shooting might spread into a third world war. He did not want the fighting to cross a threshold where NATO and Russia were openly in conflict. U.S. officials said as much. Speaking in May, Avril D. Haines, the Director of National Intelligence, stated this explicitly, saying, "We do not want to have a situation in which actors are using nuclear weapons." The thinking in Washington was that Putin would only go nuclear if he perceived an existential threat to Russia. But did that mean to the country, or merely to his regime? Possibly the second. Would a rout of Russian forces in Ukraine amount to an existential threat, as seen by Putin? Probably it would.

The Ukrainians didn't really agree with this logic. My own view was that Putin was unlikely to use a tactical nuclear weapon, given his paranoia about his personal survival, as shown by the extraordinary steps he took to avoid close-up official encounters. Also, his Kremlin colleagues enjoyed the good life, something secret offshore documents that had passed my desk laid bare. "We don't think World War Three is going to start. The Russians don't have enough power," Zagorodnyuk told me. The global risk, as seen by Kyiv, was a protracted war in which the country was made to sign an unfair peace. The Ukrainians placed their hope on getting the weapons they needed and then liberating their country rapidly—by winter 2022, Zelenskiy hoped.

Beginning in late spring, American heavy weapons began to flow. President Biden signed into law a $40 billion security assistance package. These tranches included the M777 howitzers seen in action in the Donbas, multiple launch rocket systems and artillery ammunition, as well as a coastal defense system. The Ukrainians took delivery of truck-mounted multiple rocket launchers with satellite-guided rockets. These had a range of sixty-five kilometers and were devastatingly effective. Four arrived, and then four more.

The Pentagon believed Ukraine would soon be able to turn the tide. This pivot moment didn't happen immediately. Having initially overestimated the Russian military, the United States now appeared to have underestimated it. The shipments, it had to be acknowledged, fell well short of what Ukraine hoped for. The White House sent four MLRS initially, rather than the three hundred Kyiv said it needed to beat back Russia. The Brits dispatched another three, the Norwegians four, the French CAESAR howitzers. The Russian advance continued.

Ukraine had won international backing, public support, and hearts and minds. But the grim reality was that 20 percent of its territory was occupied. The figure grew slightly every day—a road there, a hamlet here, as Russia crawled forward. Hurrying back from Zelenskiy's press conference to my Kyiv hotel in order to file a story, I reflected on the reality of life under Russian rule. Ukraine's president had dubbed the invaders *Rashist*s. The word was a combination of *Russia* and *fascists*. It caught on. Torture, rape, the murders of children: the occupiers behaved in the same way as the Nazis, eighty years before, Zelenskiy said.

Much of the south of Ukraine was lost in the early days of the invasion. Putin, it was clear, had no intention of giving this land back. Instead, his forces were busy snuffing out all and any resistance.

EIGHT

Back in the USSR

Kherson Oblast
January 2022

> Who controls the past controls the future:
> who controls the present controls the past.
>
> —GEORGE ORWELL,
>
> *1984*

The derelict restaurant looked out onto a shimmering expanse of water. There were lagoons, ducks, and a road. From a balcony on the café's castellated tower I watched as a white minivan pulled up at the far end of a bridge. Several passengers got out, rolling small cases. They walked the last section to a Ukrainian military checkpoint. My visit took place in late January 2022, a month before Moscow's invasion. The scene was tranquil, with no hint of what was to come. A cold winter wind blew.

The abandoned building where I was standing was situated in the village of Chonhar, in Ukraine's southern Kherson Oblast. Ukrainian soldiers used it as a base. It was one of three crossing points on routes connecting the Crimean Peninsula—stolen by Russia more than eight years previously—with Ukrainian government–controlled territory.

There were few obvious signs of a Russian army presence. At night Ukrainian soldiers could hear the roar and grinding of tanks as the enemy maneuvered, concealed behind a small wood. Mostly these counterparts were invisible. In the near distance was what Moscow considered to be Russia, a ragged group of houses past the bridge. There was no shooting across the front line, in contrast to daily exchanges of fire in the Donbas.

Those defending the bridge understood an attack might come at any moment. "It's not the first time the peninsula has been occupied," Mykola Chekman, a Ukrainian army photographer, reflected as we stood on the tower's upper story, reached via a concrete staircase. He peered through his binoculars. "Crimea has seen a lot of war. We are getting ready. They are getting ready." It wouldn't be like in 2014, he predicted, when Russia took Crimea without firing a shot.

Morale in the Ukrainian camp was evidently high. On a wall in what was once the café's dining room someone had scrawled the words "Putin is a prick." The officer tasked with showing me around, Ivan Arefiev, said Ukraine was receiving help from Canadian and European military instructors. "Putin dreams of making a land corridor here between Donbas and Crimea. We won't let him. We are prepared," he told me.

I toured a First World War–style trench reinforced with wooden pallets. Soldiers stood guard, rifles at the ready. They gazed out at the isthmus through mailbox-style slots. The only intruder was a ball of tumbleweed. There wasn't much in the way of heavy weaponry. I saw one armored vehicle, a BTR personnel carrier, hidden behind a fir tree. Nearby was a crumbling gateway decorated with summer grapes; a black flag featuring a Crimea map flew from the restaurant's roof.

This Ukrainian contingent seemed modest and little match for Russia's land, air, and sea forces. Most soldiers were in their early twenties; they slept in a cozy barracks warmed by a log stove. I asked what they made of Putin's thesis that Ukraine and Russia were one people. "We are moving to Europe and NATO. Russia is stuck in the Soviet past," Lieutenant Petro Yanchenko said. Why was he fighting? "So my family can live in a free country," he replied.

Yanchenko pointed out that Ukraine had land claims of its own. In the nineteenth century, Russia's southern Kuban area—just across from Crimea's Kerch Strait—was home to Ukrainian Cossacks. "It's our territory," he said. So, too, were the Donbas and the zone over the bridge, he added. There seemed little prospect that Crimea—which I had visited prior to Putin's annexation—would be returning to Ukraine anytime soon.

Chekman, the photographer, disagreed. He recalled how the peninsula had changed hands on numerous occasions. Its bloody history was all around. Chonhar had a needle-shaped memorial to Soviet dead from the Second World War. On the Russian-held side was a monument to anti-aircraft gunners. The Nazis swept through Chonhar in 1941, killing some Jewish residents. The Germans occupied Crimea for two years until the Red Army drove them out.

For locals, and for the tourist economy, Putin's more recent Crimea takeover was a disaster. The village was once a stop on the railway line to Sevastopol, as well as a rest stop for tens of thousands of vacationers crossing by car during the summer. "This place is now a *tupik*, a dead end," said a man named Viacheslav, standing at what was left of Chonhar's once-thriving roadside fish market. With no tourists and little vehicle traffic of any kind, business was slack, he said.

Viacheslav sold silvery roach fish, large smoked whitefish, and mullet, which he caught himself. His neighbor Valeriy, a coffee vendor, said life was better in the Soviet Union—the entity whose borders Putin wanted to restore. "You could buy *kolbasa* [sausage] for eight roubles," Valeriy explained. The prices were much lower than now, he said, but added that he still didn't want to go back to those days.

The only beneficiary from this Crimea standoff was nature, I concluded. In the absence of humans, Chonhar had become a peaceful wildlife haven. Its wetlands were home to gulls, hares, rabbits, wild boar, and pheasants, seen clattering amid reeds and tall yellow feather grass. The coast was home to several nature reserves; soldiers reporting for early-morning duty encountered foxes. Nobody shot the mammals or birds for fear of awakening a Russian response.

I left Chohnar wondering if Ukrainian engineers had mined the bridge in case of Russian attack.

There was no doubt that both the province and the city of Kherson, the region's administrative capital at the mouth of the Dnipro River, were Kremlin targets. Their capture would solve an issue that had dogged Crimea since 2014, exacerbating its economic difficulties and day-to-day problems: a lack of water. There were also sporadic power outages. The Russian writer Leonid Kaganov compared the annexation of Crimea to stealing an expensive cell phone without its charger. Kherson was that charger.

Before annexation, water reached Crimea via a four-hundred-kilometer-long Soviet-era canal. This network linked the Dnipro with the peninsula, and supplied residents and irrigated fields. In 2014, Ukraine built a dam to stop its flow to occupied territory. Russia responded by constructing a nineteen-kilometer road and rail bridge linking the Russian mainland and Krasnodar Krai with the Kerch Strait, but the water shortages continued. In 2021, Crimea suffered a severe drought.

The canal was therefore a strategic object, coveted by Russia. I drove past a stretch of the waterway on my way back to Kyiv, stopping off to take photos. Snow lined the canal's embankment; a chill breeze whipped over the water; the clouds were pearl gray. A little farther on, a branch of the canal had frozen over. It was a picturesque spot, with willows and dense vegetation, blanketed white. But where were the soldiers?

Outside the city of Nova Kakhovka I saw a Ukrainian army post. It was located next to the canal and beneath a highway overpass. The defenses weren't exactly impressive. There was a single guard stationed there, living in a small wood cabin. The guard had a German shepherd and was armed with a Kalashnikov.

In the first hours of invasion, Russian armored vehicles rumbled over Chonhar's bridge. The Ukrainian soldiers I had met the previous month appeared to have offered little resistance. The Russians made rapid progress. Some battalion groups went east, sweeping up the coast and the Sea of Azov. Other troops traveled north toward the city of Kherson. Beyond Kherson was the port of Mykolaiv on the Southern Buh River—and the route to Kyiv.

There was only one way to move into the center of Kherson.

For their blitzkrieg to be successful, the Russians had to capture the city's Antonivskyi Bridge. It connected the southern bank of the lower Dnipro River and the town of Oleshky with the main urban area on the other side. Russian forces quickly reached the southern end of the 1,300-meter-long road and pedestrian crossing, which is supported by girders and pillars.

What happened next has not been fully explained—a lack of preparation or something more sinister? According to Kherson residents, someone gave away the location of concealed Ukrainian positions around the bridge. The word I heard was *predatelstvo*—treachery. There was fighting. The Russians were able to knock out these defenses using mortars and air strikes. Ukrainian soldiers were killed. The bridge was mined, I was told, but the explosives were never activated.

One commander told me "some kind of failure" took place. Ukraine's presidential adviser Oleksiy Arestovych had a similar explanation for what went wrong. "We fucked up," he said. Zelenskiy fired the local head of the domestic intelligence agency, the SBU, accusing him of treason. The SBU's chief, Ivan Bakanov, was also fired because of collaboration on his watch. The National Security and Defense Council in Kyiv had anticipated the shape of a possible Kremlin offensive from Crimea and had planned accordingly. In the end, however, the Russians were able to move speedily through the Kherson region and use it as a springboard to advance on Mariupol. The south proved to be Ukraine's weakest link. Much of it was lost early on. Kherson was the first Ukrainian city to fall.

Olha Shvets, a poet from Kherson, started keeping a diary, published in *The Guardian*. "All night and all morning the air-raid sirens howled. Shells blew up. We ate ice cream," she wrote. "The Russians had just crossed Antonivskyi Bridge and were firing at civilian vehicles. Public transport had stopped, there were very few cars, and almost no people." At night she heard "enemy aircraft" and "my father's snoring."

Shvets chronicled the experiences of her family, and of her newly occupied city. She got her son to seal the windows of their kitchen with tape, and to put her glass vases and porcelain figurines in a box. "I read Harry Potter to my kids in the evenings so they don't focus on the explosions. My daughter sits half a day with her cat on her knees in the corner and keeps silent," she recorded. Kherson was blockaded; Russian troops were trying to rob grocery stores; "everyone is on edge," she added.

Another local journalist said she woke on March 1 to the "rough shout" of "Private! Into line": "Thirty soldiers with machine guns are marching through my yard," she wrote. The Russians bombed a high-rise building, killing civilians. There was shooting in many districts. A video showed bodies lying in the city's lilac park on Naftovykiv Street. The dead were "guys from territorial defense"; nearby were "unused Molotov cocktails," she noted.

Soon Kherson was entirely in Russian hands. "Armed visitors," as the mayor, Ihor Kolykhaiev, delicately put it, turned up at his executive building. He advised locals to observe the 8:00 p.m.–6:00 a.m. curfew and to go into town only during the day and with no more than one other person. Cars should move slowly, he said. Kolykhaiev said he had made no promises to these new overlords, adding that Kherson remained a Ukrainian city—at least at that moment.

Russia may have beaten the Ukrainian army, but it did not reckon on the mass uprising from the civilians left behind. Protests greeted Russian occupying forces wherever they went.

Unarmed demonstrators took to the streets of Kherson. They gathered in Melitopol, a city and municipality in the Zaporizhzhia region, and they confronted armed Russian soldiers in the Azov seaport of Henichesk, where I stayed in January in a Las Vegas–themed hotel.

Putin, it appeared, had assumed his February invasion would follow the same pattern as the one in 2014. His "little green men" were able to pacify Crimea because they enjoyed support from many residents, especially in Sevastopol, the home of Russia's Black Sea fleet. Kherson and Zaporizhzhia were different. Their populations were pro-Ukrainian. They regarded the Russians not as liberators but as unwelcome intruders—as marauding "orcs" who had rolled in from some modern-day Mordor.

There were moments of heart-stopping bravery. Video showed one man jump in front a Russian column, forcing a vehicle to swerve out of his way. In Melitopol, a group armed only with umbrellas halted a line of olive-green Z-marked trucks. They shouted: "Go home, fascists! We are unarmed!" Melitopol's mayor, Ivan Fedorov, said Putin wished to turn all of Ukraine into a "second pseudo-Belarus."

Some of these encounters between occupiers and occupied were extraordinary. In Henichesk—seized by Russia on February 24—a woman approached a newly arrived soldier wearing a white armband, as shown in a video that went viral.

She asked him, "Are you Russian? What the fuck are you doing here?"

"This conversation won't lead to anything," the soldier responded.

"You're occupiers! You are fascists! You came to our land.

What the fuck! Why did you come here with weapons?" she spat, calling him a "piece of shit."

The woman handed the soldier a small packet. "Take these seeds so sunflowers grow when you die here," she told him.

In Kherson, thousands assembled in Freedom Square outside the regional state administration building. The Russians took over the building and parked their equipment outside; machine-gunners guarded the perimeter. "I went many times with my fifteen-year-old son," Yulia Anatolivna, a Kherson artist, told me. "There were Russian guys with guns and tanks and everything." She said the crowd shouted "Go home," "Kherson is Ukraine," and—whenever soldiers dragged someone away—"Putin motherfucker." They sang patriotic songs and waved Ukrainian flags, one "many meters" long.

Yulia said she managed to leave five minutes before the Russians broke up these rallies. The Kremlin's security police fired into the air, lobbed stun grenades, and filled the square with tear gas; men in dark clothes filmed the protesters. These daily public shows of defiance went on through March, rattling the soldiers. "Nobody wants Russia. Maybe a small percentage. But very small," Yulia said. Olha, the poet, added: "Everything was fine with us until the Russian troops invaded. We didn't need to be freed from anyone."

The Russian authorities sought to bring Kherson and its surrounding villages under their comprehensive control. The city was the largest functioning regional capital under new occupation. Moscow, as Yulia put it, played a different game from the Donbas, where Mariupol and other towns were blotted out. The Kherson region was a valuable war trophy. It could feed Crimea. The region had hydropower stations and fertile agricultural land: wheat, rice, melons, and apricots, grown in cottage gardens.

The Russian government was keen to use Kherson as a laboratory, a political showcase for how the south's "return" meant positive change. Its preferred military-administrative model had been tested in the east. According to Zelenskiy, it wanted to create a "Kherson People's Republic" along the lines of the Moscow-controlled puppet governments in Donetsk and Luhansk. The plan was to hold a "referendum" on Kherson joining Russia, similar to the spurious polls held in 2014 in the separatist areas.

It was increasingly obvious, however, that there was little support for integration with the Russian Federation. Humanitarian convoys were brought in from Crimea, together with former prisoners who acted as locals and gave flowers to Russian soldiers. But even Russian state TV struggled to come up with footage of enthusiastic crowds cheering Russia. The real residents ignored the humanitarian aid.

And so the Kremlin came up with a solution. Referendum or no referendum, it would annex the Kherson and Zaporizhzhia regions and proclaim them Russian territory. They would join Crimea as a part of Russia's southern federal district. This takeover was contrary to what Putin had promised at the start of his special operation: that he did not seek to steal Ukraine's land. He did. That was always the idea. It was this century's most stunning example of naked imperialism.

Russia proceeded to use the same insidious methods employed in the Donbas. These included handing out Russian passports to Kherson residents and threatening and intimidating those who refused to accept them. Moscow introduced the rouble, first as a parallel currency, and then as a replacement for the Ukrainian hryvnia. Russian was made the official language, to be used for all matters of "national importance," as one official put it. And Kherson and Zaporizhzhia were put on Moscow time.

The most radical changes involved media and communications. In early March, Russian soldiers entered Kherson's TV center and put trip wire around it. They replaced Ukrainian channels with pro-Kremlin Russian ones. Ukrainian cell phone services and the Internet worked patchily for a while. Then they were switched off. A Crimean provider replaced them. Google and YouTube stopped working. In terms of news, as Yulia put it wryly, the choice became "Putin or Putin." There were work-arounds. Locals used virtual private networks and kept in touch with relatives by Telegram and WhatsApp.

To give this colonizing project legitimacy, Moscow needed collaborators. There was a small pool of locals from whom to recruit. Olha estimated 1,000 to 1,500 people backed the invading army, from a population of 300,000 in Kherson and 1 million in the region. "They were like mushrooms after the rain. They popped up. Ugly red mushrooms," she said. "They feel like they are masters of the situation." Locals considered these pro-Russian agitators "to be loonies," she added. Now these careerists joined the new administration, together with officials from Russia.

One was Kirill Stremousov, a former journalist who became the Kherson region's unelected "deputy head." Stremousov told Russian news agencies Kherson would live as part of the Russian Federation, its pace of development "something close to Crimea." "No one will force you to do anything. But the primordially Russian lands must return to their historical channel of cultures and values," he said. A visiting Moscow party official was more blunt. "Russia is here forever," he declared.

Collaboration was a hazardous affair. On April 20, Valery Kuleshov—a pro-Kremlin blogger who worked with Stremousov—left his Kherson apartment. It was 8:15 a.m. when he sat down in the driver's seat of his gray Mazda. A gunman raked the vehicle with automatic fire, killing Kuleshov. He had been a candidate for the job of city police chief. In Nova Kakhovka, a policeman who swapped sides was shot dead. Vitaliy Kim, the governor of Mykolaiv Oblast, said Kuleshov had deserved his fate. Wanted posters appeared, charging Stremousov with treason.

In keeping with his preference for placing former spies in key roles, Putin gave Kherson's top administrative job to a trusted intelligence operative. The new regional chief was Sergei Yeliseyev, a graduate of the FSB's academy, brought in from Kaliningrad. Yeliseyev's deputy was Alexei Kovalev, a local Kherson parliamentarian who defected to Moscow from Zelenskiy's Servant of the People party. In June, Kovalev survived an assassination attempt. Two months later, he didn't: he was shot dead in his home.

In order to consolidate power, the Kremlin used repression and terror. According to multiple witnesses, gun-wielding national guardsmen began rounding up locals suspected of having a pro-Ukrainian position. They worked from lists. Their targets included the families of soldiers, police officers and municipal workers, journalists, and participants in anti-occupation rallies. Also, village heads, council secretaries, and priests.

By the summer, 457 people had been abducted, Kyiv said. Among them were mayors from the Kherson region cities of

Nova Kakhovka, Skadovsk, Hola Prystan, and Beryslav. Others who disappeared included the chairman and deputy of the village council in Chornobaivka, where Kherson International Airport is located. Ukrainian forces repeatedly bombed the airport, killing Russian soldiers. Some forty-three law enforcement officers were seized. In Melitopol, five hundred people were taken hostage, with entire villages "filtered," its mayor said.

Olha, the poet, compared these secret police swoops to the darkest period of the Soviet era. "It's like in Stalin times. Cars arrive at night outside private houses. They break down the door, drag people out, and drive them away. It's a common situation in Kherson." A lot of people went missing, she said. Residents would wake up the next morning to find the next-door apartment ransacked and empty. Their neighbors had vanished.

The Russian authorities took away one of Olha's acquaintances, Oleksiy Yevdokymov. A physicist and member of the National Academy of Sciences of Ukraine, he shared patents with a professor in California who was nominated for a Nobel Prize. Yevdokymov appeared in a Russian video, accused of preparing acts of terrorism in connection with Moscow's Victory Day celebrations on May 9. "It was obvious they had tortured him. You could see it in his face and eyes," Olha said. The charge—clearly fabricated—was later dropped.

Another snatch squad lifted Oleh Baturin, a journalist at the Kherson newspaper *Novy Den*. An acquaintance invited him to a meeting. Waiting Russian soldiers put him in handcuffs, stuffed him in their car, and drove him to Nova Kakhovka. "They told me: 'You know, this is martial law. There is a war going on. We'll summon a tribunal and sentence you to be shot,'" Baturin said. "They began to threaten me, to describe in detail how they were going to skin me with a knife so that I would die slowly in agony."

Baturin said he was beaten several times, including in a police station where hostages were tortured with electric shocks. "They let me know clearly that I shouldn't write anymore," he told Radio Free Europe. Baturin was transferred to Kherson and held in a freezing cell. His Russian captors demanded he tell them the names of citizens organizing protests; they seemed unable to comprehend that the rallies were spontaneous. After eight days they let him go. "They want to completely suppress any manifestation of public activity," he said.

In June it was the turn of Kolykhaiev, Kherson's elected mayor. The FSB detained him when he went to work at the city council building, where his executive committee continued to function. Russian troops broke open safes, looking for documents. They seized hard drives. Kolykhaiev had refused to transfer communal enterprises to Russian jurisdiction, aides said. He was put in a bus marked with a *Z* and driven away to an unknown destination. The "ex-mayor" was "neutralized," Stremousov said.

Word of these abductions spread. Gradually the mass rallies ceased. A quiet terror descended over Kherson. Streets were mostly empty. Supplies of fuel, food, and medicines ran low; ATMs and banks stopped working; farmers supplied vegetables; bread was homemade. "The whole city was mostly moving on bicycle," Yulia, the artist, said. "We pedaled past Russian tanks. The soldiers generally wore balaclavas. You couldn't see their faces." In some raids, the occupiers took away laptops and phones, hunting for evidence of anti-Moscow activity.

Before the invasion, Olha ran a Kherson poetry festival; she met regularly with writers and artists. Ukrainians, she said, had become used to freedom. They had enjoyed it for three decades. Its sudden, brutal extinction in occupied Ukraine was a shock. Those weeks she spent in Kherson in early spring were like "living in a prison." She wrote a poem: "The Song of a Russian Occupant." It was a darkly biting ballad. There were allusions to a monster's paw—the Russian army—imagined by a soldier who thinks himself a prisoner. The poem begins:

I'm a velociraptor
A Russian looter raider
I stole that day a tractor
a bidet and a vibrator
Today the refrigerator
I've taken out of here
And tomorrow to the cemetery
I'll just lie down near

Release me please
From paw, from P.O.W.
From Russian fucking powers
'cause we're back numb
without number
In tarpaulin covers

Few believed life would improve under Russian rule; the fairy tale told by Kherson's new military-civilian administration was unconvincing. And so residents left the city. It was both a pragmatic act of personal rebellion and a matter of survival. Groups on Telegram exchanged information on what route to take and the locations of Russian checkpoints. Initially this was possible by vehicle. Later, escape involved an odyssey along back country roads, best done by bicycle.

Olha decided to flee with her two children and cat. A woman from her chat group, Ina, said her father was driving out to Mykolaiv. She arranged a lift. "Seven people and two cats traveling through a war zone in a Daewoo Lanos," she wrote in her diary. "There were four orc checkpoints, then Ukrainian checkpoints and traffic jams. We saw bombed-out houses, scorch marks from shells in the fields, and the remains of other cars on the way."

It was March 20. She traveled to Poland, then Stockholm, and finally London, where we met. Yulia, the artist, departed in April. The "green corridor" to Mykolaiv was shut down when the Russian army mined the road. The only way to leave Kherson was to go through Crimea or to head east to Zaporizhzhia. The Russians refused Ukrainian offers of humanitarian assistance. The area found itself behind a new iron curtain, swallowed up by *Russkiy Mir*.

Dressed in a three-piece suit and sporting a familiar goatee and mustache, a well-known figure returned to the port of Henichesk. He had been gone for some years. Vladimir Ilyich Lenin stood proudly once more on a pedestal, back just in time for his 152nd birthday. The communist leader's statue had been reinstalled outside the town council headquarters. Two banners flew from the building's roof: the Russian tricolor and the wartime Soviet flag with its hammer and sickle.

In each new occupied area, Russia conducted a symbolic makeover. It ripped down Ukrainian flags from city halls and other official premises. Workers scrubbed out the Ukrainian trident and repainted city signs in red, white, and blue. Monuments to Cossack leaders were demolished; mechanical diggers uprooted memorials to fallen Ukrainian servicemen. The aim was to erase all vestiges of Ukrainian statehood. After all, in Putin's Orwellian view, Ukraine had never existed, and he who controls the past controls the future.

The purge in Henichesk extended to Ukrainian officials. They, too, were rendered invisible. The town's mayor, Oleksandr Tulupov, was last seen in March. He and his colleagues posed for a photo in the town park next to a statue of Taras Shevchenko; Tulupov sported a black cap and padded jacket. It was the anniversary of Shevchenko's birth. Later that month the Russians hacked Henichesk's website and announced Tulupov had "resigned." A new "mayor," who had lived in Crimea for eight years, Gennady Sivak, replaced him.

The return of Soviet emblems was meant to drum up enthusiasm for Russia and its local proxies. Also brought back was the coat of arms for the Kherson region dating back to the early nineteenth century and the Russian Empire. It featured a two-headed black eagle similar to the one on the Russian Federation coat of arms. A plan was floated to rename a Kherson street after Vladimir Zhirinovsky, an ultranationalist Russian politician known for his clowning antics, and recently deceased.

This Great Russia mash-up didn't really work. Yuriy Sobolevskiy, a first deputy chairman in Kherson's regional council, said this statue campaign was ridiculous and ill-timed, coming amid a worsening humanitarian crisis and a squeeze on dissent. "Their motive is absolutely transparent. They try to parasitize on people's nostalgia. The problem is that these sentiments scarcely exist here," he said. The "USSR show" would go on until the Ukrainian army threw the Russians out.

Maryna—a woman living in occupied Berdiansk—told me by phone that the new authorities invited residents to a May 9 Victory Day party. She didn't go. "I was a Pioneer and in Komsomol [communist youth organizations] and I don't miss Lenin," she said. "It's the same scenario as in the Donbas. They have not come up with anything new." Russian propaganda worked on the older generation, she conceded, including her grandfather. "He doesn't believe the Russians bomb civilians. He watches Russian TV and has no other source of information."

There was no fighting in Berdiansk and little of the carnage seen down the coast in Mariupol. And yet the mood was restive. "Young people are against occupation," Maryna said. The Russians had switched off the Internet and were now trying to "zombify" residents with their fictions. "We are living in an information vacuum. It's like a terrible dream. I never believed this would happen," she told me.

Lenin's return struck me as bizarre, nonsensical. After all, Putin blamed Lenin explicitly for creating modern Ukraine. It was, critics observed, a sign of the ideological vacuum at the heart of Moscow's invasion project. "They feel there is no legitimacy to what they have done. They need some other kind of legitimacy, so they bring back Lenin and the Soviet flag. The Russian flag on its own isn't enough," Dmytro Lytvyn, Zelenskiy's speechwriter, told me in Kyiv when we discussed Russian and Ukrainian writers.

From its standpoint, Moscow was fixing the mistakes of history and reversing developments it regarded as anti-Russian. Already in the 1990s Ukraine began removing monuments to Lenin. The rest came down in 2014, in the wake of the Maidan revolution. Statues were toppled in Kharkiv, Kyiv, and elsewhere. Communist slogans were banned under "decommunization" laws passed by the Verkhovna Rada. Ukraine's occupied south was now experiencing "recommunization." It was, quite literally, going back to the USSR.

Anne Applebaum has argued Putin's methods were well-known totalitarian ones. He was replicating what Stalin's forces did in occupied Poland, the Baltic states, and the rest of Central Europe in 1939, as well in 1944 and 1945. It was an "eerily precise repeat of the NKVD [Soviet secret police] and Red Army's behavior," she told me. Arrests, murders, ethnic cleansing, the shutdown of noncommunist parties and free media . . . all took place in East Germany, Hungary, Poland, and other zones under Soviet control.

Speaking of today's Moscow, she said, "They have lists of people to arrest—mayors, museum directors, local leaders of all kinds. They systematically rape and murder civilians in order to create terror. They deport other people en masse to Russia to enhance their own depleted populations. They eradicate local symbols and put up their own." Applebaum said there was "one new twist" in Russia's Ukraine takeover: "Because modern Russia stands for nothing except corruption, nihilism, and Putin's personal power, they have brought back Soviet flags as well as Lenin statues to symbolize Russian victory."

Putin and his United Russia party also recruited literature to the cause of state ideology. The Ukrainian novelist Andrey Kurkov—my dinner host on the eve of the invasion—tweeted a photo of a new billboard in Kherson. There was a picture of the poet Alexander Pushkin, holding a feather quill and looking pensive, next to a party logo and the slogan: *Kherson—*

a city with Russian history! Its text noted that Pushkin had visited twice, in 1820 and 1824, and that his great-uncle Ivan Gannibal supervised the building of the city.

Russia's claim on southern Ukraine went back to a few decades earlier, and to the era of Catherine the Great. After defeating the Turks, Catherine's favorite Grigory Potemkin expanded Russia's borders to the Black Sea. He established a chain of cities. They included Kherson in 1778, with docks and a shipyard, conceived as a place to build vessels of war, and Mykolaiv, thirty-two kilometers upriver. He constructed a naval base farther afield at Sevastopol, in newly annexed Crimea, and he chose the site of what would become Odesa. The city was envisaged as a southern counterpart to Saint Petersburg, Peter the Great's northern imperial capital.

The Kremlin's narrative, however, was partial and self-serving. The region had a long pre- and post-Russian story. The northern Black Sea coast had Greek settlements; Kherson was named after an ancient colony founded in the fifth century B.C. in Crimea. Its name comes from Chersonesos, the Greek word for "peninsula." Other early inhabitants were nomadic; a Scythian grave was found in the place where Kherson's fortress was located, now a central park. The Ottomans occupied the area until the eighteenth century; many of its nineteenth-century settlers were Jews. Kherson's modern citizens voted in 1991 for independence from Russia. They spoke Russian and identified as Ukrainians.

Across occupied territories Moscow sought to enforce its version of history, identity, and cultural allegiance. Russian military police removed printed matter they deemed "extremist." That meant Ukrainian history books, dictionaries, and teaching materials, together with Kurkov's novels—written, ironically enough, in Russian. The books were taken from schools, libraries, and higher education institutions. They were thrown away or burned. Anything concerning Ukraine's 2004 and 2014 uprisings—liberation movements, essentially—was seen as dangerous "nationalism."

Moscow enforced a switch in schools to the Russian language and curriculum. Pupils would no longer be taught using Ukrainian textbooks. Instead imported Russian books would be used, which identified the government in Kyiv as "fascist." As part of its citizenship and education policy, Russian primers were revised to remove references to Ukraine. The country was expunged. It was even written out in its medieval form— "Ancient Rus" replaced Kyivan Rus.

Teachers faced an invidious choice. They could agree to teach the new Russian curriculum—or be fired. The authorities warned staff could be sent to Crimea for "retraining." The pro-Russian authorities called a meeting in May of Kherson's seventy-one educational institutes. Twenty people attended; fourteen got up and left; two said they had been brought at gunpoint. Pressure was applied to families. In some districts, parents were told those who objected to the new Russian-based educational system would face punishment. Their children might be sent to boarding schools; mothers would be made to do municipal cleaning work and fathers press-ganged into the "DNR" army.

In southern areas still under Ukrainian control, Putin's invasion triggered a campaign to replace Russian names and monuments. Numerous streets were named after USSR generals, air force pilots, and scientists. Metro stations commemorated Soviet victories. There were parks honoring Pushkin and Tolstoy. How might these references be interpreted today?

Was Pushkin a representative of Russian colonial culture or a universal artist? And what about Bulgakov, a writer of genius whose epoch—in Lytvyn's opinion—was over?

The debate was especially relevant to Odesa, a Russian-speaking southern Ukrainian city on the coast of the Black Sea, which the Kremlin had failed to capture. The city had a bronze bust of Pushkin, put up on the fiftieth anniversary of his death in a duel. It bore the words: PUSHKIN—CITIZEN OF ODESA. Russia's national poet had lived in the port for thirteen months from 1823 to 1824 and had written some of his verse novel *Eugene Onegin* in the city. There was another statue of him in a top hat on Pushkinska Street. Should these monuments be carted off?

According to Petro Obukhov, a deputy in Odesa's city parliament, Pushkin's bust should stay on its plinth. When we met, Obukhov explained his plan to remove some but not all Russian names from Odesa. His proposal was nuanced, I thought: a jumping-off point for debate among Odesa's residents rather than a sinister purge. He recommended keeping the names of Russian figures who had a genuine Odesa connection and removing some of those who didn't.

Under this formula Pushkin would stay. So would Catherine the Great, together with writers Nikolai Gogol and Ivan Bunin. Catherine's celebrated general Alexander Suvorov—who captured Warsaw—was on a red list. Obukhov described Suvorov as a "symbol of Russian imperial militancy." The Odesa district named after him should be renamed, he said. Obukhov wanted to sweep away names from Russian geography (Baikal, Omsk, Rostov) and those that referenced Dmitry Donskoy, a fourteenth-century Moscow prince.

Opinion polls suggested residents broadly supported these

changes. Some 44 percent were in favor of de-Russification, 36 percent were opposed, and 7 percent wanted to bring back communist-era names (this minority was largely made up of pensioners fond of the Soviet Union). The war had created fresh myths, Obukhov said; when it was finished there would be streets called "Heroes of Mariupol."

We strolled together along Prymorskiy Boulevard. This was Odesa's seaside promenade, overlooking the harbor. Acacia trees lent their shade; there was a scent of elderflower blossom; fluff from poplar trees known as *pukh* tumbled in the breeze. One lady was feeding an ownerless cat sunning itself on a wall, a representative of Odesa's feral feline population. Periodically, the Russians fired cruise missiles at the city in erratic fashion, killing civilians. That day, all was quiet.

The Ukrainian military had shut off the city's historic center. The Potemkin Steps, made famous in Sergei Eisenstein's 1925 film, *Battleship Potemkin*, were no longer accessible. Odesa's opera and ballet theater—the most beautiful in Europe, locals said—was swagged with sandbags, its French rococo exterior visible from beyond a heavily guarded cordon. The memorial to Catherine the Great was boarded up.

Many people had left Odesa. Those who remained enjoyed the spring sunshine. There were dog walkers, children on skateboards, and couples sitting on benches. When an electric sightseeing minitrain drove past, I jumped on. Tour guide Larysa Otkalenko said she probably supported the name changes. "You can't print what I think about Putin because it's rude. What I can say is his view of history is completely untrue," she told me. "Yes, Odesa is a Russian-speaking city. But it's also multinational and cosmopolitan."

As Larysa explained, the city had a rich and syncretic past, drawing on many talents. The commander who seized the Turks' Black Sea fortress, José de Ribas, was a Spaniard serving in the Russian military. The city's first governor, the Duke of Richelieu, was a French aristocrat. It was Richelieu who planted Odesa's wonderful acacia trees. A Flemish engineer, Franz de Volán, drew up its street grid. Odesa was known as Little Paris. Other foreigners who lived and settled in Odesa included Greeks, Poles, Bulgarians, Germans, and Italians.

It was once the third-largest Jewish city in the world, Larysa informed me, after New York and Warsaw. This status ended when the Nazis occupied Odesa between 1941 and 1944.

Larysa was a charming companion; we chugged past art nouveau buildings and a reconstructed cathedral. "We don't need Russia to save us. We can take care of ourselves," she said as the tour ended on Derybasivska Street, named after de Ribas, a pedestrian boulevard of cafés and bars. She offered a last observation: "History is the servant of all ages and epochs."

The drive from Odesa to Mykolaiv takes two hours along Highway M14. The region is known for its industry: shipbuilding, coal, an oil terminal at the port of Yuzhne, and an ammonia factory. But as I traveled east along the southern steppe, my overriding impression was of rampant greenery. It was late May. There were fields of sunflowers and rapeseed, grapes ripening and willow trees. We crossed a shining estuary. I spotted an oystercatcher and three white storks flying in solemn formation in a limpid sky.

On the outskirts of Mykolaiv the atmosphere darkened. The war, you sensed, was close. Soldiers checked my documents; they advised me to put on body armor and a flak jacket. To visit the city you needed to notify the authorities in advance. Beyond a checkpoint, a bridge led across the Southern Buh River into the center of town. My driver parked outside a café. An aide-de-camp appeared. We followed his vehicle to an anonymous residential building. In the distance there was a thunderous reverberation—artillery.

I had come to interview Roman Kostenko, a special forces commander turned politician and a member of Ukraine's parliament. His men had been fighting the Russians for four months by this point, across the southern front line. Mykolaiv was a hundred kilometers northwest of Kherson. The line of contact ran approximately along the administrative boundaries separating Kherson and Mykolaiv Oblasts. The Russians were twenty kilometers away from Mykolaiv's outer neighborhoods—on the doorstep, practically.

Ukraine's adversaries used this proximity to lethal effect. They shelled the city relentlessly. Some bombs landed on barracks and army targets. Most fell on residential areas. They smashed low-rise buildings, the palace of culture, the port, and the main regional administration complex, as well as universities and schools. The Ingul Hotel's central section had been transformed into a concrete pancake. Surrounding villages and towns were struck, too. According to Mykolaiv's mayor, Oleksandr Sinkevych, by midsummer the Russians had killed 121 people and wounded 534, six of them children. More than five hundred buildings were damaged.

Some 230,000 people—just under half the population—relocated elsewhere. Those who stayed lived under constant hazard, with explosions at all times of the day. The port was moribund; the local economy devastated. Mykolaiv was a city without water: shelling cut the supply. Water for washing was partially reconnected in May, but there was still a shortage of drinking water; residents went around carrying large five-liter plastic bottles, waiting in line at standpipes.

I shook hands with Kostenko, a muscly figure with a big grin and close-cut black hair, wearing a khaki T-shirt. He was something of a national legend. Javelin missiles were piled up in the hallway of his office. A powerful-looking green cylinder had been left next to a wooden shoe rack. "It's a British NLAW anti-tank weapon. We've used it," Kostenko said, adding: "We love Boris Johnson. The UK has firmly stated its position. It stands by its values and isn't afraid of Russia. And President Biden. He gives us help."

In the days after February 24, the Russians came close to capturing Mykolaiv. Some of their convoys bypassed Kherson and raced to cut off the city. At the time, Kostenko was in Kyiv. He swapped a politician's suit and tie for a uniform and drove south. By the time he reached Mykolaiv, Russian troops were camped nearby. They had struck Kulbakino air base in the southeast and were advancing from the north. "I was the last car in," Kostenko said. Citizens were preparing for bloody street-to-street fighting. They had piled up tires and were making homemade bombs.

The Ukrainian army withstood the assault and pushed the invaders back. Kostenko showed me a video he took of a Russian position on Mykolaiv's outskirts. It showed him walking through a hellish brown field. There were abandoned field guns, mangled trucks, an engine, and the bodies of enemy soldiers, scattered amid debris and shells—victims of a Ukrainian aerial barrage. "They didn't retrieve their dead. We buried them," Kostenko said of the Russians. The victorious Ukrainians seized the Russians' cannons and pointed them toward their former owners.

Since this unsuccessful pincer attack, fighting in the south had turned into a battle of rockets and artillery. There were fewer direct encounters. "It's like the Second World War with modernized tanks and weapons," Kostenko told me. The Russians had plenty of everything, he added—tanks, ammunition, reserves, Smerch and older S-300 rockets. He was confident Ukraine could win, but to do so it needed firepower: MLRS, heavy artillery, air defenses. In the meantime, his guys lived in frontline trenches under murderous 24/7 fire; most fatalities were from shrapnel. "To survive is very hard," Kostenko admitted.

The U.S., UK, and Swedish anti-tank weapons that had proved so effective in the early weeks of the war were now of little use, he explained. His fighters couldn't get close enough to lock on to enemy targets. The Russians had hidden their armored vehicles in a network of communist-era irrigation canals. For the moment, Ukraine could make only local tactical gains and had had some success, winning back a few villages. But liberating the whole of Kherson could only happen once Ukraine's Western partners had stepped up, Kostenko said.

A member of the liberal pro-European Holos Party, Kostenko suggested some European countries had not fully grasped what was happening in the south and east—a brutal struggle fought by Ukraine on behalf of the civilized world. Which allies did he mean? "Germany and France. They are behaving very cautiously. It's inexplicable. They are not calling out the enemy. We are fighting totalitarianism here," he said.

I liked Kostenko. He was smart and an optimist, too, despite his daily professional experiences of death and suffering. His personal story was compelling. The secretary of Ukraine's Committee on National Security, Defense, and Intelligence, he spent fifteen years as a soldier and alpha commander. He'd been wounded twice in late 2014 while fighting outside Donetsk. He grew up in a village in the Kherson region. During the recent occupation, Russian soldiers broke into his parents' house. They stole his parade uniform and combat medals and made off with the furniture.

According to Kostenko, Putin was determined to bring Ukraine back into Russia's political and cultural orbit. His intention was to take Mykolaiv and Odesa and to unite with the Moldovan breakaway republic of Transnistria. "They want to make us a non–sea country," he said. The Kremlin lacked popular backing in Kherson, which is why its pro-Russian administration delayed plans to hold a referendum. "Ninety-nine percent of the people are against them," he estimated.

Kostenko gave me a souvenir: a jagged metal fragment from a Russian Kalibr cruise missile warhead. He wrapped it carefully in a kitchen towel. I put it in my laptop bag. "Victory now depends on our international friends," he stressed. "We have plenty of Kalashnikovs and machine guns. If we get enough heavy arms, Russia will not be able to go any farther. The West can change the outcome of this war."

After our interview I went to meet one of Mykolaiv's long-suffering civilians. Makar Kostiuk, a Russian from Vladivostok, had moved to the city to study. He left Russia for political reasons: he was active in anti-Kremlin politics and had worked as a volunteer in Alexei Navalny's local office. Olha, the poet, had introduced me to Makar; he had published a well-received novel based on his experiences, and was part of her Kherson literary circle.

We met next to a statue of Viktor Lyagin, a Soviet NKVD intelligence officer and hero of the Soviet Union. Lyagin worked as an undercover spy at the dockyard; the Germans executed him for wartime sabotage. Mykolaiv's shipbuilding industry once employed a hundred thousand people; up until the invasion, some of its former workforce were sympathetic to Moscow. Makar was not surprised by how 2022 had turned out. "When the bombs started falling, I was working on my second novel. The explosions made me type faster," he said. A shell had landed in his courtyard, punching a hole in a stairwell window.

Mykolaiv's residents had grown used to shelling. I went with Makar to the city's theater and concert hall, where he worked as a volunteer. Built in 1824, and originally a venue for naval officers, it had been transformed into a humanitarian aid distribution center. There were clothes, shoes, and medicines. Locals filled in a form explaining what they needed. The pharmacy was well stocked but lacked mosquito repellent; insect bites were a problem for soldiers on the front line.

Those who had chosen to remain in the shell-battered city seemed upbeat. Olga Pidsosonna, a helper at the center and a major in the port's customs department, said the war felt like "one very long day." "Russia is trying to eat us. But it will break its teeth. We are a strong nation. I'm proud to be Ukrainian," she told me. The army should recover everything Moscow had taken, including Crimea. "I have relatives in Crimea. They want to be with Ukraine. They can't say this openly, of course. They are afraid."

At that moment normality seemed far off. Most shops in Mykolaiv's main Soborna Street were boarded up. A bomb had shattered the glass at a McDonald's. Even here, though, life continued. A man in Lycra cycled past me on his mountain bike; a few people were out shopping; a charity van dished out meals from a fold-up table; canned music played from pavement speakers. I chatted with an off-duty soldier, Oleh. "Russia thinks we are Russians. We don't agree. We are a separate nation, and we want to live according to our own rules," he said.

With the right weapons, Kyiv might regain the south and push the Russians back to Crimea. This was a crucial national task. If Ukraine were to become an economically successful country with a European future, it needed the Black Sea. That summer, President Zelenskiy ordered his commanders to draw up a plan and to prepare a southern offensive. Liberation would not be quick or easy. But maybe it was doable.

In the east it was another story. There the Russian military was at its most powerful and entrenched. For all their courage, Ukraine's armed forces in the spring and early summer were outmatched. They were going backward, a slow and painful retreat, explained by Kyiv as a necessary step to preserve lives and not a strategic defeat. There was another way to describe this motion, though it was less palatable to say it.

The Donbas was slipping away. It seemed almost, but not quite, lost.

NINE

The War for the East

Four days the earth was rent and torn
By bursting steel,
The houses fell about us;
Three nights we dared not sleep,
Sweating, and listening for the imminent crash
Which meant our death.
—RICHARD ALDINGTON,
"Bombardment"

The enemy was fifty meters away. From time to time voices floated from behind a concrete slab across a no-man's-land of wintry trees and scrub. Smoke was visible in a white sky. There were muddy trenches and camouflage netting. This war had been going on for years. It was a dreary, grinding, monotonous conflict, characterized by snipers and deadly bombs. For long stretches, not much happened. And then there was a gunshot and someone's luck ran out. All was quiet until it wasn't.

The Somme? Verdun? Ypres? Actually, this distinctly non-moving battle was being fought in the twenty-first century, and not in Flanders or France, but in eastern Ukraine. In some ways, Putin's invasion on February 24, 2022, wasn't an invasion as such. More accurately, it was an escalation. Or, as Biden put it, a further invasion. Some kind of qualification was needed: full-scale, bigger, avowed. Russia's war had begun in spring 2014. The 2022 version was a dramatic scaling up of an ongoing shoot-out, in which fourteen thousand people lay dead.

In December 2021, I traveled to the Donbas amid predictions by the White House that Russian divisions parked on Ukraine's borders were preparing to go in. The line separating government-controlled territory from the breakaway zone ran for 450 kilometers at that point. On the occupied side were the pro-Russian puppet territories of the DNR and LNR. The "border" went through a landscape of coal mines and chimney stacks, factories and lakes, the legacy of decades of Soviet heavy industry.

The Donbas was Putin's reason for invading Ukraine, an idée fixe in official propaganda. The region's inhabitants were Russian speakers; Moscow had come to save them from fascists and genocide, or so it said. Exiled president Viktor Yanukovych had grown up in the Donetsk region city of Yenakiieve in the shadow of a metallurgical factory; his mother was buried in the local cemetery. Like much of the Donbas, it had fallen on hard times. Pits had shut and the city's Red October mine was a ghostly ensemble of brick buildings.

The Donbas's electorate traditionally supported Yanukovych's pro-Russia Party of Regions. So did the Kremlin, which in 2004 interfered to try to keep Yanukovych in power after he lost a presidential election. The party was "long a haven for Donetsk-based mobsters and oligarchs," in the words of a 2006 U.S. diplomatic cable. Putin regarded Yanukovych as clumsy and a dummy. But Yanukovych's exit from power in the wake of the 2014 Maidan revolution was unacceptable to Moscow. It triggered Putin's annexation of Crimea and his war in the east.

In the spring of 2014, around 33 percent of Donetsk's residents wanted to join with Moscow, polls suggested. They included elderly communists who rallied in the city's Lenin Square. One activist I spoke to acknowledged Yanukovych's shortcomings as a leader: the president's corruption was legendary. The protester told me: "Yanukovych may have been a crook, but he was *our* legitimate president." As well as those nostalgic for the Soviet Union, there were other, younger, more radical pro-Russian voices prepared to use violent methods.

Poverty was also a factor, as was a feeling that life had gone downhill since the demise of the USSR. Some who took part in protests in 2014 were youths from small, depressed mining communities as well as "tourists" brought in from across the border. Russia and its spy agencies transformed these sentiments into an armed anti-Kyiv insurgency. By the time it was over, Kremlin-backed separatists controlled about a third of Donetsk and Luhansk Oblasts, which make up the Donbas, the Ukrainian government two-thirds.

At the time of my trip the conflict was frozen. The front line separated the northern outskirts of Donetsk from the Ukrainian-held city of Avdiivka. In 2017, Ukraine's land forces pushed the rebels back a few kilometers; the fight pulverized buildings and shredded trees. Ukraine's command post was located in an abandoned factory. European and American lawmakers dropped by on occasion to see the conflict for themselves; next to the checkpoint was a tablet commemorating Ukraine's fallen, a ceremonial tank, and a small military museum.

I borrowed a flak jacket and body armor and made my way into the base via a warren of underground rooms. The headquarters connected with a well-developed trench system. Someone had hung a uniform on a mannequin and a blue-and-yellow flag. "There are some similarities with the First World War. We have positions. They have positions," Oleksandr Tymoshuk, a lieutenant, told me as we stood at an observation point. He passed me his periscope. The Russians were concealed behind a spider-shaped structure, he said.

But Oleksandr said there were differences, too, compared to a century ago. Officers on the western front would send platoons out at night to glean intelligence, stealing between foxholes. Now reconnaissance was done using technology—drones and remote sensor cameras that could detect any intrusion or movement. New advanced weapons made the situation on the battlefield more complicated, he said. The Ukrainians had bought sophisticated Turkish-made Bayraktars—unmanned combat aerial vehicles. Moscow employed drones, too—a menacing danger.

"Our task is to stand here and not let anyone through. The time will come when we reclaim everything they took from us," Oleksandr said. He was dismissive of Putin's claims that Russia and Ukraine were one. "Russians can't understand Ukrainian. I understand Russian because the language has been forced on us for centuries." He and his soldiers only returned fire, he stressed, adding: "If it were up to me, I would give them back ten times what they dish out to us."

I followed a party heading to the outer front line. We threaded in single file through a former textiles warehouse. Now it was a ghostly and roofless ruin, smashed up in the battle of 2017. Cavernous brick chambers were decorated with graffiti. One message reminded those going on duty: FUCK UP AND YOU DIE; another read: OLIGARCHS! STOP PLAYING WITH WAR. Sheets of plastic flapped in the chill wind; the floor was damp; we spoke in whispers. The Russians were close, hidden across a bare field.

It was a strange intimacy. Mysha Novytskiy—a twenty-five-year-old senior lieutenant—told me that he could hear snatches of Russian from across the divide; at mealtimes enemy smoke floated over to their position. "Every day they shoot at us," he said. The quarrel between the two countries was not fixable, he thought. "Russia is stuck in the Soviet past. They think the whole world owes them something. There's no progress. Ukraine is trying to make progress, even if it's baby steps." To where? I asked. "To Europe," he replied.

For eight long years Moscow denied its troops were fighting in Ukraine. This was a big lie: Russia supplied the rebels with personnel, thousands of tons of ammunition, and weapons. Without that direct intervention, Kyiv would likely have recaptured Donetsk and Luhansk. Mysha said his military opponents were not DNR volunteers. "Of course they are Russians. The weapons they are using, the way they are behaving, they aren't a bunch of Donbas miners. They are professional career soldiers," he said.

Mysha was a charismatic guide. He took me on a tour. We walked along Tymyriazev Street, named after a Russian botanist. Its once-pleasant dachas were wrecks. The gardens survived. In summer the soldiers gathered walnuts and tomatoes,

Mysha said, as patrols padded through the empty plots. "The Ukrainian health ministry wouldn't want you to be here," he joked. In the absence of humans the natural world thrived. I saw a blue tit and crows.

The civilian cost of the Donbas conflict was vast. Residents in affected cities fled when it started. Most headed west to safety; others moved to Russia; some joined the separatists. The villages directly in range of hostile fire were mostly abandoned, their shops and post offices closed. A few stubborn seniors refused to leave. The Ukranian soldiers adopted cats and dogs that had been left behind. Three seconds before a Russian artillery attack, the animals would take cover, Mysha told me—a useful alarm signal.

The Avdiivka base had an air of permanence. Soldiers lived in bunk rooms and relaxed in a cozy mess. There was a small library. Letters and drawings from Ukrainian schoolchildren were stuck to wooden pillars. Ivan Skuratovskiy—an English-speaking lieutenant—showed me his subterranean living quarters. Two kittens dozed on his bed. Five men from the platoon he commanded had been killed. "It's really hard to take casualties. Some strings are broken in me. I've become more cynical," he said.

Those who stayed on in frontline towns got used to war. "You hear the firing. It's pretty damn loud. I try not to think about it," Olha Teslenko, a pensioner in a knitted hat, told me. Her home was close to the base, which was often bombarded. "We were afraid at first, but now we're accustomed to it," she said. "Nobody thought the war would last so long. We had hopes that peace will happen, but they are fading." As for another Russian offensive, well—she didn't want to consider it. "If you think about it, it can drive you mad. My heart is already hurting."

As my writer friend Andrey Kurkov remarked, the Donbas's fear of war and death had gradually been transformed into apathy. In the winter of 2015, Andrey made the first of three trips to the region. They resulted in his 2018 novel, *Grey Bees*, set in the gray zone between occupied and nonoccupied territory. It was a place where inhabitants were familiar with the whistle of shells. Sometimes they swept shrapnel from their yards. War was normal, he discovered. "I saw people learning to live with it, as if it were a rowdy drunken neighbor," he noted.

The book's protagonist—a disabled pensioner and devoted beekeeper—is a holdout who refuses to exit his home village after almost everyone else has gone. Those who opted to stay tried to remain inconspicuous, almost faceless. It was a way of coping with a "new, strange, and harsh reality," Andrey wrote. The Donbas's character was singular, he suggested, occupying a mythical place in the Soviet imagination. "The Russians even came up with a special designation for them, 'the people of the Donbas,' as if they were the children of mines and slag heaps, without ethnic roots," he observed.

The war's most enduring consequence in Avdiivka was to sever the town and its railway line from Donetsk, eight kilometers to the south. This rending separated neighbors and friends and split up families—sometimes leaving parents on one side and their children on the other. In a town café I met Mariia Lepilova, a former teacher whose relatives lived in Donetsk. She could no longer visit so she spoke to them on the phone. "We avoid politics and talk about our kids. People can get used to anything," she told me.

Mariia said she was forced to leave Avdiivka in 2014, when shelling made their lives unbearable. There was no power and their house was hit. "My ten-year-old daughter was very afraid. Almost everyone left," she said. Later most residents came back, with apartments rebuilt and new investment, including from the town's large coke factory, a residue of coal used as fuel. Around 22,000 people lived in Avdiivka when I visited, including soldiers. Like Mariupol, it enjoyed a mini renaissance, an advertisement for Ukrainian Donbas.

Putin's 2014 invasion changed Avdiivka's character. A younger generation identified as Ukrainian. The Donbas was strongly Russophone; after the Second World War, the USSR sent ethnic Russians to the region and practically eliminated Ukrainian-language schooling. Now the Ukrainian language was heard again in schools and shops. Children learned Ukrainian in class from the age of six or seven. Locals had become more patriotic. The lingering cultural influence of Russia was slowly fading, Mariia said.

She mourned what was lost. Residents used to visit Donetsk to go to restaurants or the cinema, or to support the city's football team, FC Shakhtar Donetsk, which played at the Donbas arena. This was one of the venues for the 2012 European Championships, hosted by Ukraine and Poland and a moment of national unity. The McDonald's in the center of Donetsk, across the square from the city's Lenin statue, was shuttered in 2014, when the separatists took over; to take her daughter now meant going to Kharkiv, three hundred kilometers away.

Mariia told me she missed the cultural life in the big city and its museum, especially its collection of Dutch paintings and Greek sculpture. "It's the city of my youth," she said. There seemed scant prospect she would return.

.   .   .

In the febrile spring of 2014, I spent several weeks reporting from Donetsk and Luhansk as Russia tore the cities from
Ukraine. I left on one of the last flights to take off from
Donetsk's international airport. A new passenger terminal had
been constructed two years before, for Euro 2012. The building was named after the composer Sergei Prokofiev, a native
of Donetsk Oblast. Its glass concourse was deserted, my plane
back to Kyiv near empty. The regional governor and local oligarch, Serhiy Taruta, fled with his entourage not long after on
a private jet.

Soon afterward, DNR fighters and Russian mercenaries
seized the airport complex. The Ukrainian army won it back;
the defenders who held it during the following months were
feted for their valor and acquired the nickname "cyborgs."
More than one hundred of them were eventually killed. In
January 2015, the DNR finally captured the site. The airport
was trashed in the exchanges; its control tower collapsed. Only
two towers survived. They stood like disembodied sentinels,
watching over a desolate and lifeless runway.

The Ukrainians, meanwhile, fell back to Pisky, a village two
kilometers from the airport, and ten kilometers from the center of Donetsk. The day after touring Avdiivka, I drove to meet
the local brigade commander in Pisky, Major Serhiy Kozachok.
I met him at his base. This was a spacious residential house,
with ground-floor offices, a canteen serving soup and cups of
tea, and a well-kept garden. No armored vehicle was available
and so we set off to the airport in the major's civilian car.

The Russians, Kozachok said, were constantly trying to stir
trouble. Their intention was to make Ukraine break the Minsk

protocols, agreed between Kyiv and Moscow in 2014 and 2015. The agreements established a buffer zone between the two parties from which heavy weapons were banned. And—in theory—a cease-fire. The Organization for Security and Co-operation in Europe, the OSCE, monitored the situation. "The other side provoke us with fire. Single shots. We're not allowed to respond. We comply with Minsk," the major said as we drove along the road.

Logically enough, Ukraine had concentrated the bulk of its forces in the Donbas. Kozachok said that his soldiers were reliable and experienced, unlike some of the volunteers who fought and died in 2014. "We know what we are doing. My men are always training. Our task is to preserve what we have as much as possible," he said. After going a short distance down a tree-lined country road, we turned left and sped up—driving between seventy and eighty miles per hour along an exposed roadway.

"They might shell us. If we move fast, it's harder for them to hit," the major explained.

This "road of life," as it was known, led to a frontline out-post on the edge of the airport. I got out, put on borrowed body armor, and followed the major along the side of a broad muddy track, taking care to tread in his footsteps. Red signs warned of mines; the fields and copses nearby were littered with unexploded ordnance. A pheasant rose out of tall yellow grass, clattering away into the gray horizon. We kept going.

After three hundred meters I heard a shot, an echoing *pop*. And then two more.

A Russian sniper was firing at us.

We quickened our pace and took cover behind an embank-ment. "They are shooting at us constantly. Snipers work during the night and day," Kozachok said. The mound where we stood was made from earth excavated when the airport was built. It resembled a gigantic anthill: there were dugouts and raised trenches; soldiers scurried up ladders leading to an upper level. *The Guardian*'s videographer Volodymyr Yurchenko scrambled up and poked his camera over the top. Another shot rang out, nearer this time. The spectral twin towers left standing at the airport were visible beyond the runway.

At this unlikely garrison and across the front, soldiers expressed the same patriotic sentiments. As Vitaliy Barabash, Avdiivka's military-civilian mayor, put it to me: "Nobody wants to be Putin's slave." All stressed otherness from Russia: a hostile foreign power. "I'm here to defend my country. It's my duty as a Ukrainian. We have a different mentality. We are Europeans, and we don't want to live in the USSR," Kozachok said.

What would he do if he met Putin, I asked? "I'd punch him on the nose," the major said.

One idea in particular characterized Russian military thinking: *razgrom*. It means crushing defeat, devastation, a rout. The best way of achieving *razgrom*, according to classical and twentieth-century Soviet doctrine, was to encircle the other side's forces. Encirclement offered the swiftest path to victory. It worked in Berlin and Stalingrad. You could bypass the enemy's strongest defense lines and sweep in around the back. The troops caught in this cauldron might surrender. Or be annihilated. It didn't really matter. Any breakout would be costly.

In March 2022, Kremlin officials announced the first phase of the so-called special operation was over. Russian units retreated from Kyiv and vacated north and northeastern Ukraine. They left through Belarus and went east. Putin's new, updated plan was more modest but still dumbfounding in its ambition: to seize the whole of the Donbas. As promised, he intended to grow the LNR and DNR in size so they reached their regional administrative borders. That meant the wipeout of Ukraine's eastern army: *razgrom*.

Moscow embarked on this second military phase in April. Russian battalion tactical groups did not seek to smash through the existing heavily defended Ukrainian front line, which included Avdiivka. Instead they went around it. They advanced from the south, moving up through territory around Mariupol. They came from the north and Kharkiv Oblast, making the captured city of Izium a strategic forward base. And they rolled west across Luhansk Oblast, taking a string of villages, including Shchastia and other minor towns.

The offensive followed the same scorched-earth method seen in Mariupol. It involved brutal and indiscriminate bombardment using air strikes, rockets, and artillery to soften up terrain. In the process, settlements were destroyed. Once there was little left but rubble, tanks were deployed. And finally infantry. The cost—civilian casualties, damaged infrastructure, a shattered urban environment, no utilities or means of life—was irrelevant.

What mattered was territory. And the completion of Putin's great expansionist task.

Much of Luhansk fell in the first weeks. This was land closest to Russia. Thereafter progress was slow, often amounting to a kilometer or two a day. But this tortoise-like advance was not the same as failure. When I arrived in the Donbas in June 2022, Russia was squeezing the city of Sievierodonetsk, the administrative capital of Ukrainian-controlled Luhansk, and was bombarding the next-door city of Lysychansk, on the opposite side of the Siverskiy Donets River. The Russian army was firing rockets at Sloviansk and Kramatorsk, both major Ukrainian bases and the next axis of attack.

The war was being waged regardless of losses on the Russian side. The Kremlin appeared entirely indifferent to the deaths of its servicemen. In May, at least four hundred Russian soldiers were killed while trying to build a pontoon bridge over the Siverskiy Donets near the village of Bilohorivka. It was an encircling action meant to cut off Lysychansk; Ukrainian artillery wiped out Russian armored vehicles as they tried to cross; bodies lay amid mud and fallen branches.

Despite these reversals the front line was creeping closer. The Russian army began bombarding Sloviansk in late April, the city's deputy mayor, Yuriy Pidlisniy, told me. We met in the lobby of the city's main administration building; a Ukrainian flag flew above the square. At his suggestion we went outside and sat on a bench decorated with graffiti. It was an enclosed spot. If a shell landed nearby, we would probably survive, I reflected, but a cruise missile strike? Not so much.

The Russians were eleven kilometers away. "They've hit us with Iskander missiles, air strikes, and Smerch rockets," Pidlisniy said. The enemy had shelled Sviatohirska Lavra, north of Sloviansk, killing a nun and burning down the wooden All Saints monastery. I had visited the religious site in 2014; the monastery was built on a steep hill with a series of caves overlooking the fast-flowing Siverskiy Donets. Families used to visit carrying brown wicker baskets filled with Easter eggs and cake; Russia's war, in part driven by the Orthodox faith, had put it to flame.

The omens were grim. Might Sloviansk avoid the fate of Mariupol and other urban areas the Russians had flattened and overrun? "I believe in our army. We need to stay and hold on. I hope there are enough forces," Pidlisniy said. He added: "It's hard to know why Putin decided to attack. Russia has an imperial complex. It thinks Mother Russia sits on top of the world. And without Ukraine in its sphere of influence Russia is not an empire. Also, Putin thinks he doesn't have much time left."

In the distance there was a loud thump. The noise came from outgoing Ukrainian artillery, the deputy mayor assured me. "If it's incoming, you feel it in your legs. The ground vibrates." At that moment he received an alert on his cell phone and broke off to make a short phone call. One of his staff sounded the air raid siren, which blared across the city from his office roof. These warnings were frequent; locals largely ignored them, he said.

Pidlisniy said he kept telling residents to leave Sloviansk. About 25,000 people out of its population of approximately 100,000 had stubbornly declined his advice, he said. Many were elderly and didn't want to go. Others pleaded sick relatives or much-loved pets. "One woman told me she had to look after her cats. A bomb killed them," he recounted grimly. Male pensioners would refuse evacuation only to change their minds when it was too late.

Conditions inside the city were getting worse, he went on. There was no gas or water and only intermittent electricity. With gasoline costly, people got around on bikes. Some who left at the start of the invasion returned despite the risks, after running out of money. The local economy was trashed. Soldiers queued outside a café in Sloviansk's market to buy cost-price 60 hryvnia ($1.60) kebabs; one stall-holder, Lubov

Petrovna, who was selling dill, told me she had packed her car and would flee if the situation got worse.

The Kremlin was evidently determined to seize Sloviansk, even if that meant wrecking it. Again, it was politics; the city had symbolic value. In 2014, a Russian militia led by Igor Girkin, the former GRU colonel also known as Strelkov, seized the administration building and occupied Sloviansk for three months. It was a time of terror and kidnappings. Gunmen imprisoned a U.S. journalist, as well as European military observers from the OSCE, who were being kept in a basement. Pidlisniy described the separatists as "drunks, drug addicts, and *lumpenproletariat*."

During this wild period, a shadowy masked group hijacked Ukrainian armored vehicles at Kramatorsk's railway station. It drove them to Sloviansk. I followed in a rented car and caught up with the column after it parked outside city hall and the White Nights café. I asked one special operative in a balaclava where he was from. "Russia," he replied. He said he had just come from Simferopol. How were things in annexed Crimea? "*Zamechatelno*," he said—splendid. The old ladies were happy with their higher Russian pensions, he added.

Some citizens in 2014 supported Girkin's soldiers of fortune. His ragtag followers included a troupe of mysterious pro-Kremlin "Cossacks" who posed outside the administration building and a self-appointed "mayor." One middle-aged commando with a bushy beard told me he had come to Sloviansk "to help." "We don't want Ukraine. Ukraine doesn't exist for us. There are no people called Ukrainians," he declared. "There are just Slav people who used to be in Kyivan Rus before Jews like Trotsky divided us. . . . We should all be together again," he stressed.

Others were appalled at this alien takeover. Visiting Slo-viansk was an unsettling experience. Masked youths, mostly armed with sticks, set up roadblocks using piles of tires. Closer to the city the barricades got bigger. One morning I saw a group of women, in the main elderly, holding gold-framed icons; they bowed and prayed by the road—volunteer human shields. Another time a drunken DNR commander stopped me at the same checkpoint on the bridge and waved a pistol in my face. "Get out of here!" he screamed. He punched my car, leaving a dent.

The occupation ended when the Ukrainian army evicted Girkin and his deadly pantomime militia. Girkin was named the DNR's "defense minister"; later he fell out with the Kremlin and became a hawkish critic of its Donbas campaign. Incredibly, a minority of Sloviansk residents was sympathetic to Russia in 2022, Pidlisniy said, even after the experience of 2014, and Bucha and Mariupol. "It's not straightforward. I know a lot of ethnic Russians who support Ukraine and Ukrainians who back Putin," he told me.

A recent Russian missile attack killed three people and wounded several others, the deputy mayor said. It took place at night. Projectiles slammed into a street named after Yaroslav the Wise, the eleventh-century grand prince of Kyiv. When I reached the neighborhood, I found a grisly mess. A burnt-out Lada sat in the road. The blast blew out balconies and splat-tered walls with holes. Glass showered a communal garden. A white-painted school at the end of the road was also damaged.

Worst hit was apartment building number 10. I spoke to residents sitting outside next to a walnut tree. Vitaliy Kolesny-chenko said he had been asleep with his wife, Neliia, when their building was struck. "We live on the third floor. It was dark. There was a huge explosion. It blew off our bathroom door. I saw yellow and green smoke," he said. He added: "I looked for my wife. She had gone very quiet. She said: 'My legs, my legs.'"

Vitaliy, a handicapped pensioner, was unable to do much. He said he found a flashlight and tried to drag his wife out. Rescue workers arrived and carried her away. She died en route to the hospital in Kramatorsk, the garrison city down the road. A twenty-one-year-old soldier who had been living across the hall was killed, too. Vitaliy showed me a photo of Neliia on his phone. "We were married for one month short of thirty years. There was nothing like this in the USSR. We were brothers," he lamented.

On the fifth floor at number 10, I found another scene of heartbreak. Alona Boivet and her husband, Viktor, fled Sloviansk in April days after their marriage. Alona's mother, Oksana, had returned in a car to the couple's debris-strewn apartment. She sobbed as she retrieved her daughter's wedding dress and shoes. Male family members stoically patched up a window frame, blown in three days before. Through the open gap you could see swifts, hurtling around a sultry sky.

The building's inhabitants blamed Moscow for bringing war to Sloviansk for a second time. "The mayor's office should send a commission to value the damage and help us but they haven't," Vitaliy's neighbor Olena Voitenko said. "And then Russia should pay for all of this. I am ethnic Russian, but my homeland is Ukraine. I didn't ask them to come here. My daughter lives in the DNR and is zombified. We can't talk anymore." What would happen next? "They will never take Sloviansk," Olena predicted.

A terrible battle was drawing near. In the meantime, there

was normal life. On the way out of Sloviansk, I stopped by the bridge where the commander once waved a pistol at me. Boys were swimming in the Kazennyi Torets River, a tributary of the Siverskiy Donets; a gull flapped languidly over green osier trees. A large-wheeled armored carrier rolled into view. Its driver jumped out and introduced himself as Slava Vladimirovich. He stripped to his underpants and plunged into the water.

"In battle there is nowhere to wash," he explained, wringing out his wet khaki T-shirt.

Slava dried off and showed me his vehicle. On the roof was a joystick-controlled machine gun. Shrapnel had dented the transporter's right side. There was a crack in a porthole-like window, although the spacious interior was undamaged. Slava said he had been rescuing noncombatants from Lysychansk, one of the last slabs of Ukrainian-held territory in Luhansk Oblast. "A Russian rocket landed twenty meters from us. We were okay, but two civilians were killed. We were supposed to evacuate ten people. Only three turned up," he said. There was no water and long queues at distribution points. "Poor people are afraid of losing what little they have," Slava said.

He was optimistic his side would prevail. Slava was a member of Ukraine's volunteer Donbas battalion. At the time Ukrainian forces were clinging onto the western industrial suburb of Sievierodonetsk and the Azot chemical factory; there was fierce street-to-street fighting. The battle had gone on for seven weeks; everyone was exhausted. According to Luhansk's governor, Serhiy Haidai, the enemy was taking heavy losses. "The Russians don't have any reserves or motivation. A country of 140 million and they lack infantry!" Slava exclaimed. "Nobody wants to die for that idiot Putin. He's a bloodthirsty dog."

Slava was an amusing and energetic character, tanned after days at the front, closer in age to forty than twenty, and far from a professional soldier, I discovered. He fought in 2014, went back to civilian life, and rejoined the army in 2022. He painted the Donbas as a luckless, history-cursed place. The Germans and Soviets had fought across the same territory, which, eighty years later, the Ukrainians and Russians were brutally contesting. "Why did God punish me by making me be born here?" he asked wryly.

Could Ukraine win? Slava thought for a moment. "A difficult question. After fifty thousand people have died there is no victory. War is absolute madness," he said.

Traveling across the Donbas that summer, two things struck me. One was that civilians remained in their homes, even when the circumstances of war made life dangerous and almost impossible. In Kramatorsk, the coordinating capital of Ukrainian-controlled Donetsk Oblast, much of the population carried on as before. Around half of the customers in a supermarket were soldiers and police; the rest were ordinary shoppers. Under wartime regulations, alcohol in the Donbas was banned. At a checkpoint I spotted vodka bottles laid out on the road— a confiscated consignment of bootleg booze.

The evidence of Russia's destructive intent was abundant. An airstrike had ripped the side from school number 15's sports hall, its basketball hoops exposed as if the building were a monstrous doll's house. The apparent intended target was the neighboring police station. I inspected a ten-meter-wide water-filled crater. Russian warplanes had bombed high-rise buildings in other parts of Kramatorsk, gouging holes into the earth. And yet still residents stayed—or as one put it to me, "tried to live."

My other conclusion: Ukraine was at the time outmatched in this post–February 24 kinetic conflict. The Russian army was bigger, better equipped, superior in most respects. It had fifty-four battalion tactical groups on a Donbas front stretching from Balakliia in the north to Kostiantynivka in the south. Each comprised five thousand men. One group for every 5.6 kilometers. This was an extraordinary concentration of forces. After disarray in February around Kyiv, the Kremlin executed a different strategy in the east. You might call it a condensed assault.

In military terms these microtactics made little sense. Sievierodonetsk was a city of 150,000 people, founded in 1934. It had factories, a palace and concert hall used for figure-skating competitions, twenty schools, and two fountains in the main square, one of which played music. It was not Kyiv or Kharkiv or Dnipro. Explosions could be heard in Sievierodonetsk from the beginning of the invasion, and much of its population had departed in minibuses and cars. A few of those who remained supported the separatists.

The Kremlin's grueling two-month push to capture the city was driven by politics. Once Sievierodonetsk and Lysychansk fell, Putin could credibly claim he had "liberated" the whole of Luhansk Oblast.

A victory! Proof to the Russian public that his special operation was a success, and a humiliation for America and its allies, their political and military support to Kyiv ineffective.

In case Russia's former international partners had missed the point, the authorities in Moscow renamed the square outside the British embassy on Smolenskaya after the Luhansk

People's Republic. Ditto the land outside the U.S. embassy, which became Donetsk People's Republic Square. The Russian divisions rolling through the Donbas countryside were thus carrying out a mission of high state importance.

Despite its battlefield advantages, Russia's invasion force had weaknesses. Chief among them was low morale among its troops. Unlike their Ukrainian counterparts, many were reluctant to fight. They complained of bad leadership, tiredness, and a lack of professionalism. A top-heavy command structure meant units were unable to make real-time tactical decisions and had to wait for orders from the general staff. Over time, Russian military groups became undermanned and degraded.

Set against this was a blunt fact: Ukraine's defenders were outgunned.

They were trying to hold ground with Soviet-manufactured heavy artillery and rocket launchers. These existed, but not in great quantities. On the road to the Donbas front line, military traffic was visible. I counted armored personnel carriers, fuel trucks, engineering and logistics units, and ambulances. Civilian cars had been painted green and pressed into military service. One column had broken down; a sergeant bashed a tank tread with a hammer. Soldiers waited in the afternoon sunshine.

There was no sign at this juncture of the game-changing long-range multiple launch rocket systems promised by the Pentagon. The impression was of a medium-sized army, improvised at times, doing its valiant best against a mighty foe. "Now it's a lot of rockets and artillery," Maksym, a Ukrainian officer, told me. His supply convoy had stopped on a grassy shoulder for a short break. "In 2014, the Russians didn't want people to know it was them. It had to look like Donetsk People's Republic," he explained.

The war was taking place across a sprawling area. Outside Sloviansk, two Ukrainian Mi-8 helicopters flew very low above the ground; black smoke plumed from a village in the hazy distance to the north. A few civilian cars moved around the edge of the city. And public transport: a number 6 trolley bus. Closer to the Russian line there was only army movement. We passed a checkpoint made from breeze-blocks and followed Highway E40 to the frontline city of Bakhmut. The road was a supply route to Siversk and Lysychansk.

It was an uncanny journey. A vast defensive trench had been dug on one side of the road. A minicolumn was going to the front. Soldiers sat on ammunition boxes inside a covered truck; others traveled in a boxlike Niva car with taped-up windows. The atmosphere grew spookier. I saw a Ukrainian Smerch launcher; the words WELCOME TO HELL were written on its side in Cyrillic letters. And, sitting majestically on a loader, a spectacular Malka artillery piece, with a twelve-meter-long gun that fired 203mm rounds.

I traveled to Bakhmut with my *Guardian* colleague Isobel Koshiw. Unbeknown to us, Zelenskiy was nearby, visiting Lysychansk and the salt mine town of Soledar. He handed out medals, posed with a Ukrainian regimental flag, and paid tribute to the courage and indomitability of Ukraine's heroes, living and dead. It was a brave trip. Dangerous for sure.

On the outskirts of Bakhmut we saw an elderly woman at work in a field of grazing cows, as if the war were someone else's affair. Most of the city's inhabitants had evacuated. The fighting was close: no more than seven miles away. There was a constant whump from artillery. Outside Bakhmut's hospital we found Ukrainian soldiers smoking and resting in a shaded yard.

Doctors treated the wounded from Lysychansk and other hot spots; the dead went elsewhere.

"We are mostly dealing with fractures," Danylo Shapovalov, a forty-seven-year-old vascular surgeon, told me, adding that he was able to talk because of a lull in the shooting. "We get everything. Wounds to legs, the spine, arms." One challenge was transporting the injured quickly from the battlefield to a stabilization point. His job was to stop blood loss so soldiers didn't die; other medical staff did amputations. According to Danylo, the Russians were less concerned about casualties. "They don't know how to fight. They simply throw people into battle," he opined.

The war had taken a psychological toll. A young army medic, Lieutenant Oleksandr Voronin, said his personality had changed—and not for the better. "The first time you are in a battle you are afraid. You see a tank and it's terrible," he said. "After a while you get used to it, you don't feel it. It's like going into a trance. Your objective is to kill the enemy. You can't do this if you have a normal psyche. You become different. My parents tell me I'm disconnected from reality."

Voronin recounted how he spent three weeks in Rubizhne, the scene of intense fighting in April and May. The city, near Sievierodonetsk, fell to Russian forces. The battle resembled the highly mechanized warfare of World War II, he suggested—with Moscow enjoying more weapons. Russian firing was relentless, from 6:00 a.m. until 11:00 p.m., and in all directions. Voronin said three rocket-propelled grenades hit his armored vehicle as he left the city, causing it to flip over; he was lightly injured. "We will win because it's our land," he insisted.

Despite this optimism you had to recognize that Russia's

proxy-run empire was growing. Volodymyr Romanovych, a fifty-two-year-old driver, said the newly conquered areas of Luhansk could expect rapid de-Ukrainization. Romanovych said he was from the city of Sverdlovsk, eight kilometers from the Russian border in Luhansk Oblast. When separatists took over the city government in 2014, he decided to stay. The LNR purged Ukrainian from the curriculum at the school his children attended, changed names and maps, and rewrote history, he said.

Romanovych said Russia's GRU and FSB spy agencies competed for influence inside the LNR and DNR. The local separatists were opportunists and mafia guys, who "destroyed everything." By way of example he cited what had happened to the coal industry: the LNR promised miners higher wages but stole most of the money, so salaries fell. Meanwhile, Russia looted Sverdlovsk's chief factory, shipping engineering parts across the border. "The separatists suspected me because I was born in western Ukraine. Eventually they told me: 'You stayed, so you must be okay.'"

He added: "I hated what they did. The LNR is like an old version of the Soviet Union. Everything is going backward."

In 2017, Romanovych returned with his family to Ukraine via the Russian city of Belgorod. Since February he worked as a volunteer, delivering fuel to the front line and riding in a battered minivan, parked outside the hospital. "We need heavy weapons and artillery. Without that we can't beat them," he said. "We need ambulances. In fact we need everything. We've only got old Soviet stuff." And what about casualties? "They are losing more men than us. Most of them are without body armor. They don't collect their own corpses."

The Russians, it was clear, were determined to capture

Bakhmut, whatever the price. Not far from the military hospital I met Hlib and Lina, walking up a deserted street. They were on their way to visit Lina's sick grandfather, who refused to evacuate. Up until 2016, the city had been known as Artemivsk, named for a Bolshevik revolutionary. It was, she said, a wonderful place—with colorful flower beds, fifteen factories, a winery, a micro-district of high-rise apartments, a central library. . . .

The conversation ended abruptly. Gunfire rattled out from across the road. It was unclear who was firing at whom, or why. Hlib and Lina apologized and hurried off. We drove out of Bakhmut, past the main council office and 1950s neoclassical buildings. How much longer would they stand? On the highway back to Sloviansk I came across the same Smerch rocket launcher I had seen earlier. It had just unleashed its lethal cargo from a nearby wood.

The rockets were gone. They had left muddy trails in the air, like strips of sepia paper hung from the bright heavens.

It was a bucolic spot. The Privolia sanatorium looked out over the gleaming Siverskiy Donets River. A short drive down the road were the cities of Rubizhne and, a little farther south, Lysychansk. Guests stayed in a five-story 1970s complex with twin bedrooms. A steep forest path descended through pines and beeches to a floodplain recreation area. There were two cabins painted in fading blue and turquoise, a summer house, and a sandy beach. A sign pinned to a tree read: NO SWIM-MING.

On the far bank was thick vegetation: a shimmer of impassable green. The health clinic and dispensary was once used as a recreation center for Soviet miners, one of several holiday hotels in the area. There was a nature reserve. Families came to the area to camp; friends to relax, drink beer, and grill shashlik. The river was a popular place to fish. Latterly, Privolia was boarded up. Teenagers broke in and wrote their names on the walls of the dining room; grass crept over the outdoor tennis court.

And then the Ukrainian army arrived.

The troops were billeted at Privolia to stop the enemy from traversing the river. Bilohorivka—the scene of the pontoon bridge wipeout—was a few kilometers to the southwest. If the Russians crossed the Siverskiy Donets, their armored units could move down and close off the road leading to Lysychansk. They would be able to cut off Ukraine's last toehold in Luhansk Oblast, a twenty-five-kilometer-deep and fifteen-kilometer-wide salient surrounded on three sides by pressing Russian forces.

One of the defenders sent to Privolia was Ivan Tetichko, a twenty-four-year-old volunteer and car mechanic. It was 6:00 p.m. on May 31, 2022, and Ivan was sitting in the wooden summer house smoking a cigarette, together with another solider, Vitia. All was calm. And then suddenly it wasn't—mortars began raining down on the recreation zone from across the river. A bullet flew past. It hit Vitia in the arm. The Russians were staging an ambush.

Ivan dove to his right into a shallow two-man trench; Vitia flung himself to the left and lay down in the other dugout. A Ukrainian soldier, Andrushka, tried to help them. "A sniper shot him and he died. Then our sergeant Oleh broke cover from one of the cabins and tried to reach us. A bullet took half his head off, and he collapsed almost on top of me. The sniper got Vitia as well and killed him," Ivan said.

The holiday camp became a place of ghoulish nightmare. "There were bullets everywhere. Shots every five seconds, explosions," Ivan recalled. "I ran out of cartridges. I tried to grab Oleh's rifle. And then I got hit. A bullet fragment caught me in the eye. Blood was flowing. My ears were ringing and I was concussed. I came to my senses and tried to drag Oleh back to the cabin. But I couldn't see properly."

Ivan said he ran out of ammunition. He had two grenades with him. He threw one of them, not to hit the Russians concealed on the opposite bank but as a distraction.

And then he waited for death.

"I took the pin out of the other grenade. I thought: 'If they come, I can blow myself up and take two or three of them with me,'" he said.

The Russians didn't cross the river. After fifteen or twenty minutes, they disappeared as rapidly as they had come. Ukrainian reinforcements arrived from the sanatorium, running down the forest steps. They prized the grenade from Ivan's hand and pulled him out of the trench. He was bleeding and blind in his right eye. He told me his story in June, while he was receiving treatment in the ophthalmic department of a hospital in Dnipro. He was crying—with his good eye; his hands trembled as he talked of his dead comrades.

Like many of Ukraine's soldiers, Ivan had scarcely any military training before he was dispatched to the front, far away from his home in Zakarpattia, in western Ukraine. Was this appropriate? Did his lack of experience matter? "You learn very quickly on the job," he answered. He said he was fighting for his two children and for his community, unlike the Russians who were killing for money. He called them *tvari*—wretches, creatures. "We have a strong heart and spirit but not enough weapons," he said.

Doctors at the hospital said they had treated more than a hundred patients with similar eye injuries. A month on, Ivan still couldn't see with one eye. He was expected to recover. Physically, that was: the deaths of his friends evidently haunted him. "I think I was very lucky. I'm still alive," he said.

The question of how many Olehs and Vitias were being killed in battle was a sensitive one. The figures were high— 100 soldiers a day in May, with 500 injured, Zelenskiy admitted. Oleksiy Arestovych, a military adviser to Zelenskiy's chief of staff, told *The Guardian* the number was higher: 150 a day and 800 wounded. Many of those killed were core personnel; Arestovych said his Facebook page was filled with photos of the dead. Ukraine was losing most men in the Donbas, the "most complicated" front, as the president dubbed it. It was also taking continuous losses in fighting north of Kharkiv and in the south. By summer, the death toll exceeded 10,000, not including civilians.

Ukrainian social media channels accentuated positive stories. Video showed soldiers returning from battle and proposing to their girlfriends. Or hugging their children after months away. The defense ministry released daily footage of successful precision artillery and air strikes. It showed tanks vanishing in puffs of smoke and the flaming wreckage of downed Sukhoi fighter jets. There are before and after shots of Russian depots and military installations.

There was other gruesome footage, which was never broadcast. Anton Gerashchenko, a former deputy interior minister, who has a large following on the social media platform Telegram, showed me the aftermath of a Russian "cassette" or cluster bomb strike on a Ukrainian position in the east. A wailing soldier runs between corpses of his fellow servicemen, too many to count, strewn over a wide grassy area. "No, no, fucking no," he cries. Gerashchenko's point: Ukraine lacked basic armored vehicles. It needed them from the West in addition to much-desired long-range U.S. missile systems.

Whatever the sacrifice, Zelenskiy had little choice but to fight on. After months of intense resistance in the Donbas, his commander in chief, Valerii Zaluzhnyi, made the decision to retreat from Luhansk Oblast—that is, the remaining sliver under Kyiv's control. It was a pragmatic step, done to minimize casualties and to preserve ground forces for future encounters. Ukrainian divisions, Gerashchenko told me, had typically lost around half of their soldiers killed or wounded, including a large proportion of officers.

The Russians filled the vacuum. The LNR declared that it had taken control of Sievierodonetsk and Lysychansk. Both were flame-blackened wastelands. Around eight thousand people were left in Sievierodonetsk, cooking on open fires amid the rubble. In July, Moscow declared an operational pause. Its next targets were Sloviansk, Kramatorsk, and Bakhmut. Putin had made territorial gains, Zelenskiy the opposite. Neither was defeated, and Moscow's February blitzkrieg was beginning to resemble a forever war.

Away from the battlefield the conflict was transforming Russia itself. Over three decades Moscow had experienced various forms of government: a semi-democracy, soft authoritarian rule, and a thuggish mafia state. Putin's special military operation meant a return at home to something not seen on the

TEN

The Captive Mind

Moscow
March 2022

> All the crushing might of an armed state is hurled against
> any man who refuses to accept the New Faith.
>
> —CZESŁAW MIŁOSZ,
> *The Captive Mind*

Every morning, when opposition activist Vladimir Kara-Murza woke up in his Moscow apartment, he would have a cup of coffee and begin perusing Russia's last pockets of independent news. They included the radio station Echo of Moscow, founded in 1990, and the popular online TV channel Rain. There was also the newspaper *Novaya Gazeta*; in 2021, its editor Dmitry Muratov—a bearded figure beholden to no one—won the Nobel Peace Prize together with the Filipino American journalist Maria Ressa.

These outlets offered an alternative perspective to ubiquitous state propaganda. Additionally, there was Facebook, used by millions of Russians, as well as Twitter and Instagram. Social media and these few independent news sources provided real information about a regime that had no qualms about lying; indeed, the KGB regarded the concept of truth itself as a ludicrous bourgeois construct. In the Kremlin's relativistic universe, what mattered was the story you told. Control that story and society would surely follow.

Putin's onslaught against Ukraine threw up new challenges, however. His sovereign version of what was going on next door was wildly at odds with reality. To shore up this far-fetched account, the presidential administration resorted to drastic measures, unprecedented since Russia's modern independence. Almost overnight, it closed down accurate sources of news. All of them. A strange, unsettling silence descended on Moscow and the Russian Federation.

"A new iron curtain descended in front of my eyes. Everything was shut down," Kara-Murza told me when we spoke a month after the invasion began.

The era of nonofficial reporting in Russia ended with dizzying speed.

In early March, Putin signed two draconian media laws: No. 31-FZ and No. 32-FZ. Their target was "fake news." What Russia's president meant by this were truthful broadcasts and newspaper articles about the bloody war in Ukraine. Reporting on what was actually happening there—the flattening of peaceful cities, the murder of civilians, the mutilation and execution of bound captives, a litany of dreadful crimes—was forbidden.

Under an amended criminal code, disseminating "false information"—in this case, real news—was a criminal offense. Likewise, anything that disparaged the soldiers carrying out the Kremlin's orders constituted "spreading false information about the actions of Russia's military." It further outlawed criticizing any Russian state body: the foreign ministry, FSB, the national guard, the prosecutor's office, and so on.

The penalties for violating these new measures were extreme: fifteen years in jail for circulating "fake" information, five for scorning the army. On February 24, Russia's media watchdog, Roskomnadzor, told outlets that the only sources they were permitted to cite were defense ministry press releases. Also, the war wasn't a war. It was a special military operation, the agency said. Anyone deviating from the phrase would be liable to prosecution.

Kremlin censorship was not exactly a new phenomenon. In 1934, one of my *Guardian* predecessors in Russia, Malcolm Muggeridge, wrote a satirical novel about the strict rules reporters had to follow. Called *Winter in Moscow*, it described how journalists would submit their articles to a beady-eyed Bolshevik censor. Anything that "displeased the Dictatorship of the Proletariat," as Muggeridge put it, was cut out. Amid an absence of actual facts for most of the Cold War, Kremlinology was born. Indirect clues such as who was standing next to whom at Red Square parades were used to interpret internal Soviet politics: who was up and who was down.

From the late 1950s, real information began to trickle in. It arrived in the shape of broadcasts from Radio Liberty, Voice of America, Deutsche Welle, and smaller stations—all of them jammed. There were books published in the West and smuggled into Russia, as well as samizdat, or "self-published" literature, passed illicitly around kitchen tables. Only a limited number of people, mostly the intelligentsia, were able to access these sources. For the rest there was untrue Soviet official information.

By the end of the 1980s, restrictions were eased. Previously forbidden literary works were published, including Boris Pasternak's *Doctor Zhivago*. In the first years of postcommunism under Boris Yeltsin, the press enjoyed widespread freedom, including the freedom to criticize the president.

This stopped abruptly with Putin, who early in his premiership eliminated independent TV. The Kremlin sought greater control of information. State channels played a foundational role in boosting his regime and strengthening its grip. There was flattering daily coverage of the president, domestic and international messaging that was favorable to the government, and a blacklist for the opposition. Critics didn't appear on federal shows; they were nonentities. Propaganda helped shore up popular support for Russia's ruling structures, especially among the older generation.

In contrast with television, papers and news websites had greater latitude. Critical comment was possible. As a correspondent living in Moscow between 2007 and 2011, during the years when Putin was prime minister and Dmitry Medvedev president, I would leaf through a range of publications. Sitting in the *Guardian*'s cramped low-ceilinged office near Belorussky station, I read *Novaya Gazeta*, the English-language *Moscow Times*, and the business dailies *Kommersant* and *Vedomosti*, at the time both semi-independent.

Most other titles reflected the Kremlin line. There was the tabloid *Komsomolskaya Pravda* and the utterly dull broadsheets *Izvestiya* and *Rossiyskaya Gazeta*. State news agencies such as ITAR-TASS put out the approved headlines. And there was Russia Today, later rebranded RT, run by Margarita Simonyan, one of Putin's most influential apologists. RT grew into the Kremlin's chief influence platform abroad, broadcasting in English, French, German, Spanish, and Arabic.

It purported to offer "alternative" views on current affairs. Typically, RT's on-screen guests came from the far left and far right. They included Brexit campaigners like Nigel Farage, antiestablishment American and British leftists, and assorted conspiracy theorists. RT viewers learned little about Russia today, ironically. That was never the intention: the idea was to boost pro-Kremlin narratives and to undermine moderate Western thinking. After February 24, the European Union, Canada, and the United Kingdom blocked RT broadcasts; Apple and Microsoft did the same.

Novaya Gazeta's survival was always something of a mystery. There was ample evidence the authorities disliked the paper intensely. Six of its journalists were murdered. The most famous was Anna Politkovskaya, a powerful critic of Putin's and of Ramzan Kadyrov, Chechnya's thug president. She was shot in October 2006 in her Moscow apartment building, not far from the *Guardian*'s bureau. Her alleged killers were arrested; the mastermind behind her execution was never found, as was invariably the case in other murky assassinations of reporters and opposition leaders.

Why did the Kremlin tolerate a few liberal outlets? *Novaya Gazeta*'s deputy editor Andrei Lipsky believed his paper allowed the authorities to rebut foreign criticism that there was no freedom of speech in Russia. It gave genuine information to senior officials, who were locked in a continuous and exhausting battle for position, money, and influence. "*Novaya Gazeta* lies on the table of the presidential administration and all regional governors. Putin reads it or people read it for him," he told me.

The new post-invasion laws had a chilling effect on press freedom, not only for Russian journalists but also for their foreign counterparts. Talented correspondents made their reputations in Moscow throughout the Soviet period and in the tumultuous years afterward—among them *New Yorker* editor David Remnick, the author of *Lenin's Tomb*; Canada's deputy prime minister Chrystia Freeland, a *Financial Times* reporter in the 1990s; *Guardian* journalist turned novelist and essayist James Meek; and many others.

There were drawbacks to a traditional Moscow posting: interminable hours, a meager diet, a lack of toilet paper, and the grueling physical environment of post–Cold War Moscow—a drab, gray metropolis of Stalin-era skyscrapers and multilane boulevards. There were joys, too: snow falling on wooden palaces, the surrealistic domes of Saint Basil's Cathedral, and the Tretyakov Gallery, with its astounding collection of nineteenth-century Russian realist art. And the friendships and conversations, often forged over late-night vodka, more intense, elemental, and philosophical than those at home.

But now this distinguished epoch of reporting—of interpreting Russia to a curious outside public, in sun and storm—was over, or so it appeared. Leading Western news organizations responded by yanking their staff from Moscow. *The New York Times* announced it was temporarily closing its bureau. Bloomberg News suspended operations. *The Washington Post* said it would scratch bylines and locations from its Russia articles. France 24 told its news crews to book flights out. Reporters relocated to Riga and Istanbul. Some later came back to Moscow, hoping to work around the rules. Many didn't.

My own exit had taken place a decade earlier. Expulsion was a traditional weapon used by the Russian foreign ministry's press department for journalists deemed to have crossed a line. In communist times, the authorities frequently slung out

American correspondents; the KGB bugged their offices and, in the 1970s, slashed the tires of reporters seeking to meet with dissidents. These crude methods stopped briefly with the USSR's collapse, only to start up again during Putin's tenure in the Kremlin.

In my case, that meant living in a third-rate espionage thriller. FSB spies broke into our family home, leaving behind easy-to-find clues; bugs were installed; my phone was tapped; suspicious young men in cheap leather jackets and brown shoes followed me around the icy streets of the Russian capital. There were nasty hints from foreign ministry officials, as well as a summons to visit Lefortovo prison, the FSB's sinister investigation and pretrial detention facility in Moscow, previously run by the KGB. Lefortovo was a chilling place, a drab, yellow three-story building encircled with spiraling razor wire.

The reason for this low-level state harassment was never spelled out. Probably it was to do with my reporting. I pursued topics regarded as taboo. Among them was the question of Putin's personal wealth and the role played by the FSB in Alexander Litvinenko's teapot murder in London. I traveled to the North Caucasus, where federal and local security forces were rooting out an Islamist insurgency. They used brutal methods, including filtration, which in 2022 Russia would use again in occupied Ukraine.

In February 2011, the Federal Migration Service stopped me when I flew back to Moscow. My visa was annulled and I was deported. A border guard informed me: "For you, Russia is closed." In 2022, my persona non grata status was confirmed when the foreign ministry published a list of twenty-nine UK nationals banned from Russia. It included five colleagues, among them the *Guardian*'s editor in chief, Katharine Viner.

Similar lists were published for North America, featuring the former U.S. ambassador to Moscow Michael McFaul and 398 members of Congress.

Russia was now closed to a large swath of Western observers and politicians. The only story the home media were allowed to share was a virtuous fable, shouted by Russian state TV anchors. It said the Kremlin was not to blame for hostilities in Ukraine. Rather, Moscow was forced to defend its security interests and to take action against the U.S.-controlled neo-Nazis swarming Kyiv. Russia was a victim of Western aggression. Its *spets op* was clinical and proportionate. No civilians had been hurt. To say otherwise was to lie.

Orwell had imagined this shrill reversal of things in his portrait of high Stalinism. War was peace, freedom was slavery, ignorance was strength.

These developments were explicitly political. Russia's Duma rushed through the new "fakes" legislation. The administration had seen off previous antigovernment protests, including mass demonstrations in 2011 and 2012 against Putin's return as president, and pro-Navalny rallies as recently as 2021. Authorities were determined to prevent future unrest. A sinister campaign began. Russians who spoke out against the war were arrested. A wider crackdown was launched against scientists, lawyers, and others suspected of having contact with the West. The FSB inherited many of its domestic functions from the KGB. Increasingly, Putin's spy agency began to resemble the NKVD, Stalin's secret police, enjoying a greater degree of control over the population than in the late Soviet period.

The Putin regime had long been repressive, but not totalitarian. What qualified as totalitarianism might be debated; the political theorist Hannah Arendt defined it as a systematic reliance on terror. The Stalin era fit this definition. It was a place of fear and of purges; of arbitrary large-scale murders and knocks on the door at night, with suspects taken away by shadowy state agents, never to return; of prison camps and gulags, administered by a colossal security bureaucracy.

Prior to 2022, Putin had not quite taken Russia to that point. But his wartime state was at least as restrictive and controlling as Leonid Brezhnev's Soviet Union. His regime was moving even further in the direction of the 1930s, using mechanisms of coercion and intimidation. As David Clark, a former senior adviser to the British foreign office, put it to me, Moscow had gone "an extra 15 to 20 percent" in the direction of tyranny. It was a further stage in Russia's neo-Soviet regression.

Vladimir Kara-Murza was well aware of the dangers—to truth tellers in general and to him personally. He was a prominent opposition leader well known on both sides of the Atlantic. Educated in England, he had read history at Trinity Hall, Cambridge, where contemporaries recalled him as brilliant. He worked for Open Russia, a pro-democracy organization financed by Mikhail Khodorkovsky, the oligarch arrested in Siberia in 2003 and jailed by Putin. Kara-Murza moved to the United States, where he lived with his wife, Evgenia, and their three children in a Northern Virginia suburb.

Kara-Murza played an instrumental role in rallying support for action to be taken against corrupt Russian officials. He lobbied for targeted personal sanctions against Putin's inner circle—the cronies and billionaire friends who enriched themselves at the expense of the Russian taxpayer. These measures exploited a weakness in Putin's kleptocratic system. The elite hid its assets in the West: yachts, luxury property, vineyards. They used dollar-denominated bank accounts.

Kara-Murza spoke on Capitol Hill and testified before Congress and European parliaments. He became friends with the Republican senator John McCain. He blogged for *World Affairs*, a U.S. journal, and was a contributing writer to *The Washington Post*, writing lucid columns about developments within Russia. And, remarkably, he continued to spend time in Moscow, his home city—despite the assassination in February 2015 of his friend and mentor, the charismatic Putin critic Boris Nemtsov, who was godfather to Kara-Murza's younger daughter. Nemtsov had been investigating Russia's covert war in eastern Ukraine when assassins gunned him down in front of the Kremlin. It looked like a state-approved hit.

Three months later, it was Kara-Murza's turn. After a trip to the provinces, he was poisoned by suspected FSB operatives in Moscow. He collapsed during a meeting at the news agency RIA Novosti and lost consciousness. His symptoms—a sudden, incapacitating illness leading to immediate multiple organ failure—were troubling and mysterious. An ambulance took him to the hospital. Doctors put him on life support. Evgenia Kara-Murza told me his chances of survival were estimated at 5 percent.

Remarkably, he beat the odds. His strange illness and its cause remained undiagnosed. He recuperated in the United States and relearned how to walk with a cane. In 2017, back in Moscow, he was poisoned a second time. The symptoms were identical; the same doctor put him on a ventilator. Russia's investigative committee refused to open a case. Journalists from Bellingcat revealed that the FSB team that poisoned

Navalny shadowed Kara-Murza, too, tailing him for months. Their weapon: a biotoxin similar to the Novichok nerve agent.

In March 2022, Kara-Murza called me. He was visiting London, about to return to Russia, appalled at the invasion and thinking about what the war might mean for his country's development. We discussed his campaign to name a street in London after his late friend Nemtsov, which local Conservatives opposed. We also talked about Kara-Murza's shabby treatment by UK border agents. Officers had taken him aside at Luton Airport and grilled him for forty minutes in a holding room.

Putin's all-out attack on Ukraine was a huge strategic blunder, Kara-Murza felt. It "sped everything up." The president and his acolytes looked vulnerable, in a way that opened up the possibility of democratic change. "There has not been a single failed war that has not led to significant change at home," Kara-Murza remarked. When this happened, it would be "swift and sudden." An optimist, he was certain Russia would one day be free.

The Kremlin liked to portray its Ukraine operation as a continuation of the 1940–1945 struggle against German fascism. For Kara-Murza a more fitting comparison was with previous "small victorious wars." He mentioned the decade-long Soviet debacle in Afghanistan. There was Russia's humiliating defeat in the 1904–1905 war with Japan, which saw the tsar's eastern fleet sunk. And—going further back—Nicholas I's 1853–1856 Crimean War. All ended in defeat—as well as upheaval, reform, and modernization.

The Russian public was not universally behind Putin's invasion, he sensed, despite propaganda. "My personal impression walking the streets and riding the metro is it's half and half," he told me. Support was lower than in 2014, when 80 or 90 percent backed the takeover of Crimea. Preparations had to begin for a post-Putin era, he said. Russia would need to be de-Putinized, state institutions rebuilt, a Marshall Plan enacted. The transformation would be analogous to West Germany's post-1945 reconstruction.

Kara-Murza reserved his bitterest comments for the West. He and Nemtsov, a deputy prime minister under Boris Yeltsin, had spent hours with policy makers explaining Putin's intentions. Their thesis: internal repression ends in external aggression, inevitably. "We tried to warn the West what this man was about. He brought back the Soviet anthem in 2000, destroyed media and elections, invaded Georgia, and stole Crimea. Why did the West do nothing? He was going to invade Ukraine from the beginning," he said. "I'm a historian. This is the only way the appeasement of dictators goes."

What made Kara-Murza different from many other opposition figures was his willingness to speak out from Russia itself. In London that March, friends urged him not to return. They included Bill Browder, the fund manager and human rights campaigner. Kara-Murza worked with Browder to promote the Magnitsky Act, named after Browder's tax adviser Sergei Magnitsky, who exposed a fraud by senior Russian officials, was arrested, and died in jail in Moscow in 2009. The U.S. Congress passed the act in 2012; other countries followed. "I begged Vladimir not to go," Browder told me later that summer.

Kara-Murza shrugged off these requests. He was a patriot who refused to be intimidated or to accept banishment. As the Polish writer and poet Czesław Miłosz put it, exile was an abyss, the "worst of all misfortunes, for it meant sterility and inaction." In Kara-Murza's view, it was important to share the same risks and challenges as other Russians who stood up to Putin. In April, he went back to Moscow. The following day he spoke out, telling CNN the Putin administration was "a regime of murderers." It was a "tragedy" that it took a war in Europe for the West to figure this out, he said.

The reckoning was quick, and grimly predictable. When he returned home on a Monday evening and began parking his car, five or six officers from Moscow's internal affairs directorate grabbed him outside the entrance and bundled him into a minivan. They took his phone and drove him to Khamovniki police station. He was sentenced to fifteen days in jail for "changing the trajectory of his movement" when arrested, and, subsequently, for disseminating "fake news" and "working for an undesirable foreign outfit."

Taken to a special detention center, Kara-Murza found himself in the company of other "politicals"—political prisoners locked up after the invasion. They included two women picked up for writing antiwar graffiti, students from Moscow's higher school of economics who took part in an antiwar demonstration, and a young man and woman who staged a protest over the murders in Bucha. The scene was reminiscent of the 1970s, when jails and psychiatric facilities overflowed with dissidents and refuseniks.

This repression was extensive. According to OVD-Info, a Russian independent human rights project, by summer 2022 police agents had arrested 16,380 people for their antiwar stance. More than sixty criminal cases were initiated under the new laws. Those detained included a physicist, a respected liberal economist, and a professional hockey player. The physicist

Dmitry Kolker was accused of sharing state secrets with China. He was taken from his hospital bed in the city of Novosibirsk, where he was being treated for terminal cancer. He died three days later in Lefortovo prison.

There seemed little prospect Kara-Murza would get out. The view from his cell, he wrote, was a barbed wire fence; the exercise yard was covered by a roof, with only a narrow strip of sky. The only glimpse he got of the sun and of foliage was during the ten seconds it took to escort him from a windowless prison van into the detainee holding room of Moscow's Basmanny district court. After each trip he was driven back to jail, his detention prolonged for two more months. The authorities seemed reluctant to put him on trial, knowing he would publicly denounce Putin's invasion. At a court appearance in August, he sat in a cage with a glass window, reading a copy of Solzhenitsyn's *Gulag Archipelago*.

Police state, mafia state, shadow state, spy state . . . the Russian government in its 2022 incarnation was all these things. Those not zombified by broadcasts on Kremlin-run Channel One or NTV had an impossible choice: stay and risk imprisonment or leave and face an uncertain life in exile. Nobody knew how long this might last. Months, years, decades?

Alexey Kovalyov always knew the day would arrive when he would have to flee Russia. What he had not anticipated is how quickly it would all happen: his old life collapsing in an instant, a sudden sundering, as if it had been a mirage all along.

Smart, opinionated, and waspish, Kovalyov was investigations editor at Meduza, an independent news website published in Russian and English. Although Meduza was based in

Latvia, it was not exile media as such. Several of its journalists, including Kovalyov, continued to work from Moscow, even as the climate grew chillier and after Russia's justice ministry branded the publication a "foreign agent" in 2021. His plan was to stay in the capital for as long as possible.

The writing was on the wall when Meduza published an editorial on February 24 condemning the invasion in unambiguous terms. It accused Putin of lying and said the president had failed to grasp the essentials of history. The simplest way to turn neighboring states against Russia was to intrude in their lives—as with the Soviets' 1940 takeover of the Baltics, the 1956 invasion of Hungary, and the 1968 crushing of the Prague Spring. "Let's stop this. It's never too late to end a war," the editorial said, bewailing the "shame" Putin had heaped on Russia's citizens.

The mood in Moscow that February was one of shell shock, Alexey told me. Muscovites walked around glued to their phones, silent; they felt fearful and anxious. Graffiti and messages reading NO TO WAR sprang up during the night; the next morning, city utility workers scrubbed them off. At Meduza, Kovalyov worked 24/7, surfing the wave of dark news. The invasion was "a waking nightmare, horrible and absurd," he wrote in a piece for *The New York Times*, and, for Russia, a "crushing moral defeat."

Those who shared these sentiments were not just the usual critics. Major public figures, artists, and leading reporters spoke out against the war. There were demonstrations in St. Petersburg, Putin's home city, where crowds chanted peace slogans in front of police vehicles. In Moscow, protesters laid flowers on the Kyiv monument near Red Square dedicated to the heroism of Soviet Ukrainian soldiers. A million people signed a petition to end the war. There was feminist resistance. Newspapers were mocked up to look like daily free sheets, with antiwar articles printed next to recipes and sudoku puzzles.

A harsh response from the Kremlin looked likely. Putin accused the West of trying to divide Russia and to provoke "a civil confrontation." Those calling for peace were "scum and traitors," he said; Russians should spit them out "like a fly that goes accidentally into your mouth." A "cleansing" of society was needed, he added. What did this mean? There were rumors the Kremlin was going to introduce martial law, that Russia's borders were closing, and there would be Soviet-style exit visas.

These predictions turned out to be wrong. The overall thrust was correct: a state clampdown was coming. Roskomnadzor blocked access to Meduza's website, snuffing out its journalism. Kovalyov received a message from his boss: time to go. A quick search on Google revealed it would cost two thousand euros to fly to Tbilisi, Georgia. Too much. So he got in a car and drove through the night, taking with him a few "panic-packed bags" and his French bulldog, Tyrion.

He tweeted: "Felt a massive door slam shut behind my back. Barely had enough time to call my parents. Crazy times." He was better off, he acknowledged, than the millions of Ukrainians waiting for asylum and stuck by the roadside.

Nine hundred kilometers later, he arrived at a normally sleepy rural crossing point at the northern border with Estonia. Two women guards were dumbfounded by the numbers waiting to leave—a great exodus of Moscow's creative class. Hundreds of journalists and activists were departing, a human tide to rival the flight of foreign capital and companies. There was a queue of cars and trucks. After four hours, Kovalyov was across and on his way to Riga.

There, he might be a proper journalist again, in a Russian-speaking city. But the world had changed. It was no longer possible to talk to sources inside Russia; for them it was too dangerous to be associated with Meduza, or indeed with any opposition media.

Kovalyov said he was skeptical of opinion polls that suggested the war enjoyed popular support—with 68 percent reportedly backing the special operation and the alleged "denazification" of Ukraine. In his assessment, a relatively small minority actively and enthusiastically backed the war. An equivalent number was passionately opposed. The majority acquiesced and went along with Putin's war lie, taking their cue from state media, which played an outsize role in shaping opinion.

Even as the curtain came down on independent news, Russians were still able to access real information via virtual private networks. Most chose not to do so. The difficulty was not the technology: it was psychological. "It's one extra click. But you are asking Russians to admit complicity in a mistake of historic proportions, to have their world turned upside down. It would involve recognizing that their country isn't a force for good and has committed horrible war crimes," Kovalyov said. The majority preferred to watch official TV.

Was Putin's Russia fascist? I wondered. There were certainly similarities with fascist regimes of the past: a cult of personality; the militarization of society; ubiquitous swastika-like Z symbols. At the same time, state propaganda had failed to persuade most Russians to embrace the war fully, as shown by the fact that volunteers weren't exactly queuing up outside recruitment offices. On the battlefield, the lack of combat infantry was a problem; some of those signing up for tours of duty were men in their forties with debt problems.

"People don't buy all that stuff. If it is a fascist dictatorship, it's a pretty shitty one," Kovalyov posited, suggesting the Kremlin lacked the resources to control a country as big and diverse as Russia.

As the war continued, the prospect of civil unrest diminished. The protests fizzled out; to hold a placard was a brave but doomed gesture. The growing tally of dead Russian soldiers had little impact on Moscow residents, Kovalyov suggested. Most of those killed came from faraway ethnic regions—the republic of Buryatia in eastern Siberia and the mountainous Muslim republic of Dagestan. The Kremlin was ensuring it was the village poor doing the dying. In the capital, life was near normal. The rouble bounced back, cafés and bars were open, and the effect of sanctions had yet to be felt. "People don't see that many downsides. The economy runs like clockwork," Kovalyov noted.

As for when he might be able to return to Russia, that was wholly unclear. It was not going to happen while Putin remained alive. "There is a strong possibility that even if he suddenly croaks whoever comes next will be worse," Kovalyov hypothesized. This was a plausible scenario. Were, say, Nikolai Patrushev to take over—the hard-line head of Russia's security council—one could well imagine Russia would carry on in a similarly gloomy vein.

.   .   .

It was 11:42 a.m., a bright morning in June 2022, and Andrei Soldatov was drinking coffee on the southern coast of the Adriatic Sea. He had flown from London to Montenegro with his partner and cowriter, Irina Borogan. They had tracked Russia's security services for two decades and were the authors of three well-received books. These were *The New Nobility*—a phrase Putin used when he came to power to describe his fellow KGB-trained intelligence officers—and *The Red Web*, a study of the Kremlin's attempts to master the Internet. Their most recent work, *The Compatriots*, deals with the cat-and-mouse relationship between the Kremlin and Russian émigrés. I had met Soldatov and Borogan in Moscow in 2007; we became good friends.

This trip mixed business and pleasure—meetings with journalistic sources, and a few days relaxing in a rustic stone farmhouse. Soldatov and Borogan's hotel in the town of Bar looked onto a marina and a harbor from which boats sailed to Italy. There were beaches, olive and lemon groves, and an ancient monastery.

Soldatov's phone started buzzing. One message, then four more. At first he dismissed the alerts as some sort of phishing attack or scam. They came from VTB, his bank in Moscow. Soldatov hadn't been back to Russia in a while: not since September 2020, when he and Borogan locked up their apartment for the final time and moved to London. The texts informed him his bank account at home had been frozen. The sum of 7,898 roubles was confiscated. Reason: court order.

What was happening? A further text from UralSib, a Moscow commercial bank where Soldatov had a second account, enlightened him. It said his cash had been seized pursuant to an *ugolovnoye delo* lodged by the authorities against him—that is, a criminal action. Helpfully, there was a case number. Soldatov flipped open his laptop, clicked on the interior ministry website, and entered the details. Bingo.

Staring back at him was a familiar face: his own. His mug shot appeared on a page of international fugitives sought by Russia's investigative committee. A lawyer in Moscow offered his services and hurried on Soldatov's behalf to the Basmanny court. A bundle of papers laid out the charges. Prosecutors accused him of spreading fake news concerning the war in Ukraine and had correspondingly seized his assets.

(I later asked Borogan why the authorities had not charged her with anything. Her answer: old-fashioned Russian sexism.)

The episode was alarming. It marked a further brazen stage in the Kremlin's pursuit of journalists seen as engaging in "anti-state" activities. Soldatov might have been out of reach, but like most émigrés, he had family in Russia. His father, a former deputy minister and an early Internet pioneer, was already under house arrest on an unrelated matter.

The court papers revealed intriguing details. The FSB's internal security department initiated his case in mid-March. This was three days after Soldatov and Borogan published a scoop on their investigative website Agentura.ru, which monitors Russia's spy agencies. The article said that Sergei Beseda, an influential general, had been arrested. Beseda was chief of the FSB's Fifth Service, a special body dealing with foreign intelligence. Seemingly, Beseda had made serious operative errors in Ukraine.

Beseda was locked up in Lefortovo and kept in the prison's lower depths. Other inmates included high-ranking Azov fighters captured in Mariupol and senior Ukrainian intelligence officers. The FSB ensured prisoners did not encounter each other as they moved along an etiolated corridor or were escorted in a Victorian-style lift to boxlike interrogation rooms. For Beseda, it was an unhappy and sudden fall, similar to the fate of the character Nikolai Rubashov, a Bolshevik general arrested for treason, in Arthur Koestler's novel *Darkness at Noon*. Later the FSB released Beseda, Soldatov reported. This was a "truly Stalinist twist" designed to show that everything was going according to plan.

Beseda's department was the only one out of twelve directly involved in secret preparation for the war. It was supposed to cultivate pro-Moscow political figures inside Ukraine. Putin's plan was to use the FSB as a special operations force that would consolidate administrative power once the Russian military swept in. An FSB-sponsored puppet government was primed to take over in Kyiv, and safe houses were prepared. It appeared Beseda was being scapegoated for wrong intelligence and for the mission's overall failure.

He wasn't the only one. Other senior officials found themselves arrested, in what looked like a minipurge. In July, three top interior ministry generals were accused of embezzlement, together with a deputy head from Russia's national guard in charge of special forces. Apparently, nobody was entirely safe in the new martial era. Putin didn't consult the FSB's rank and file ahead of his invasion. The agency quickly got behind the project. Officers based at the Lubyanka—the FSB's forbidding Moscow headquarters—were told to get ready for three-month tours of the occupied territories.

What prospect, I asked Soldatov and Borogan, of a palace coup? Their answer: zero, nada, forget it. "Unfortunately, it's out of the question," Soldatov told me. The FSB had undercover officers stationed inside army units. At home, counterintelligence and counterterrorism departments led the crackdown on street protests. In Ukraine, FSB special forces and the military counterintelligence branch ran filtration camps; part of what they were doing, beyond stirring fear in the local population, was seeking to recruit Ukrainians as FSB agents to send back behind enemy lines. They also prepared show trials of captured fighters.

The agency was playing a different, more comprehensive role in Russia's war effort than the one originally anticipated. There were criminal cases against activists and writers living abroad, demonstrative arrests at home. In July and August, the authorities detained Ilya Yashin, another well-known opposition leader, and Yevgeny Roizman, the former mayor of Yekaterinburg. They were accused of spreading fake news. These arrests scarcely encouraged exiles to return.

Would Soldatov and Borogan ever see Moscow again? Well, maybe. "I don't think it will last any longer than five years," Borogan replied.

In a nineteenth-century building in the heart of Kyiv, Ilya Ponomarev gave me a tour of his new TV studio. There were cameras and a presenter, Olga Volkova, getting ready to interview a military expert. In a neighboring room, reporters were busy posting content to Telegram, YouTube, and Facebook. The studio had two flags as a backdrop. One was familiar: the blue and yellow of Ukraine. The other less so: a white-and-blue-striped flag.

"It's the Russian tricolor minus the blood," Ponomarev explained. A Russian antiwar activist living in Berlin had come up with the idea, he said, adding: "I love it." In medieval times the flag flew above Veliky Novgorod, one of Russia's oldest cities, known as the cradle of national democracy. Its citizens enjoyed representative rule. Until, that was, Ivan the Terrible took over and imposed the kind of despotism that became the country's system of government for centuries.

Ponomarev was once a member of Russia's lower house of parliament. He was known for his freethinking left-wing views. In 2014, he was the sole elected representative to vote against the annexation of Crimea. His fellow deputies tried to throw him out of the Duma. Then, while he was away in California on a trip, the Kremlin barred him from reentering his own country. Bailiffs froze his accounts. Ponomarev had been a technology entrepreneur, but chucked out of his hotel and with twenty-one dollars in cash in his pocket, he slept in his car. Friends helped him find a job as an investment adviser based in San Jose.

In 2016, Ponomarev moved to Kyiv and three years later became a Ukrainian citizen. From exile he expended his energies on one seemingly impossible goal: to get rid of Putin. His newest media initiative was February Morning, a Ukraine-based Russian-language TV channel and news portal aimed exclusively at an audience living inside Russia. It launched in March 2022. Its seventy staff members were Ukrainian and Russian, some based in provincial Russian towns as part of an underground stringer network.

The swiftest way to end Russia's bloody war was to bring down the regime in Moscow, Ponomarev told me. With Putin alive and in the Kremlin, there was every prospect the conflict would drag on for years, even decades. "Our job at the end of the day is an uprising of the masses," he said. "To achieve a mass movement, we need individuals to see they are not acting alone." Another Russian revolution, in short—one that would use violent methods to sweep away the president and his decadent entourage of spies and crooks.

He conceded it would be difficult to persuade Russians conditioned by years of TV propaganda to turn on their government. They did not know the full truth about what was going on in Ukraine, nor did they show much interest in finding out. How could his channel reach Russia's masses and then persuade them they were the victims of a fake version of history? They would have to overcome brainwashing, trauma, and a persistent imperial complex, he recognized.

But he said there were two distinct groups that formed a promising constituency. The first consisted of young urban liberals. These were the supporters of Navalny, Internet-savvy hipsters, and members of Russia's intelligentsia who got their news from Meduza, *Novaya Gazeta*, and TV Rain—or used to before the great switch-off. Given the choice between joining an insurrection against state power and leaving the country, most would choose the second option. Many already had.

The second group was a frustrated working class. Unlike their middle-class peers, they were still in Russia. They were fed up with corruption and misrule—so angry, in fact, they were prepared to carry out acts of civil disobedience. Since February, activists had burned down army recruitment offices and torched cars belonging to local pro-war politicians. Some who hurled Molotovs were left-wing radicals and communists. Others were right-wing populists who voted for the ultranationalist Liberal Democrats.

Ponomarev said he claimed "limited" credit for these nighttime attacks. February Morning's Telegram channel circulated videos filmed at the scenes of these incidents. The channel offered tips on bomb-making and how to thwart the FSB by turning off mobile phone geolocation settings. These "small tricks" were taught in the early Putin era at radical summer camps, he told me. He described his own politics as "left-libertarian anarchist." In his view Russia should become a decentralized state, a place where local communities make decisions.

So far, Ponomarev said, he financed the station himself, to the tune of fifty thousand dollars a month, using funds amassed from his job in Silicon Valley. The channel wanted to build a second studio on its balcony, which overlooked a steep cobbled street near the Maidan and the Renaissance Hotel. He was looking for Western sources of funding. But he said London and Washington were wary of calling openly for "regime change" in Russia, even though that is what they wished to happen.

The journalists I spoke to at the channel had few illusions as to the challenges they faced. "It's a long journey," editor Larysa Rybalchenko told me. But necessary: the Russians had occupied her home city of Svitlodarsk in the Donbas, she said. The biggest obstacle, seemingly, was how to overcome the captive mind. "Nobody inside Russia wants to believe that we are the fascists," Ponomarev said. He described his opponents in the Kremlin as "unfortunately really smart" and said they had successfully marginalized leftists and nationalists.

How real was Ponomarev's partisan army? In August, Darya Dugina, the thirty-year-old daughter of the Russian fascist philosopher Aleksandr Dugin, was blown up by a car bomb on the outskirts of Moscow. Dugin was a close Putin ally who frequently called for violence against Ukrainians. The FSB said

Kyiv's secret services were behind the murder. Ponomarev ascribed it to a previously unknown group operating inside Russia, the National Republican Army. There wasn't much evidence to support either claim.

And what about the elites? They were dissatisfied with Putin but not "scared enough," in Ponomarev's opinion. A century earlier, left-wing social revolutionaries had helped overthrow the tsar. Russia's new anti-Putin revolution had yet to gain real momentum. Until it did, the country's ruling classes—its oligarchs, bankers, and top bureaucrats—were unlikely to break with Putin or to move decisively against his war in Ukraine. "They need to see the ghost of 1917," Ponomarev told me.

In the absence of social upheaval in Russia, it was down to Ukrainians to ensure the survival of their state. They had one secret weapon. It wasn't an advanced American rocket system nor a shoulder-carried missile; it was a mode of social organization. Russians were vertical in their thinking, always looking feudally upward. Ukrainians were horizontal—a collective or superorganism. This millions-strong decentralized network was working tirelessly toward a shared and shimmering goal: victory.

ELEVEN

Horizontal

Snake Island
February 2022

> Russian warship, go fuck yourself.
>
> —UKRAINIAN BORDER GUARD TO THE
>
> FLAGSHIP CARRIER *MOSKVA*

In his twelve years in the border service, Bohdan Hotskiy had seen many wild places. In his view, Ukraine was the most beautiful country in the world. It had the sea and mountains, forests and steppes, marshes and abundant lakes. All was perfect, and so complete in its perfection that Hotskiy—a twenty-nine-year-old captain—had never felt the inclination to go abroad. After all, why bother? "We have everything," he told me. We met in August in the town of Izmail, his current base, next to the Romanian border.

Hotskiy's career meant moving around. In late 2021, he had received orders to deploy to a new maritime location. He was to command a force of twenty-eight men. They were being sent to a strategically important mini-territory thirty-five kilometers off the coast and east of the Danube River estuary. It was a rocky outpost in the Black Sea. An ancient place known in Ukrainian as *Ostriv Zmiinyi*. English translation: Snake Island.

The island was associated with warriorship and legend. The Greeks knew it as White Island, after its rock formations, or—as one story had it—the color of the serpents that lived there. According to mythology, it was where the spirit of Achilles went after his death at Troy. In some versions, Helen of Troy joined him. A cult of Achilles arose and the hero's spirit was said to roam the isle. Sailors were advised never to sleep there, lest they anger the gods.

In classical times, the island was a point along the trade route that connected Greece with early Pontic settlements along the northern Black Sea. In 2011, divers found the wreck of a vessel that had sunk off Snake Island in the fourth century BCE. It had set off from the Aegean and the island of Skopelos. Its cargo—three thousand amphorae, neatly stacked and containing wine and olive oil—was found in transparent waters, together with an anchor.

In the modern age, rival powers contested the island: the Ottomans, the Russian Empire, and the Germans. A lighthouse was built in the nineteenth century on the spot where a temple to Achilles once stood. There were wrecks from the First and Second World Wars—a Russian destroyer, *Leytenant Zatsarenny*, sunk in 1917 by a German mine; a Soviet submarine, resting at a depth of thirty-five meters; and a grain ship bound for Europe.

Hotskiy arrived just before Christmas, at a time of new imperial threat. It was obvious that the territory would be hard to defend in the event of a large-scale Russian attack. So great was the concern that Zelenskiy came to see for himself, dropping in twice by helicopter. Fifty soldiers were sent as reinforcements. The island's population grew to eighty, including the border service men and two janitors. There were dogs, feral cats, and seagulls.

The captain made himself at home. "It's a beautiful place. You can see the sea all around. In winter it's very cold. There's a permanent wind," Hotskiy said.

It took thirty minutes to walk around the whole territory. The settlement included accommodation blocks and a radio station. There was a museum, closed to the public since the events of 2014, with ancient Greek stones, an old compass, and seascape paintings. And a modern pier. The guards lived in a dormitory with showers and a kitchen; it had a library with books by Jack London, the American author of the adventure novel *The Call of the Wild*. During the long nights, Hotskiy had time to read. The men received extra rations. "We had everything we needed," he recalled.

Hotskiy said that he and his colleagues hoped there would not be a conflict but prepared for one anyway. There were daily drills. Then at 4:00 a.m. on February 24, as the first airstrikes hit Kyiv, war arrived in the form of the Russian patrol boat *Vasily Bykov*. It came from the northwest. Hotskiy ordered his guards to grab their weapons and take up positions. They had no heavy arms of any kind, he said—only sniper rifles and grenades.

The ship told the island's defenders to surrender. They ignored the message.

As dawn broke, Hotskiy peered through his binoculars. The *Vasily Bykov* was visible just a mile offshore—a sleek gray corvette. The ship's radio operator repeated his earlier order: Give up, lay down your weapons! At 10:00 a.m., the first missile came crashing into the island. "I didn't know if it was a warning," Hotskiy said. "I was too busy to be scared. People were looking to me for decisions."

What followed was a one-sided encounter. A second Russian ship came from the south. It was the *Moskva*, the flagship of Russia's Black Sea fleet, newly dispatched from Sevastopol and the most powerful vessel in the region. It was almost two hundred meters long, had a crew of 510, and was equipped with guided cruise missiles and anti-aircraft systems. It was essentially a Soviet-built gun platform, capable of mincing anything in its path.

"The *Moskva* started hitting us with artillery. It was too far away, and we couldn't shoot back at it," Hotskiy told me. "Then warplanes started bombing us. We took cover in hiding places." The *Moskva* repeated the message delivered by the *Vasily Bykov*. The Russian officers appeared to be under the impression Hotskiy and his men would swap sides, as many Crimea-based Ukrainian colleagues had done in 2014.

"They were promising us jobs, money, a career in Russia," Hotskiy recounted. "No one was ready to accept their offer. We were not going to give up." Around midday, Hotskiy found himself in the radio transmission station, together with two other border service colleagues whom he declined to name. This was a secure area. He drew me a map of the building— a room of medium size, modern in design, with beige walls and two office tables, near the island's lighthouse.

On the wall were three monitors. The screens showed marine traffic in the vicinity and a live video feed of the island's surroundings. The immediate picture was grim: the island was encircled by Russian boats. It was clear that with the whole of Ukraine under massive attack, no help was coming. One of the captain's colleagues was monitoring transmissions. He sat crouched in front of a handheld radio connected to long antennas.

The radio could be used for encrypted naval traffic. At that point it was set to channel 16—an international frequency available to any boat within sixty nautical miles, broadcast on 156.8 MHz. The public channel was used for calling ships and for sending distress signals. The common language of communication was English. The radio set crackled to life.

On the other end of the line was an urgent voice speaking in Russian. It was the *Moskva*; the caller's tone was booming and portentous.

The exchange went like this:

Russian warship: "Snake Island. I, Russian warship, repeat the offer: lay down your arms and surrender, or you will be bombed. Have you understood me? Do you copy?"

First border guard to second border guard: "Well, that's it then. Or do we need to tell them to fuck off back?"

Second border guard to first border guard: "Might as well."
First border guard: "Russian warship, go fuck yourself."

The guard who made the remark was wearily matter-of-fact. The conversation lasted no more than thirty seconds. "At the time no one thought much of it. It was the first thing that came into his head," Hotskiy told me. "Nobody knew the phrase was going to be so famous. We didn't pay attention. Now, of course, we can laugh about it."

Soon after the conversation, the Ukrainian command lost contact with the island. It assumed all its defenders had been killed. Zelenskiy awarded a posthumous honor to Hotskiy and his comrades. They became "Heroes of Ukraine." The audio clip was released, and the Ukrainian public listened with sadness and pride. They were hearing the words of valiant ghosts, martyrs who gave their lives to defend Ukraine. Or so everyone thought.

A few days later it emerged that the guards were alive, albeit in Russian captivity. There was rejoicing. And "Russian warship, go fuck yourself" went viral. It became a national slogan, a meme, and a symbol of Ukraine's defiance in the face of Russian hubris and invasion. The five words went on a great journey, traveling far beyond the retransmission station where they were first uttered. They perfectly summed up Ukraine's response to Russia's overweening assault, to its arrogance and presumption—go fuck yourself.

The phrase was soon ubiquitous: it appeared on billboards, on electronic road signs above traffic junctions, in cafés, in shops, on municipal government buildings, on the back and front windshields of innumerable cars, on the uniforms of soldiers fighting and dying on the front line, on the khaki flak jacket of one of Zelenskiy's personal bodyguards, and on packets of coffee.

It became a popular anthem sung by the Ukrainian band Botashe. The song's lyrics suggested Russia was not fighting against individuals or a state, but against a family and an invincible human collective:

Russian warship go fuck yourself
My whole country here is a great family
No one ever needed you
You do things that disgust the entire world

Demonstrators who attended rallies abroad in support of Ukraine wrote the slogan on placards. Some had Ukrainian connections, others were international well-wishers expressing solidarity. For English-speakers, the original—*idi na khuy!*—was tricky to say. *Khuy* means "penis"; it appears to come from ancient Slavic. The root *khu* means "shoot" or "offshoot," and is also the basis of the words for "(pine) needle" and "tail." Whatever the etymology, the sentiment was understandable.

I came across my favorite version at a checkpoint outside Dnipro. Someone had dug what looked like a grave by the side of the road, in a weed-covered spot next to a traffic barrier. I drove past, then stopped the car and doubled back incredulously, wondering if what I had seen was real. At this inconspicuous spot there was indeed a mound of earth. And a genuine headstone: Vladimir Putin's.

The tombstone had the Russian president's face engraved upon it and a span of years, 1952—2022. Written in Ukrainian in large capital letters were the words "Go fuck yourself." Beneath, in smaller letters: "Never forgive, never forget."

Why did the phrase take off? There was a bureaucratic reason. Ukraine's national agency on civil service issues ruled that government employees and local officials could use the phrase without breaking ethical guidelines. Exceptionally crude swearing known as *Russky Mat* was allowed. "Go fuck yourself" became sayable, discussable, and part of sanctioned discourse. Zelenskiy stopped short of using the words himself but alluded to them in several speeches, employing a dramatic pause.

The plucky "fuck off" of the Snake Island defenders did nothing to alter the grim facts out in the Black Sea. The bombardment continued all day: from the *Moskva* and *Vasily Bykov* came thunderous booms. At around 6:00 p.m., two groups of

Russian commandos stormed the island in darkness, Hotskiy said. Eighty enemy soldiers swarmed along the pier. A second party landed close to the lighthouse, shinning up the cliffs.

He was reluctant to explain what happened next. Outnumbered and cut off, and with the situation hopeless, the garrison appears to have laid down its weapons. Hotskiy said his captors blindfolded him. He and other border service personnel were loaded into a service tugboat and brought to the naval base in Sevastopol—a journey of nearly twenty-four hours. "They didn't say anything. We didn't see anything," he said.

They spent the next two weeks in a barracks located somewhere in the port area. The conditions were tolerable. Hotskiy said he had no idea what was happening back home—if Kyiv had fallen, whether the Russians had steamrollered Ukrainian resistance.

In early March, Hotskiy was blindfolded again, put on a plane, and taken to Stary Oskol, a Russian city in Belgorod Oblast. His colleagues were dispersed. He found himself in a prison, locked in a cell with "two guys from Kharkiv." "It was a terrible place, worse than before. There were bars. I had no idea what had happened to my relatives, whether they were alive." He assumed he would remain in Russia for a long time.

Then, one day in mid-April, the door swung open. Hotskiy was taken out and flown back to Crimea, where he was driven from the peninsula in a Kamaz truck through the occupied south to a crossing point in the Zaporizhzhia region. When his blindfold was removed, he learned his name was on a prisoner exchange list. The Russians handed over nine border guards, including Hotskiy. Nineteen of his colleagues are still in captivity, their whereabouts unknown, together with the soldiers from the island.

The captain learned he was now a national hero and had been promoted to the rank of major. Zelenskiy also gave a medal to Roman Hrybov, the border service employee credited with telling the Russian warship to go fuck itself. There are doubts, however, as to whether Hrybov is really the one who spoke the famous phrase. Hotskiy hinted that the full story has yet to be told. It might be revealed once everyone is back from Russia, he said.

We spent an hour chatting on a bench in a sunny park, not far from the Danube River and Izmail's port. Hotskiy is a modest and diffident person, tall and a little awkward, his dark hair receding into an arrow shape. We ate a lunch of kebabs and Greek salad in a garden café. Hotskiy smiled but was taciturn. Meal over, he picked up his Kalashnikov and went to work. My sense was that being in Russia, his first experience abroad, haunted him.

The queue outside Kyiv's central post office was spectacular. It was no ordinary line: the procession began on the steps of the branch's columned arcade, stretched along Independence Square, then went all the way up Borysa Hrinchenka, a street named after the compiler of the first Ukrainian dictionary. It kept going. Thousands of people stood under a muzzy April sky, evidently prepared to wait for hours.

The building belonged to the national postal service, Ukrposhta. Close to the entrance there was a commotion. Scuffles broke out as one desperate woman tried to force her way into the high-ceilinged neoclassical vestibule. The inside of the post office, constructed in the early 1950s in monumental socialist style, was thronged. The stained-glass windows were decorated with the names of Ukrainian cities; light fell onto staff pinched in behind counters.

What was going on? Three days earlier, Ukrposhta's general director, Igor Smelyansky, had released a new stamp. It showed a Ukrainian soldier giving the middle finger to a large floating object: the battleship *Moskva*. The colors of sea and land reflected the national flag. On the margins of the perforated sheet were the words "Russian warship go . . ." and "Glory to Ukraine, to the heroes, glory."

Smelyansky left his office and descended into the hubbub. He was recognized; those waiting below greeted him like a rock star. He grinned and chatted, posed for selfies, and walked cheerfully along the queue, stopping every two hundred meters or so to make the same short speech. "Don't worry. We have seventy thousand stamps on sale today. Sixteen for each person! Just be patient. Enough for everybody," he told the crowd. They responded with claps and cries of "Slava Ukraini!"

"People are in love with it. It reflects the mood around the world toward Russia," Smelyansky told me. He said he thought up the idea of a stamp in the first days of the war and asked the public for suggestions. A short list of fifty designs was put to a vote. The warship was the triumphant winner. "It was democratic, just like Ukraine," he explained. "Even when the air-raid sirens sound, people refuse to leave their place in the line."

The postal service issued a million *Moskva* warship stamps. Seven hundred thousand went on sale across Ukraine, with two hundred thousand reserved for Kherson, Crimea, and other occupied areas. Another hundred thousand were sold online, including to foreign buyers. The general director said a "Russian warship" T-shirt—he was wearing a prototype, the stamp design printed on a black background—would go into mass production.

The stamp was a sensation, a must-have piece of history, seemingly imbued with supernatural powers. It went on sale on April 12, 2022; two days later, a pair of Ukrainian Neptune anti-ship cruise missiles slammed into the *Moskva*. Russia had not anticipated such an attack; indeed, it appeared to think it impossible. It was Kyiv's most audacious strike since Putin's invasion had begun, a stunning coup de théâtre.

Images filmed in the aftermath show a plume of thick black smoke rising from the dying vessel. The ship's lifeboats are deployed. How many of its crew survived is uncertain. The missile cruiser lists to port; two fire hoses shoot streams of water into the air; the area around the bridge is in flames. Rescue ships attend. "What the fuck are you doing?" a voice cries to the person filming these few seconds of video.

What is now known is that the badly damaged *Moskva* sank while being towed back to Sevastopol. An embarrassed Kremlin claimed a fire had broken out, causing munitions to explode. The cruiser went down in stormy seas, it said. Ukrainian officials I spoke to were publicly coy about what happened and privately jubilant. The *Moskva* was the first Russian flagship to be sunk since the 1905 Russo-Japanese War and the largest Russian vessel to be lost in conflict since 1945.

It had descended to the bottom of the Black Sea, joining sailing ships and barques from antique times.

Or, put another way, the *Moskva* had fucked off, the words from Snake Island a curse and a prophecy.

Smelyansky wasted no time in capitalizing on the predictive powers of philately. He showed me designs for successor stamps, to be chosen again by popular decision. One fea-

tured police dragging away Putin, and the words "War criminal arrested." Another depicted a burning Red Square. The
winner—with eight hundred thousand votes cast in its favor—
was a Ukrainian tractor serenely towing a destroyed Russian
tank with the slogan "Good evening, we are from Ukraine."

In the summer, Ukrposhta released an image of a boy and a
girl gazing at the Crimean Bridge. The Russian edifice was on
fire; two orange clouds burned next to its arches. This event
had not at that point actually happened. It was a statement of
intent, a vatic stamp-tiding that sooner or later the crossing
over the Kerch Strait would be joining the doomed *Moskva* at
the bottom of the Black Sea.

Sitting in his executive office, Smelyansky described how
he got the post office director's job in a hard-fought process
that would have been unthinkable in Russia, a hotbed of nepo-
tism. A Ukrainian American, he had an MBA from George-
town University and a law degree from George Washington
University. He applied from the United States, beat forty-nine
other candidates, and returned to Kyiv in 2016 to take up the
position.

"We should win this war. We will win it," he asserted. "The
Russians don't know what they are fighting for. Their bullshit
keeps changing, from denazification to freeing the Donbas."
Smelyansky gave me sixteen stamps and a signed envelope,
with an instruction to pass them to Boris Johnson. An aide
brought in an XL "Russian warship" T-shirt for the United
Kingdom's then prime minister; I pointed out tactfully he
might require an XXL.

Down in the packed central hall, I talked to Nataliia
Tkachenko, who said she managed to buy stamps on the first
day they were released. "It's a symbol. It shows our inner patri-

otism. I feel this," she added. "Snake Island didn't surrender. I'm not going to surrender. Nor is my husband. Take a look at the queue. The stamp is a bit of paper. It may be small but it's powerful, just like Ukraine."

On my way out, I also spoke to Viktor Fyodorovych, a Kharkiv pensioner who was buying stamps for his relatives. They were stuck in a bomb shelter, he told me, and couldn't venture out. "I'm sixty-three years old. I've never felt so much pride before in our nation. It's a symbol of our courage and steadfastness. Putin is mad." Viktor paused and then clarified: "Scratch that. Better to say he is a bad worm."

The previous month I had been staying in a downtown flat on Taras Shevchenko Avenue in Lviv, Ukraine's largest western city. Lviv is about sixty-five kilometers from the Polish border. It was a safe haven for refugees fleeing from other parts of the country. Its elegant streets—featuring classical and baroque architecture, a legacy of its rich Polish and Hapsburg past—were full of displaced people. Some were affluent, others desperate.

Millions were on the move. Many were going west, to Poland, Slovakia, Hungary, Moldova, and Romania. The route to the border followed the M10 highway, passing through an expanse of pine forest. Along the way were checkpoints manned by soldiers and local militiamen wearing hi-vis jackets. There were sandbags, machine-gun posts, and logs piled next to braziers.

Western Ukraine was largely spared the grievous Russian attacks seen elsewhere. Nonetheless, the war felt close. There were echoes of previous historical struggles: visible alongside blue and yellow was the red-and-black flag of the Ukrainian insurgent army, which fought against Soviet forces during the Second World War. Roadside signs read "Russian warship, go fuck yourself" and "It's our home. We will bury you in it."

Near the Polish-Ukrainian border town of Krakovets I found a twelve-kilometer-long traffic queue. On that day in March, the line was thirteen hundred vehicles long, plus five hundred pedestrians. It began on a desolate stretch of road surrounded by yellow scrub and fir trees. Many cars had signs with the word *dyeti*—children—written on their windshields. Some mothers emerged from taxis and walked the last few kilometers, dragging along children and suitcases.

"Putin has gone bonkers. He wants Ukraine to be part of his imperium," Lyudmyla Lyskevska said, stretching her legs as snowflakes swirled. "He's managed to unite the whole country against him." Lyudmyla told me she spent four days on the road, sleeping in her car. She was part of a three-car family convoy. Over the course of our twenty-minute conversation, the group advanced a hundred meters. They had been queuing for twenty hours. Behind her, more vehicles arrived.

A pensioner, she said she had fled from Zaporizhzhia and left with her daughter, son-in-law, three grandkids, and a dog. Many of those exiting had relatives in Russia. Lyudmyla said she had quarreled with her sister, who lived with her Russian husband in Saint Petersburg. She said, "I rang them up. He told me the Kremlin was only bombing military infrastructure. I asked him to stop watching Russian TV and said, 'Our people are dying.' They didn't believe me."

The border crossing was busy in both directions. In the early weeks after the invasion, more than sixty thousand Ukrainian expatriates returned home, moving east. Most were young men who had come to defend their homeland. Inside the country, Zelenskiy banned males aged eighteen to sixty from leaving. Some of the fathers I talked to in the Krakovets line told me that after seeing off their families, they would go home and take up arms.

Going in search of coffee one morning on Taras Shevchenko Avenue, I noticed a group of recruits standing outside Lviv's territorial defense center. Some were in military uniform. Others wore civilian clothes and baseball hats and carried shiny backpacks. Nearby was a branch of McDonald's, temporarily closed, and a bronze statue of Volodymyr Ivasyuk, a popular Ukrainian singer-songwriter of the 1970s.

"Raise your hand if you have a car," their new commander barked. The volunteers split into groups and introduced themselves. Some lived nearby; others had come from abroad. "History is happening right now. I don't want to be on the sidelines," Vitaliy, a thirty-five-year-old founder of a Lviv IT start-up, told me.

Vitaliy said his firm's fifteen employees began weapons training in mid-February. He volunteered for the army on day one of the invasion. The recruits were off to learn combat first aid and other skills at an undisclosed location outside Lviv, before being sent as reinforcements to the front. "It's unquestionable. There's no other choice. Everyone is going to fight for Ukraine. We are going to win because of people power," he told me.

Each morning the roll call next to the Ivasyuk statue was repeated with new willing faces. It was an affecting scene. The commander spoke of anti-tank missiles and Stingers, supplied by the United States and the United Kingdom. He referred to the enemy as *Moskali* and shouted, "Glory to Ukraine"; a roar came back: "To the heroes, glory." I watched excited young men climb into Vitaliy's Nissan SUV and go off to learn how to shoot. A blue-and-yellow flag stuck out of the SUV's front window, attached to a wooden pole.

How many, I wondered, would come back?

This bottom-up patriotic activity was typical of what was going on across Ukraine in the aftermath of Russia's invasion. Volunteers helped the war effort in myriad ways. They offered accommodations to those whom bombardment made homeless. Grandmothers cooked borshch for refugees and donated food; the same ladies made camouflage nets for the army while singing songs. Their teenage grandchildren took a break from homework to make bombs.

I toured a former factory site in Lviv and found a dozen students and young professionals at work around a wooden table. They wore masks and gloves and were busy making Molotov cocktails. The room smelled strongly of gasoline and paint remover—two of the ingredients, along with polystyrene and silver dust. Bottles were stacked in a corner, one labeled "Apple juice 1996"; there were flowered linen squares to be torn into strips and used as fuses.

Daniil Mediakovskiy, a twenty-year-old history student at Lviv's university, broke off to chat. He had spent the previous two days working on the basement production line. Shouldn't he be studying? "It's practical history. It's time for this right now," he told me, loading a Molotov into a crate. Daniil said his mother woke him early when the invasion started. After twenty-four hours doom-scrolling on social media, he decided to volunteer.

The Molotov cocktail was named after Stalin's foreign minister, Vyacheslav Molotov. The students called their 2022 version a "Bandera smoothie," a reference to the militant nationalist Stepan Bandera. "My parents know about the bombs. I haven't told my granny. She's worried enough about things already," Daniil said. He acknowledged his improvised weapon would probably not halt a Russian tank. But he stressed: "It will break Russian soldiers mentally and show them they're not welcome here."

One of the smoothie bottles fell and smashed. The collective broke off for ten minutes to allow time for the fumes to disperse. Tips on how to use the bombs went around on Facebook and Instagram. The finished cocktails were loaded into car trunks, fifteen hundred a day. They were distributed via contacts; who exactly, the students declined to say. Some were stored nearby in case Russia tried to storm Lviv—something the city's mayor, Andriy Sadovyi, told me was Russia's eventual plan.

Back in my rented flat, I dialed Alex Riabchyn, a former deputy in Kyiv and adviser to the CEO of the state gas firm Naftogaz. Relocated to Lviv, he was buying Kevlar vests for the Ukrainian army. It was one of many private business initiatives that sprang up in the days and weeks after the invasion. Entrepreneurs imported protective gear and uniforms; Ukrainians based in Silicon Valley flew home to apply their tech skills to military logistics; gamers and geeks became skilled drone operators.

Riabchyn said volunteers played a crucial part in the struggle for national survival. Ukraine had strong civil society bonds, connecting families, churches, and small enterprises. This made the country more like Greece or Italy than Russia, he said. "We are good at self-organization. There are a huge number of horizontal links. It's what differentiates us from Moscow."

Russia has a vertical tradition and is a place of strong institutions. When Putin said something, Russians listened. But in Ukraine, institutions are weak and rulers mistrusted. "We don't obey the state. It killed people in the Holodomor [Stalin's famine] and gulags. And so people here rely on their family and friends." Riabchyn added: "Ukraine is an army of ants. Everyone does what they can in this war. You feel the energy."

I found Riabchyn's argument compelling. We agreed that Kyiv had broken away from Moscow in the years since independence—first slowly, then with greater tempo. In the 1990s and early 2000s, it was quite like Russia; Russian state television was still widely watched and played an important role in shaping popular attitudes. Post-Soviet oligarchs were in charge of politics and decision-making.

With Russia's invasion of Ukraine, the two mentalities collided. As Andrey Kurkov suggested to me, Ukrainians were freedom-loving individualists who disliked being told what to do, habitually rejected their leaders, and had lived for many centuries in a state of what he called "organized anarchy." They were rebels by nature, caustic and disrespectful.

In contrast, Russians came from an autocratic system. They bowed to authority, followed orders, and loved the tsar—unless they didn't like him, in which case they killed him. The Soviet state and its modern successor revolved around a single party, and a dictator. The Kremlin's preferred method of negotiation was to use bullying force and to show who was master and who the slave. The *Moskva*'s ultimatum embodied this imperious attitude.

These views clashed during the Maidan uprising of 2004—

a grassroots street movement that led to political change and a return to the consensual model of government, familiar from Cossack times. When Yanukovych became president in 2010, he tried to rule like a tsar, in Russian style. The result was another Maidan and the popular revolution of 2013–2014. According to Riabchyn, the "spirit of the Maidan" came back in 2022. Civil society was enjoying an unprecedented moment.

The question was, which structure would prevail: the lateral network of the Ukrainian ant army or the vertical hierarchy of the lumbering Russian state? It is a battle that has pitted group ingenuity against a behemoth. Riabchyn was optimistic. He told me Ukraine's previous differences had melted away, amid what he called the "fellowship of the Maidan." How long, I wondered, might this brotherhood last? "We are prepared for a long siege," he replied.

Back in Kyiv, and mulling this conversation, I met with the philosopher Volodymyr Yermolenko. I wondered to what extent the legacy of the ancient Greeks had influenced contemporary Ukraine. According to Yermolenko, his country's decentralized political culture had deep historical roots. These predated the experiences of the Maidan and might be traced all the way back to Aristotle's idea of the *polis*, a city-state ruled not by kings but by a self-contained body of citizens.

Intellectuals who helped bring about the Ukrainian nation were interested in the Classical world, he said. One of them was Ivan Kotliarevsky, a founding father of modern Ukrainian literature, who in the 1790s wrote a satirical version of Virgil's *Aeneid*. Its characters speak in vernacular Ukrainian. Another influential personality was the historian Mykhailo

Drahomanov, who taught at Kyiv's Saint Volodymyr—now Shevchenko—University.

Drahomanov was a socialist and political thinker. He developed the idea of a community known as a *hromada*. The concept took its inspiration from Aristotle's city-states, where politics emerged at a local level. "A leitmotiv of Ukrainian literature, historiography, and philosophy is opposition to the centralized idea of state and universe," Yermolenko told me. In summary, Ukrainians were good at organizing. They opposed authority in whatever shape it took—the Polish-Lithuanian Commonwealth; Russia in the eighteenth and nineteenth centuries; and today's neo-imperial Kremlin. Putin missed this in his long pseudo-essay.

I met Yermolenko in a coffee bar around the corner from the national pedagogical university, named after Drahomanov. As well as teaching philosophy at Kyiv-Mohyla Academy, Eastern Europe's oldest academic institution, Yermolenko is a journalist and editor in chief of UkraineWorld. He hosts an English-language podcast. Before we parted, Yermolenko went to his car, opened the trunk, and gave me copy of a book of essays by Ukrainian intellectuals that he had edited, published in 2019.

His own text was a thoughtful meditation on the Ukrainian steppe and the European imagination. He examined Lord Byron's poem *Mazeppa*, written in 1819, about the rebellious Cossack leader Ivan Mazepa. It tells the story of the young Mazepa, who fell in love with a married noblewoman from the Polish court. Her enraged husband had Mazepa tied to a horse and sent out into the steppe, a journey that took him to the brink of death and despair.

The poem describes the tortures that Mazepa suffers on his three-day journey. They include "cold, hunger, sorrow, shame,

distress." And it notes the Cossacks' ability to strike unexpectedly at enemies, a serpentlike talent:

Sprung from a race whose rising blood
When stirr'd beyond its calmer mood,
And trodden hard upon, is like
The rattle-snake's, in act to strike

Russia's four-month occupation of Snake Island turned out
to be a cursed experience. The naval command in Moscow
made the outpost into a minifortress, to which it transferred
missile batteries, anti-aircraft guns, radar, and reconnaissance
vehicles. The military-strategic goal was to control airspace in
the northwestern part of the Black Sea and to enforce a blockade of Ukrainian ships to stop them from leaving Odesa and
other Black Sea ports.

But the evil spirits said to roam the isle appeared to have
returned—or so you might imagine. The Ukrainians used
Bayraktar drones to strike the Russian contingent from the
sky. The unmanned aerial vehicles blew up a helicopter delivering supplies and disabled a patrol vessel. Long-range rockets
hurtled into the pier, its coordinates well known. Drone footage showed the Z-marked vehicles parked there disappearing
in a roiling inferno.

In late June, the Russians packed up and left. The Kremlin
said it was abandoning Snake Island as a "goodwill gesture."
This was a significant Ukrainian victory. A week later, special
forces commandos set off from the coast on a nighttime mission. Engineers found a mine-free sea path; the group walked
at dawn across the island and raised the Ukrainian flag. They

logged Russian hardware, rescued a cat, and departed in boats before Moscow's ships counterattacked.

A day later, Russia pummeled the island with phosphorus munitions. The museum—with its amphorae and other Greek relics—was destroyed, its exhibits turned to dust. The lighthouse was gone, too. Russia, it seemed, was indifferent to the damage it caused to communities and to Ukrainian culture.

That summer, as Moscow's military setbacks mounted, Putin resorted to a tactic that had served him well before. An old trick with a new and glowing twist.

The strategy was blackmail. Russia would use the threat of a nuclear meltdown to menace the world.

TWELVE

A Proven State

Zaporizhzhia Nuclear Power Station
August 2022

Our enemies will die, as the dew does in the sunshine,
And we, too, brothers, we'll live happily in our land.
—LYRICS FROM UKRAINE'S NATIONAL ANTHEM

From afar, it resembled a strange pagan temple. Six reactors loomed over the Dnipro River like solemn idols. Alongside them were power lines, chimneys, and cooling towers—two of them. This was the Zaporizhzhia nuclear power plant (ZNPP). It had once symbolized progress and scientific ingenuity: man's mastery of the atom. The nuclear station was Europe's biggest, considerably larger than Chornobyl, and a godlike giver of light and heat. Its electricity powered millions of households across Ukraine.

By the time I arrived to gaze upon it in August, on a bright, hazy morning, the station was barely working. In early March 2022, Russian forces seized the facility and the adjoining city of Enerhodar, where the ZNPP's workers lived. A long armored column broke through a barricade and began shelling the plant. A fire started close to one of the reactors. The Russians moved in.

Moscow's attempts to push farther north stalled. Six months later, the station was on the front line. It was situated on the Dnipro's left bank and the Kakhovka Reservoir. Ukrainian employees continued to carry out safety and technical functions. Only now they did their jobs under conditions of enormous stress and the barrel of a Russian gun.

The Kremlin put into action an audacious plan. The intention was to sever the plant from the Ukrainian grid and reconfigure it so its electricity flowed to Crimea. The peninsula's infrastructure had always been connected to the rest of Ukraine, and it had suffered power shortages in the years since annexation. The operation was dangerous, technically complex, and quite risky, experts warned, with little guarantee of success.

Putin was attempting to do something unknown to history: to steal a civil nuclear plant from another state. It was a ghoulish and surreal heist, watched over by Russia's state nuclear energy company, Rosatom.

When the Russians had first stormed the ZNPP, two of its six reactors were offline. Ukrainian employees shut down a third when a power line was damaged. Soon, only two were on and then just one, and then none.

With each day, the situation grew more concerning. In March, Zelenskiy raised the alarm over the ZNPP with Ukraine's partners. By summer, the international community was following developments with growing horror. More than forty countries urged Russia to give the plant back to Ukraine. Kyiv accused Moscow of blackmail and nuclear terrorism and asked the United States and its allies to intervene. Putin ignored those appeals. What might he do next?

He probably would not blow up Europe. The modern pressurized water reactors had thick walls designed to protect against earthquakes—though not against artillery shells. The fallout from an explosion would contaminate Russia and Crimea as well as the rest of Ukraine, depending on which way the wind blew. A more likely scenario was an accident or mishap, a repeat of the 1986 Chornobyl disaster, when reactor number 4 exploded, spewing radiation over Belarus, Ukraine, and Scandinavia. As Mykhailo Podolyak, Zelenskiy's senior adviser, said to me: "Russia could easily fuck things up."

The Kremlin's behavior earlier that spring didn't inspire confidence. As Podolyak pointed out, Russian troops dug trenches in Chornobyl's highly toxic red zone. They took staff hostage, militarized the exclusion area, and ran thousands of vehicles through the forest toward Kyiv. "They don't know what they are doing. Russian personnel have a very low level of training," Podolyak said, adding that the chances of a Europe-wide catastrophe were real.

On the Dnipro, Russia transformed the ZNPP into a fullblown military base. It moved hardware inside turbine halls 1 and 2—armored vehicles, personnel, drones, and ammunition. Special trucks with Z markings were parked 150 meters from a reactor. The complex was mined. Multiple launch rocket systems were positioned around the territory and in the nearby settlements of Vodiane and Kamyanka.

And then, in August, Putin upped the stakes.

According to the Ukrainians, his forces resumed shelling the ZNPP. The purpose was to destroy power lines and disconnect the plant forever from the Ukrainian grid—and to blame

Kyiv and accuse it of recklessness. A shell punched a hole in the roof of the building that housed fresh nuclear fuel. Another projectile hit a solid radioactive waste storage facility. Windows were blown out. There was damage to a turbine oil tank and to a container with a radiation monitoring system.

A Ukrainian worker was hurt and a shift rotation canceled. Sources I spoke to who were familiar with the plant said these attacks were done in consultation with Russian nuclear experts. They gave advice to the Russian army on which areas were "safe" to hit. Kremlin channels then showed pictures of the damage and attributed it to Ukraine's armed forces. It was a deadly game of radiological Russian roulette.

In effectively weaponizing ZNPP, Moscow, it seemed, was deliberately blurring the distinction between its tactical nuclear arsenal and a civil nuclear facility—in this case one hijacked from Ukraine. Threats to strike the United States and Europe with long-range nuclear missiles were a staple of Russian TV discussion shows. Instead of seeking to calm the situation down, the Kremlin played up the threat of a disaster at the ZNPP. The aim was to intimidate the White House and force concessions.

Blackmail, then. Russia's foreign ministry spokesperson Maria Zakharova boldly admitted as much. Moscow was deeply unhappy with European Union plans to ban or reduce visas for Russian citizens, a move that would disproportionately affect Russian government officials and their families, who enjoyed holidays in Italy, France, and Spain. Zakharova warned: "Radiation doesn't need a visa to cross borders. If something happens at Zaporizhzhia, it will not be about visas, passports, or borders."

As well as nuclear threats, Moscow turned off the supply

of gas to Germany—a move long expected. It shut down the Nord Stream 1 pipeline "for a few days" because of alleged technical problems. And then said the supply would only resume when the West lifted its sanctions. A deal to allow Ukraine to export grain to the Middle East and Africa from its Black Sea ports appeared to be holding, despite Putin, who agreed to it, voicing unhappiness. He claimed, wrongly, that the grain was exclusively going to Europe. It was clear that Moscow was engaged in a multivector crusade. There was the military operation in Ukraine and an adjacent energy and food war designed to bring Europe to its knees.

When the International Atomic Energy Agency visited the Zaporizhzhia station in September, it found a dangerous mess. At one point the delegation, led by the agency's chief, Rafael Grossi, had to seek shelter because of shelling. Grossi reported safety breaches, wrung-out Ukrainian staff, and the presence of Russian army vehicles, including on the overpass connecting reactor units. He called on both militaries to withdraw and for the ZNPP to be turned into a secure zone.

There was little prospect Putin would agree. He had no intention of demilitarizing the nuclear power plant and handing it back to Energoatom, Ukraine's state nuclear energy company. Putin regarded nuclear blackmail as an effective international tool. His calculation: in a game of brinkmanship, his weaker democratic enemies would always blink.

And if the station blew up: well, sorry, that was Ukraine's fault.

Oleksandr devoted his life to atomic power. For him, the Zaporizhzhia nuclear power plant was more than just a workplace. It was, he said, a source of pride and destiny. Oleksandr was one of Enerhodar's fifty thousand inhabitants. The city was built in the seventies and eighties to provide housing for the plant's eleven-thousand-strong workforce. There were schools, a palace of culture, tennis courts. It was a community of the future, with a magical name: *Enerhodar* means "gift of energy."

Highly educated professionals like Oleksandr made careers at the station. Their role involved looking for anomalies; the plant's six reactors had to work in perfect harmony. Generating electricity involved a highly sensitive chain—fuel rods, steam, turbines, and power transmission. If there was a deviation from the norm, staff had to take corrective action. They were dealing with a fallible system, after all. Equipment could malfunction; humans err.

By the time Russia began its mechanized buildup around Ukraine in late 2021, Oleksandr had resigned. He was in touch with friends and former colleagues who were still active at the plant and who worked with its director, Igor Murashov. The city was home to many nuclear pensioners, as Oleksandr called them. No one from his social circle believed Putin would attack. As engineers, they viewed the situation rationally: a countrywide invasion made no sense.

When the attack began and the initial shock wore off, Oleksandr and his friends and colleagues were confident it would not affect Enerhodar or the plant. Their faith was based on exceptionalism: a belief that the Russians would recognize the station as an essential place, staffed by serious people. Surely, they would ignore it. This, too, turned out to be wrong. When the Russians took over, it felt like a double occupation, of city and workplace, Oleksandr told me when we spoke in August by phone.

Almost immediately, the young city's character began to

change. Educational facilities closed. Boys continued to play basketball every day in the playground opposite his house, but the number of voices diminished as families fled Russian rule. Enerhodar became a city of disappearing children. The streets were emptier. Those who remained spent less time outdoors; they gave up on pastimes such as jogging and swimming.

At the same time, new flags and posters arrived. The occupiers hung Russian tricolors above city hall and the building that used to belong to the SBU, Ukraine's intelligence service. A new hero appeared: Russia's unsmiling president, together with his proclamation that Russia and Ukraine were a single people. The billboards featured portraits of Soviet generals from the Second World War and communist-era heroes. "People pass by indifferently," Oleksandr observed.

No one he knew approved of Russia's arrival. He acknowledged a handful of residents might support the new administration—for career reasons, mostly—but said they were a small and deluded minority. Early on, protesters held a peaceful pro-Ukraine rally. Russian soldiers broke up the demonstration with stun grenades and automatic weapons. After that, people withdrew into themselves and waited for better times.

Life continued. Shops reopened, with higher prices than before and goods imported from Crimea. Large stores came back with new names. And the city's market was flooded with cheap fruit and vegetables—sold by villagers who were unable to transport their produce to other areas. Enerhodar got a Russian newspaper, the *Zaporizhzhya Vestnik*. Its front page reported on an impending "referendum" to join Russia. In the main square, an election tent appeared.

By this point, after six months of occupation, Oleksandr's faith that the city and its nuclear station would go back to normal was melting away. More and more people were leaving; the men typically stayed behind, sending their wives and kids to Ukrainian-held territory or abroad. "My neighbor could not stand it and evacuated his children. You can struggle with your own fears, but it is impossible to cope with fear in the eyes of your children," Oleksandr said.

The reason for this renewed exodus was simple. The Russians were firing on the nuclear facility and the city's outskirts. Enerhodar had always been supplied with cold and hot water, as well as power, because of its proximity to the plant. Suddenly the city was without electricity for several hours at a time.

Zaporizhzhia thermal power station, the largest in Ukraine, shut down due to damage to the railway bridge and the resultant impossibility of delivering coal.

Could Ukraine be responsible for shelling the ZNPP, as claimed by Moscow? "It's like believing the sun goes around the earth. It's impossible, absolutely impossible. It's our plant, our territory, our people," Oleksandr told me. "I still believe the Russians are not crazy and they will not get to the point of catastrophe. But the plant is in a bad situation. It can't be operated in such conditions." Station workers have been kidnapped, he said, including people he knew.

The Russian attack on Enerhodar was cynically calculated. One shell landed in a park, killing a man out walking his dog. Another later crashed into city hall. Meanwhile, from mid-July on, Russian forces began using the nuclear power station and surrounding territory to bombard Ukrainian-controlled cities on the opposite bank of the Dnipro River: Nikopol and Marhanets. Oleksandr followed what happened on Telegram: how many people killed and injured, how many houses destroyed.

The turbine halls and nuclear reactors offered perfect cover for the Russian attackers. They were an impregnable shield, rendering Ukraine's armed forces unable to fire back. If they did so, they would endanger the plant, run the risk of killing Ukrainian civilians, and validate Russia's propagandist narrative that Kyiv was an irresponsible international actor. Russia bombed a lot. It attacked mostly in the early hours of the morning and sometimes during the day.

On the morning of the International Atomic Energy Agency's visit, Enerhodar came under heavy fire. "The most terrible day of my life," Oleksandr said. "The explosions were near our house. We were hiding in a corridor between two walls. I knew that I could die at any moment."

I asked if he might keep a diary. He wrote:

Every night we hear the roar of artillery salvos. Sometimes the Russians drive their artillery so close that it sounds like shooting in a neighboring yard. Windowpanes tremble. It feels like the whole house is shaking. Even those who do not believe in God pray for their salvation. Sometimes it happens in the middle of the night. An ordinary person cannot distinguish the sounds of artillery salvo and shell burst.

Therefore, every time it seems that this is an explosion and the next projectile will hit your house. Involuntarily, the question arises: What kind of mothers raised these people? For many years, these cities of Nikopol and Marhanets perceived our nuclear plant as a source of mortal danger. Now real death is flying from us to them. We can only commiserate with them.

He added: "Of course, I see only a part of the overall tragic picture, but this part is sufficient to say: this must not be in the modern world!" He concluded on a note of optimism: "Nevertheless, we continue to believe that all this will end soon."

From where I stood in Nikopol, I could see the ZNPP on the far bank of the Dnipro. It was five kilometers away. Or, measured in rocket terms, fifteen seconds: the time it took for a Grad fired from the plant to fly over the deep blue water and fall among the city's high-rise buildings and chestnut tree–lined boulevards. A short interval between life and death, I contemplated. There was little chance for residents to take cover. Long enough to mutter a prayer or to crouch in a gloomy hallway.

I arrived in Nikopol in August, a few hours after a devastating nighttime barrage. This latest Russian attack killed three people and wounded several others, including a thirteen-year-old girl who was taken to the hospital. Around 120 incendiary devices fell in the district. The day before, thirteen people died in Marhanets, the mining town down the road. All the victims were civilians. These were the latest casualties from Putin's rolling war.

The damage was spectacular. An upper corner had been scooped out of a five-story residential building on Viktor Usov Street, as if swiped by a monster. Police sealed off the area with tape. A Grad rocket lay placidly on a grassy sidewalk shoulder, broken in two. There was a tail section complete with fins. A prosecutor compiling a list of war crimes emerged from a doorway, holding a couple of files.

"I can't explain why they did this. Wherever Russians are, there is only ruin, pain, dirt, and tears," eyewitness Vitaliy

Chornozob said. Vitaliy lived next door to the apartment that got hit. He said he was there at midnight when the missile crashed into his building. He rescued his neighbors—a woman and her son—but was unable to dig out the woman's eighty-year-old father. "He was dead under two meters of concrete. We couldn't get to him," he told me.

Why were the Russians obliterating Nikopol? "It's jealousy," another resident, Yana Sokolova, suggested. "They can't handle the fact that we live better than they do. We are free people and they are slaves. They want to make us that way, too." And what about the ZNPP? "You can see the plant from all over town. The Russians are hiding there and shooting at us. They are firing at point-blank range. It's inhumane. Putin is terrorist number one," she said.

Yana clutched a cup of coffee and peered at the damage next door. It had been another sleepless night; the Grad knocked out the Internet, but her flat and ground-floor shop were unscathed. The nocturnal attacks—in their fourth week at this point—were done to sow panic in the civilian population, she thought. "They want us to tell our government to capitulate because we are afraid. We won't. We're not going anywhere."

Before the invasion, traveling from Nikopol to Enerhodar involved, in summer, a short scenic trip by ferry or year-round a longer drive along the banks of the Soviet-built reservoir. The city was once a Cossack stronghold and the center of a self-governing area known as the Zaporozhian Sich. In modern times, it was home to a hundred thousand people. It was a Russian-speaking city with an industrial tube and metallurgy factory: the kind of place Putin had vowed to "save." For months, Nikopol was a safe haven for refugees fleeing the fighting in the Donbas. And then in mid-July, without explanation, the Russians started attacking the town. About half of its residents fled. Among those who remained, some left before evening curfew and bedded down in tents in the woods to reduce the chance of being killed. They would drive back to town each morning.

Grads are notoriously inaccurate; they scatter over a radius of five hundred to seven hundred meters. Further up Viktor Usov Street, a missile had careened into a third-story property, leaving a neat hole shaped like two pieces of Lego. I went to see, but as I did, Nikopol's air-raid siren sounded. I hurried to the mayor's office and took cover in its shelter. By coincidence, the damaged apartment's owner, Sasha Suvorov, was there filing a police report. He said that he had been working late at his computer when he heard the wump of an outgoing missile. "I knew they come from Enerhodar, so I moved to the other side of my flat," he said. "I calmly went to an archway. A few seconds later, all I could see was dust."

His survival seemed improbable. Why was he alive? Sasha said he must have been born under a lucky star. He showed me photos of his ruined home: a metal tube lay in a jumbled living room, its doors askew. He was applying for compensation. "I would like to leave Nikopol," he said. "First, I need to get plywood to cover up the gap."

Many of those who had packed up and gone had moved to Kryvyi Rih, the nearest big city, forty miles to the northwest. Its military administrator, Oleksandr Vilkul, said Moscow's behavior around the ZNPP resembled that of a death cult. "It's complete madness," he said. Vilkul was a former deputy prime minister in charge of emergency situations. He had toured Enerhodar several times. In his view, Russia had become a "totalitarian sect," run by a mad dictator obsessed with his place in history.

"They believe in Lenin, victory in the Second World War, and the nuclear arsenal," he said. "Nuclear has become a religious faith for them. Their god is the nuclear button." He added: "I always understood Russia was a dangerous neighbor. I didn't think it would become a crazy monster. Unfortunately, most Russians support him. Putin wants to take his place alongside Peter the Great and Stalin." How would the war end? "Like Hitler, Putin will destroy his own country," Vilkul predicted.

The siren fell silent, and with no additional damage reported, I completed my tour of frontline Nikopol. One rocket had dropped on the city's war memorial and park. I saw a deep crater in the alley of heroes, a few meters from a needle-shaped monument and a wall inscribed with the names of soldiers who fell in the Second World War. The chaotic strike was another example of the ideological emptiness of Putin's invasion, ostensibly carried out to remind a lost province of its glorious Soviet past.

Many of Putin's victims were pensioners who grew up in the USSR. Across the road, a Grad had plonked itself on a residential block, killing an elderly woman. Her body had been taken away; a crane was parked outside, and municipal workers who were trying to make the building safe tossed masonry down from a ravaged top story. Three schools and more than forty private buildings were damaged in the same raid, as well as cars and shops.

"Peaceful people live here. They don't have any weapons. They just want to stay in their own homes," Anna Sidilova, the property's manager, told me, watching the cleanup. "We go to bed and don't know if we will wake up the next day."

She was tearful and upset. I asked her what punishment

Putin should face. "The same," she said, pointing at the vaporized apartment. "Deprivation of everything he has."

From the ninth floor of the administration building, the view stretched for miles. I was in Mykolaiv, three hundred kilometers west of Nikopol. Beneath was the wharf where the *Moskva* had been built in the seventies. Another rusting missile cruiser, *Moskva*'s sister ship, *Ukraina*, was moored in the dockyard on the Southern Buh River. It was completed as the USSR collapsed, and the cruiser was never fitted out. Beyond the city, smoke rose on the horizon. It was coming from the direction of Kherson, the target of a tantalizing Ukrainian counteroffensive.

Dmytro Pletenchuk—a public-affairs officer and naval captain—gave me a tour of the wrecked building. We began on the ground floor, where he showed me his collection of enemy munitions. Propped against the wall of an office were Grads and cluster bombs. "I'm thinking about opening a bar for veterans when the war is over," he said. "My friend was killed fighting in Kharkiv. He used to run one. We could use these as decorations."

In March, a Russian air missile slammed into the regional state headquarters, killing thirty-seven people and injuring many more. Pletenchuk had been on his way to work. The security guards in reception miraculously survived. Colleagues having breakfast in the canteen were less fortunate. There were bloodstains still visible on the stairs and in an upstairs corridor, splashed on a wall. We crunched over broken glass. The workplace was noiseless and ghostly; the horror felt fresh.

"We fight with idiots. It's good for us, but they have nuclear weapons," Pletenchuk said, gesturing toward the place where a colleague had died while fetching a cup of coffee. Next door was a meeting room with tourist brochures and a picture of the Eiffel Tower. He added: "It's a problem for the whole world. Russia is like a monkey with a grenade—it's ooh, ooh, ooh. We don't know what they are going to do. And they are playing with the grenade."

Ukrainians had always resisted Russian imperialism, he said, including his grandfather, whom Stalin had sent to Siberia. Tour over, Pletenchuk disappeared and returned with a present for me—a Ukrainian flag rescued from the ruins.

Could Ukraine really win the war? I asked him. "Yeah. We have motivation. Russians don't have this. They don't want to die in this country. We are fighting for our homeland. They fight for washing machines. It's different," he replied.

I went back to Mykolaiv in August after hearing rumors that Ukraine was about to launch a major attack against Russian positions. The expectation was this would happen in the south. Zelenskiy had ordered his generals to capture Kherson and push its occupiers out. The most promising front was the territory on the right bank of the Dnipro River—the city of Kherson and surrounding villages and towns. This bulge of land was a vulnerability and a contested zone that might just determine the outcome of the war.

The region's governor, Vitaliy Kim, was politely evasive when I asked him about the timing of Ukraine's advance. A confident media performer, Kim had a national and international profile. He survived the 9:00 a.m. Russian airstrike on his office because he overslept. "It's just a question of time," he told me. "We have a will to win back our people and our territories, so we are on our way." He added: "We are counting the war not in days but in victims. So if we get more weapons, it will happen faster."

Since my previous visit to Mykolaiv in May, the dynamics on the battlefield had changed. This was largely thanks to the White House. In early summer, the Biden administration delivered a High Mobility Artillery Rocket System to Ukraine, known as HIMARS, first twelve units and then four more. A precision weapon with a seventy-five-kilometer range, mounted on a truck, it could shoot and scoot: deliver a pod of six rockets in five minutes and drive off at high speed. Russian S-300 and S-400 air defenses were useless against it.

Defense experts described the arrival of HIMARS as a game changer and critical enabler. Ukrainians celebrated it in social media videos and memes. The system contributed to the already widespread belief that Ukraine would win the war sooner or later. Roman Lozynskyi, a special forces officer and parliamentary deputy, showed me a film he had shot on his phone of a HIMARS crew in action in July somewhere in the Mykolaiv region.

A HIMARS-launched rocket streaks above a ghostly treeline and up into the black canopy of night. The noise is shattering. More rockets follow it into the heavens, one burning white parabola after another. "It's extremely powerful. Our soldiers see HIMARS, and they feel proud of our capacity to fight," Lozynskyi said. "It's important for our spirits." How did he feel personally? "Whoa!" he answered, waving his arms in triumph.

The weapon's impact was immediate. The Ukrainians set about bombing targets deep behind enemy lines. They struck ammunition depots, command posts, and defensive batteries. They began taking out bridges and cutting off lines of supply and retreat. HIMARS rockets repeatedly whacked Kherson's

Antonivskyi Bridge. They also knocked out other crossing points over the Dnipro: a sluice bridge at the Kakhovka hydroelectric power plant, west of Nikopol, and the Daryivskyi Bridge over the Inhulets River. Advanced Western technology enabled Ukraine to approach military parity with Moscow. If the Russians had once fired a hundred shells a day, they were now launching around twenty, Roman Kostenko, the special forces commander I had met before, told me in August.

By summer, Washington's security assistance to Kyiv had climbed to $12.7 billion. Controversially, the United States was refusing to supply Army Tactical Missile System (ATACMS) ammunition, which could be used in HIMARS launchers and have a 185-mile range. This was down to Biden administration policy, not logistics. Kostenko said Ukraine wanted this special weapon: "It would dramatically change our position in the south." Russia's Crimean Bridge, the gateway to Kherson, would be the first target, he added.

The Russian army responded with new tactics. Engineers built pontoon bridges; weapons and military convoys were moved together with civilian vehicles on barges. Soldiers dug trenches and rebased themselves in private homes. The strikes continued. In July, HIMARS wiped out a freight train carrying armored equipment in the Kherson region town of Brylivka. Moscow pulled back to the village of Myrne and moved its local military headquarters out of range.

Despite these successes, Ukrainian commanders told me that capturing Kherson would not be easy. "We have more weapons. But they are not enough to comprehensively beat the enemy," Kostenko said.

According to Kostenko, Ukraine's armed forces did not need to storm Kherson head-on, an operation that would feature large-scale military and civilian casualties. He laid out a more subtle approach: Russia's position on the right bank would be slowly degraded, and its troops cut off. Deoccupation would happen step-by-step. "To liberate Kherson, we don't need to attack Kherson. If we control the bridge, they have no logistics. If they make a pontoon bridge, we can destroy it," he explained.

It was a typical August scene: beach, sea, and kids with floaties splashing around in the shallows. Close to the sunny shoreline, families relaxed in wooden cabins with white ruched curtains. They read, chatted, scrolled on their phones. It was easy for those on holiday in the resort of Novofedorivka, on the west coast of Crimea, to ignore the special operation. It was taking place somewhere to the north, far away, a matter for officials and Moscow generals.

Around 3:00 p.m., however, something unexpected happened. There was an explosion in the near distance, followed by a second loud blast. Adults stopped what they were doing and gawped; the children carried on as before. A black mushroom cloud rose into the sky, its shape growing and mutating. There were orange flashes, further explosions, and the whine of police and emergency vehicles. The smoke columns wrapped themselves together, a ragged arras darkening the sky.

The blasts were emanating from Saky airfield, used by Russia's air force to inflict misery and destruction across southern Ukraine. It was alight. Ten warplanes were destroyed, satellite images confirmed, and an unknown number of air force personnel killed, including pilots. The airstrip was full of blackened objects. Cars parked on its perimeter were turned into smoking shells. In the town, windows were shattered.

A week later, a similar mysterious and devastating event took place in Dzhankoi, a railway hub in the north of the peninsula used to transport equipment to the occupied south. An ammunition dump and electrical substation blew up. On the same day, more kabooms were reported, coming from a military airfield in the village of Hvardiiske, not far from the regional capital of Simferopol. Sukhoi jets working with the Russian navy were based there.

War had come to Crimea. These events sparked panic and terror in an area Russia thought untouchable. At Novofedorivka, families made a hasty exit, scattering over the boardwalks. The explosions at Saky airfield went on for an hour; by the time they had subsided, the beach was deserted. Cars streamed over the bridge back to Russia, as many as thirty-eight thousand leaving in a single day. Traffic backed up for several kilometers. There were queues outside Simferopol's train station.

Russia's ministry of defense shrugged off these setbacks, blaming them on local sabotage. Initially, Ukraine's government did not claim responsibility, instead offering theories as to who might be behind them. They included disaffected Russian army officers and partisans. A more probable explanation was that undercover operatives working for military intelligence had carried out these hits using kamikaze drones. Or they were the work of Neptune missiles.

The destruction of Saky airfield was a sensation, as unforeseen by the Kremlin as the sinking of the *Moskva*. Zelenskiy declared that Ukraine intended to liberate Crimea, a peninsula that used to be a popular holiday destination for all Ukrainians. Russia had made it dangerous, degraded, and unfree, he said. He mentioned its ethnic Turkic Tatar residents, whom

Putin's intelligence agencies had persecuted since 2014. Zelenskiy promised more attacks. He urged residents to stay away
from Russian bases.

Zelenskiy's aides enjoyed the moment and poked fun at a
Russian claim that the blasts might have been caused by a care-
less serviceman dropping a cigarette butt—impossible unless
Moscow had "different physics," Zelenskiy's adviser Mykhailo
Podolyak said. Crimea was seeing "demilitarization in action,"
he added wryly. Another adviser, Oleksiy Arestovych, tweeted
a photoshopped image. It showed him relaxing on a lounge
chair with explosions in the background and the words:
"Morning in Dzhankoi."

In late August, Ukraine launched its long-awaited campaign
to recapture the south. Its ongoing operation entered a new
stage. The offensive did not resemble the tactics used by Moscow in the past—a big military column, used like a bulldozer.
The Ukrainian counteroffensive was more patient and sought
to grind down enemy logistics and create chaos within Russian
forces, similar to the scenario in the Kyiv region in February
and March.

Zelenskiy's administration had for months been telegraph-
ing an intention to attack occupied Kherson. This seemed
counterintuitive: Why tell the enemy what you are up to? The
Kremlin responded by bringing in reinforcements and extra
battalions. Some twenty thousand soldiers were deployed
on the right bank of the Dnipro River. This was what Valerii
Zaluzhnyi, the commander in chief of Ukrainian forces, had
intended: to lure large numbers of uniformed adversaries into
an unfavorable position and encircle them.

The counteroffensive wrecked the Kremlin's attempt to

fold these stolen regions into the Russian state. Kherson's pro-Moscow authorities paused plans to hold a "referendum" in September because of the fighting. The new school year—conducted with a Russian curriculum, the Ukrainian language banned—was disrupted, too. Partisan activity in the south stepped up. Local collaborators were blown up. Others decamped to Russia.

At first the details were scant because of operational secrecy. Then it emerged that Ukraine's armed forces were pressing all across the Kherson region front line. "We are taking the oxygen out of their defense. It's a game play," one source told me. "We are creating a situation where they have no ammunition, artillery, and tanks." The source was confident Russia would eventually abandon Kherson, realizing the position was unsustainable and pulling out group by group.

One successful push took place northeast of Kherson, in an area between the Dnipro and Inhulets Rivers. There, Ukraine's forces breached the first line of the Russian defense. Ukraine got back the village of Vysokopillya six months after the Russians first came in and said they were staying for good.

In Vysokopillya, three Ukrainian soldiers clambered onto the roof of the village hospital. Above them was a moody sky of undulating clouds. They raised the blue-and-yellow flag. It was an act of reclamation. And a statement of intent.

The attack on the Kherson front was one of the greatest deception exercises in modern warfare. Yes, the operation was genuine. But it masked a stunning and much bigger counteroffensive around the city of Kharkiv in the northeast of the country. There, Ukrainian troops assembled unnoticed, punching through flimsy Russian defensive lines and advancing into territory held by Moscow for six months. Many Russian soldiers had been sent to the south; those left behind suddenly found themselves overwhelmed and swamped.

In early September, Ukraine's armed forces recaptured almost all of Kharkiv Oblast. They freed more than approximately eight thousand square kilometers of territory in a few astonishing days. It had taken Russia four months to capture a comparable area during its grinding assault in the east. The Ukrainians liberated towns and villages all the way up to the international border with Russia. First, they encircled Balakliia, raising the national flag. Then they pressed north into Kupiansk, a rail and supply hub. After that, they secured Izium, a major Russian base and arms depot that had been at the heart of the Kremlin's operation to conquer the Donbas.

The Russians fled. Their retreat was chaotic and disorderly: a pell-mell affair. Military units were abandoned, left without officers and communications. Some soldiers called their relatives and asked them to make inquiries in Moscow as to where they should go next. Others grabbed bicycles and scooters and pedaled off in the direction of home. Many departed in civilian clothes, leaving behind their tanks and armored vehicles, or were taken prisoner.

The local population, almost all of it, welcomed this liberation. They hugged the Ukrainian soldiers and stood by the side of the road, cheering, waving, and kneeling in homage as triumphant Ukrainian convoys went past. Old ladies wept and offered pancakes. The troops tore down enemy posters with the words "We are one people with Russia" from billboards and stomped on the Russian tricolor. They restored the Ukrainian colors to border posts, radio masts, and town halls. The mood was jubilant. Even optimistic Ukrainians had thought this scenario—of swift success and total Russian collapse—unlikely.

For Putin, the rout was an extraordinary humiliation. Russia's ministry of defense claimed it was carrying out a "planned" transfer of units to separatist areas, relocating them east of the Oskil River, about ten miles from Izium. Far-right nationalist bloggers were furious. They accused the military leadership in Moscow of incompetence. The evidence was there for anyone to see. The Ukrainian side took possession of T-80 tanks, ammunition stores, and other equipment left behind by the retreating invaders during their flight from Izium. The supplies were a gift from "Russian Lend Lease," Ukrainians joked on social media.

The war appeared to have reached a dramatic tipping point. Putin's forces continued to occupy about a fifth of Ukraine. But his demoralized soldiery was, it was pretty obvious, reluctant to fight on. The number of deserters increased, after months of poor food and shoddy clothing. The momentum was with Ukraine, overwhelmingly. It was actively prosecuting the war on its own terms: the place of battle and the tempo of events. It had a psychological advantage. "The Putin regime is in a situation called zugzwang in chess—in which any moves they make lead to a deterioration in their position," Zelenskiy's adviser Arestovych remarked in September. He added: "Now *we* play them." All of this augured well for further gains.

It was a formidable sight. Russian military hardware had taken over the Ukrainian capital's Mykhailivska Square. A Pantsir self-propelled artillery system, infantry fighting vehicles, and a T-72 tank sat beneath the golden domes of Saint Michael's monastery. But this wasn't the triumphant parade Putin had imagined when he pushed the button on total invasion. It was an exhibition of destroyed Russian war machines sent by the man in the Kremlin during his failed attempt to seize Kyiv.

I went to take a look. The scene was different from the dank February day when Russia launched its air-to-ground attack. Back then, the historic center of Kyiv had been near deserted, its denizens stupefied and afraid. By the fall of 2022, life and laughter had returned. Sightseers clambered on the turrets and smiled and posed for selfies. They waved Ukrainian flags. A young man did energetic pull-ups from a gun barrel on a tank. Children clambered over a graveyard of burned-out enemy junk.

The ancient city had survived. It was itself again, a place of street murals and cafés, metro kiosks and dog walkers, cobblestone boulevards and grass-scented parks. I walked down Andriivskyi Descent. There was Bulgakov's butter-colored mansion at number 13, next to graffiti-covered walls and antique shops. Around the corner, the "alley of artists" offered a grand view of the Dnipro. Below me, I saw a woodpecker. It disappeared into the trees of Volodymyrska Hill.

This great capital was not part of the Russian Federation. Nor was there much prospect Kyiv would be joining Putin's imperium anytime soon, despite predictions in Moscow that the city would fall in three days. Zelenskiy, the charismatic leader who had stayed in Kyiv during its blackest hours, remained in his sandbagged Bankova Street office—*Ya tut*. His country had impressed the world with its heroism and resilience. Against the odds, it had held off and humbled a superior opponent.

It remained to be seen how much territory Ukraine might eventually win back. The counteroffensive around Kharkiv felt like a watershed, the moment when the possibility of a Ukrainian victory became tangible. As the first anniversary of Europe's biggest war for eighty years approached, one fact was clear: Russia had basically lost. Lost in the sense that its armed forces had failed to achieve Putin's main strategic objectives. These were nothing less than the extermination of Ukraine as a self-governing entity. Putin's plan was to extinguish the country, to replace its leadership with puppets, and to incorporate its lands into a new pan-Russia.

And lost, what's more, on the battlefield. Russia's army was the second-most powerful in the world, at least in theory. Some American commentators argued in February that there was no point in arming Ukraine since its crushing defeat was inevitable. The reverse was now the case: with further Western weapons, Ukraine's armed forces had a good chance of repeating their successes elsewhere, in the northeast, in the south, and possibly even in Crimea. The Zelenskiy government set out its peace terms: all its territory back, compensation, security guarantees, trials for war crimes.

Putin, of course, had not gone away. Nor had his vindictiveness. He could make trouble for Ukraine for years and decades to come. In September, he doubled down. He announced a partial mobilization at home and sham "votes" on union with Russia in occupied areas of Ukraine. The fuzziness of his aims—denazification, demilitarization—meant that the Kremlin's veteran dictator had plenty of room to maneuver. Victory could still mean "liberating" all of the Donbas. Or simply hanging on to occupied southern Ukraine. Or a further tactical withdrawal, while the Russian army regrouped. And then at some point another attack.

Moscow believed time was on its side. The West's resolve to support and arm Ukraine would weaken, Putin believed, especially as energy prices spiked and the cost of living rose. His calculation was that democratic leaders would have to respond to popular pressure over gas deliveries and prices. The Americans and the Europeans would strong-arm Kyiv to accept a disadvantageous truce on Russia's terms.

This scenario looked unlikely. The anti-Kremlin coalition was holding up, and there was no prospect Ukraine would agree to a cease-fire before a full Russian military departure. Putin's gamble on a quick victory hadn't paid off. Russia looked internally weaker and perhaps more brittle than at any other point since 1991. Its regime had failed, and the painful consequences of its reckless invasion would continue to be felt. Russia's president was not the great gatherer, a reunifier of empire, but a foolish despot lost in fantasy.

Ukraine had not won the war—or not yet. More trials lay ahead. But it was what you might call a proven state. It was one of history's survivors: of two world wars, Stalin's famines, the Great Terror, and the Chornobyl explosion. Then nearly a decade of subversion and occupation by Russia: first in the east, and then with a full-blown invasion. Ukraine had not yet perished, as the words of the national anthem put it. The hope lived on: of a free people living happily in their land.

ACKNOWLEDGMENTS

The author would like to thank the following people:

Pete Adlington

Edward Allen

Anne Applebaum

Ian Bahrami

Chris Barter

Peter Beaumont

Julian Borger

Liudmyla Buimister

Maggie Carr

Christopher Cherry

Adam Coll

Fiona Crosby

Ksenia D.

Sarah Davison-Aitkins

Martin Dewhirst

Julie Ertl

Vasyl Filipchuk

Susie Finlay

Owen Gibson

Emma Graham-Harrison

Nataliya Gumenyuk

Felicity Harding

John Harding

Laura Hassan

Suzanne Herz

Mariia Hlazunova

Nick Hopkins

Olesia Horiainova

Scott Horton

Chris Howard-Woods

Tim Judah

Masha Karp

Anna Kaufman

Mark Kessler

Isobel Koshiw

Alex Kovzhun

Daniel Kovzhun

Andrey Kurkov

Serhii Kuzan

Mallory Ladd

ACKNOWLEDGMENTS

Katie Lamborn

Susanna Lea

Serhiy Leshchenko

Annie Locke

Dmytro Lytvyn

Alessio Mamo

Artem Mazhulin

Una McKeown

Mark McKinnon

Sean McTernan

James Meek

Pedro Nelson

Jussi Niemeläinen

Daniel Novack

Petro Obukhov

Anne Owen

Madeline Partner

Barbara Richard

James Rothwell

Dan Sabbagh

Olha Shvets

Josh Smith

Ihor Solovey

Mollie Stewart

Sara Talbot

Oliver Taplin

Phoebe Taplin

Anastasia Taylor-Lind

Jan Thompson

Lorenzo Tondo

Katharine Viner

Ed Vulliamy

Shaun Walker

Rima Weinberg

Andrew Wilson

Jamie Wilson

Patrick Wintour

Volodymyr Yermolenko

Volodymyr Yurchenko

Andriy Zagorodnyuk

Dmytro Zhmailo

Christopher Zucker

COLLUSION

Secret Meetings, Dirty Money, and How Russia Helped Donald Trump Win

December 2016. Luke Harding, the *Guardian* reporter and former Moscow bureau chief, quietly meets former MI6 officer Christopher Steele in a London pub to discuss President-elect Donald Trump's Russia connections. A month later, Steele's now-famous dossier sparks what may be the biggest scandal of the modern era. The names of the Americans involved are well known—Paul Manafort, Michael Flynn, Jared Kushner, George Papadopoulos, Carter Page—but here Harding also shines a light on powerful Russian figures such as Aras Agalarov, Natalia Veselnitskaya, and Sergey Kislyak, whose motivations and instructions may have been coming from the highest echelons of the Kremlin. Drawing on new material and his expert understanding of Moscow and its players, Harding takes the reader through every bizarre and disquieting detail of the "Trump-Russia" story—an event so huge it involves international espionage, offshore banks, sketchy real estate deals, the Miss Universe pageant, mobsters, money laundering, poisoned dissidents, computer hacking, and the most shocking election in American history.

Political Science

THE SNOWDEN FILES
The Inside Story of the World's Most Wanted Man

It began with a tantalizing anonymous email: "I am a senior member of the intelligence community." What followed was the most spectacular intelligence breach ever, brought about by one extraordinary man. Edward Snowden was a twenty-nine-year-old computer genius working for the National Security Agency when he shocked the world by exposing the near-universal mass surveillance programs of the United States government. His whistleblowing has shaken the leaders of nations worldwide and generated a passionate public debate on the dangers of global monitoring and the threat to individual privacy. In a tour de force of investigative journalism that reads like a spy novel, award-winning *Guardian* reporter Luke Harding tells Snowden's astonishing story—from the day he left his glamorous girlfriend in Honolulu, carrying a hard drive full of secrets, to the weeks of his secret-spilling in Hong Kong, to his battle for asylum and his exile in Moscow. For the first time, Harding brings together the many sources and strands of the story—touching on everything from concerns about domestic spying to the complicity of the tech sector—while also placing us in the room with Edward Snowden himself. The result is a gripping insider narrative—and a necessary and timely account of what is at stake for all of us in the new digital age.

ALSO AVAILABLE
A Very Expensive Poison

VINTAGE BOOKS
Available wherever books are sold.
vintagebooks.com